James Bowling Mozley

Sermons Preached Before the University of Oxford

And on Various Occasions

James Bowling Mozley

Sermons Preached Before the University of Oxford
And on Various Occasions

ISBN/EAN: 9783744744362

Printed in Europe, USA, Canada, Australia, Japan

Cover: Foto ©Thomas Meinert / pixelio.de

More available books at **www.hansebooks.com**

SERMONS

PREACHED BEFORE THE

UNIVERSITY OF OXFORD

AND ON VARIOUS OCCASIONS

BY

J. B. MOZLEY, D.D.

REGIUS PROFESSOR OF DIVINITY, OXFORD, AND
CANON OF CHRIST CHURCH

RIVINGTONS

London, Oxford, and Cambridge

MDCCCLXXVI

TO

THE VERY REVEREND

RICHARD WILLIAM CHURCH, M.A., D.C.L.

DEAN OF ST. PAUL'S

This Volume

IN GRATEFUL RECOLLECTION OF A LONG FRIENDSHIP

IS DEDICATED

BY THE AUTHOR.

ADVERTISEMENT.

OF the following Sermons, the six first were preached by the Author before the University in his turn as Select Preacher; the seventh in his own turn, the eighth and ninth as Canon of Christ Church.

Of those that follow, six were preached in the Cathedrals of Worcester and Christ Church, and the three last on public occasions at Lancing College.

CONTENTS.

SERMON I.
The Roman Council.
(Preached Sunday Afternoon, November 7, 1869.

"*My Kingdom is not of this world.*"—JOHN XVIII. 36   1

SERMON II.
The Pharisees.
(Preached Sunday Afternoon, November 28, 1869.)

"*For I say unto you, that except your righteousness shall exceed the righteousness of the scribes and Pharisees, ye shall in no case enter into the Kingdom of Heaven.*"— MATTHEW V. 20   28

SERMON III.
Eternal Life.
(Preached Sunday Afternoon, February 20, 1870.)

"*For we are saved by hope: but hope that is seen is not hope: for what a man seeth, why doth he yet hope for.*"— ROMANS VIII. 24   52

SERMON IV.

The Reversal of Human Judgment.

(Preached Sunday Afternoon, December 11, 1870.)

"*Many that are first shall be last; and the last shall be first.*"—MATTHEW XIX. 30 82

SERMON V.

War.

(Preached Sunday Morning, March 12, 1871.)

"*Nation shall rise against nation, and kingdom against kingdom.*"—MATTHEW XXIV. 7 110

SERMON VI.

Nature.

(Preached Sunday Afternoon, May 7, 1871.)

"*Thou art become exceeding glorious; Thou art clothed with majesty and honour. Thou deckest thyself with light as it were with a garment: and spreadest out the heavens like a curtain.*"—PSALM CIV. 1, 2 138

SERMON VII.

The Work of the Spirit on the Natural Man.

(Preached on Whitsunday, May 27, 1860.)

"*The wind bloweth where it listeth, and thou hearest the sound thereof, but canst not tell whence it cometh, and whither it goeth: so is every one that is born of the Spirit.*"—JOHN III. 8 164

SERMON VIII.

The Atonement.

(Preached Sunday Morning, November 2, 1873.)

"*Sacrifice and offering Thou wouldest not, but a body hast Thou prepared me.*"—HEBREWS X. 5 . . . 183

SERMON IX.

Our Duty to Equals.

(Preached February 1, 1874.)

"*Condescend to men of low estate. . . . Provide things honest in the sight of all men.*"—ROMANS XII. 16, 17 . 208

SERMON X.

The Peaceful Temper.

"*Follow peace with all men, and holiness, without which no man shall see the Lord.*"—HEBREWS XII. 14 . . 231

SERMON XI.

The Strength of Wishes.

"*Ask, and it shall be given you; seek, and ye shall find; knock, and it shall be opened unto you: for every one that asketh receiveth; and he that seeketh findeth; and to him that knocketh it shall be opened.*"—MATTHEW VII. 7, 8 242

SERMON XII.
The Unspoken Judgment of Mankind.

"*I said, I will take heed to my ways, that I offend not with my tongue: I will keep my mouth as it were with a bridle, while the ungodly is in my sight.*"—PSALM XXXIX. 1, 2 253

SERMON XIII.
The True Test of Spiritual Birth.

"*Marvel not that I said unto thee, Ye must be born again. The wind bloweth where it listeth, and thou hearest the sound thereof, but canst not tell whence it cometh, and whither it goeth: so is every one that is born of the Spirit.*"—JOHN III. 7, 8 265

SERMON XIV.
Ascension Day.

"*Christ is not entered into the holy places made with hands, which are the figures of the true; but into heaven itself, now to appear in the presence of God for us.*"—HEBREWS IX. 24 277

SERMON XV.
Gratitude.

"*And Jesus answering said, Were there not ten cleansed? but where are the nine? There are not found that returned to give glory to God, save this stranger.*"—LUKE XVII. 17 288

SERMON XVI.

The Principle of Emulation.

Preached on the Anniversary (May 6th) of the Founding of Lancing College.

PAGE

"*Neither do men light a candle, and put it under a bushel, but on a candlestick; and it giveth light unto all that are in the house. Let your light so shine before men, that they may see your good works, and glorify your Father Which is in heaven.*"—MATTHEW V. 15, 16 . 298

SERMON XVII.

Religion the First Choice.

Preached on the Anniversary of the Founding of Lancing College.

"*But seek ye first the Kingdom of God, and His righteousness; and all these things shall be added unto you.*"— MATTHEW VI. 33 313

SERMON XVIII.

The Influence of Dogmatic Teaching on Education.

Preached at Lancing College (October 26, 1875) on the Opening of the Crypt.

"*The Church of the living God, the pillar and ground of the truth.*"—1 TIMOTHY III. 15 332

THE ROMAN COUNCIL.

St. John xviii. 36.

"My Kingdom is not of this world."

THIS is a text which has, as it were, looked at the Church ever since the Church was founded. It is like an eye fixed upon her, from which she cannot escape : she has in times past thought she has escaped from it, she has acted according to her own will, and taken her own way in claiming earthly sovereignty, in wielding the arms of this world, and converting herself into a kingdom of force ; but that eye has been upon her: go where she will, and in whatever divergent paths, and branches of those paths, and circuits of those paths,—that eye has been upon her. It was upon her when St. Augustine, contrary to his first and natural convictions, which he confesses he did violence to, called in the imperial arms to suppress the Donatists : it was upon her when Gregory VII. in her behalf claimed the monarchy of the world, and exercised the rights of such a monarchy : it was upon her, and more sternly, when by simple carnage she suppressed the Reformation in Italy, Spain, and France : it was upon her when she sat in the judicial halls of the Inquisition ; upon her very tribunal,

B

while her eye was fixed upon the subjects of her power, that eye was looking upon her: it was upon her afterwards when she kept up prohibitions, penalties, imprisonments, and the like, in behalf of her own faith: and it is looking upon her now—now, when the circuit of her worldly power seems to be accomplished, when the whole cycle is over; and when, after ages of earthly supremacy, from which she has lately step by step descended, the order of things has all but rolled back again upon its hinges, and the Church stands face to face again with Christ in the judgment-hall, saying, "My Kingdom is not of this world." That saying has looked through history, through all the successive phases of the Church's worldly position, and now sees itself issuing out of the long period of its contradiction, into its great verification. It has accomplished itself simply by the course of events. As a matter of fact, it is found impossible that the government of the world can be conducted upon the contrary principle. We have tried the principle of the Church being a kingdom of this world, appealing to force, in any shape, and we find by experiment— long experiment certainly, but not the less, on the contrary, so much the more certain—that it does not answer, that things cannot go on, and that another ground must be taken. It is thus that God teaches us by events; He lets us go as long as we like in our own way, till our own way becomes an absurdity and a contradiction; till it refutes itself, and we have to extricate ourselves out of it as we can.

The very earliest Christianity, that which is coeval

with the fountain-head, is thus the most modern in its tone, the most harmonising with the claims of advancing society in its political aspect. It is the political Christianity of a later age, nay, of an age almost close to our own, that is now antiquated and obsolete, the Christianity which was propped up by civil penalties; but the Christianity of the Gospel is indeed as modern in its spirit as if it had arisen to-day. See its maxims, its principles on this great subject; they are the maxims, the principles of the present day. It abjures force, it throws itself upon moral influence for its propagation and maintenance. What more could it have done to have been in keeping with latest time? These are the very watchwords that we now boast of, and by which we think we have excelled all antiquity. We have excelled a later antiquity, but not the earliest and first. That now meets us and stretches out its hands to us over a long interval. There is nothing obsolete in the original spirit of the Gospel, nothing in its truths, it is old and it is new too. And how does such a thought lead us up to the Divine Mind of the Founder, spanning all time, from the day of His own sojourn in the flesh to the end; sending forth a religion whose original political maxims we have even now to fall back upon, after a long departure, as the only ones that the modern world can act upon; those, viz., that are contained in the fundamental law, " My Kingdom is not of this world."

I am led, in connection with this subject, to make some remarks on the approaching Council of the Roman Church, the programme of which is no secret to us, viz., that it will convert the Papal Infallibility into a dogma, and adopt the Papal condemnation of the Theses of the Syllabus. And there will be no need to remind any one here of what those Theses are, viz., that some are assertions of a certain class of civil rights, which we call the rights of conscience, rights which the modern world universally recognises, and which are in all civilised countries regarded as the inalienable property of the individual ; that some others again are assertions with respect to the Christian Church, viz., that no temporal power, or use of force, resides in the Church, by any right of its original foundation. These propositions are condemned in the Syllabus.

Two sets of divines, indeed, dispute beforehand as to what will be the effect of the decrees of the Council upon the political relations of citizens, and whether they will produce any disturbance of those relations. The Theological Faculty of Munich, in reply to the question of the Bavarian Government, declares, upon the assumption on which the questions are based— viz., that the truths affirmed will be made articles of faith—that they will. On the other hand, a section of the faculty, instead of replying to the questions of the government upon the assumption on which they are based, denies the assumption. The Papal Infallibility, it is admitted, will be converted into an article of faith ; but inasmuch as the dogma of the infallibility will not, it is said, commit the Church to the sphere of that infallibility, this dogma will contain no material of collision with the civil power. On the other hand, the condemnations of the Syllabus, which do come into the province of politics, and so of their own nature do tend to collision with the civil power—these, it is mysteriously and obliquely intimated, will not be found in effect to be articles of faith, *i.e.*, to be binding upon the belief of every individual Christian.

It is indeed remarkable to see the great alteration in the point of view with which a council in primitive times was looked at, and with which a council is now, from within the bosom of the Church. Then there was a kind of impetuous rush, on the part of the whole Church, into the embraces of a council,—a forward leap into the belief of its doctrines, and almost in advance of them. Now the great advantage seems to be, not how much of a council's result there is necessary to be believed, but how little. There is a studious solicitude to reduce this obligation. We see already the line and rule at work, to mark accurately the scale of belief. This is promulgated by the Council as true, and must be believed: that is promulgated by the Council as true, and need not be believed. We see a staff of theologians preceding the Council like judicious pioneers, in order to construct a road of escape for the body of the faithful from its decrees. We see them preparing their structure beforehand to act as a receptacle of these decrees, to accommodate them for the encounter with the outer world; we see them projecting by anticipation, before the Council, a dissolving medium, to stand waiting, ready prepared to receive the dicta when they come out. Without, however, going more into this question, it will be enough for us that this will be the full and formal teaching of the Church, of which she will accept the entire responsibility; and which she will promulgate as by her very theory absolutely true. What internal accommodations will be made within the body for the unbelief of a large section of it ; and how the personal authorities of the Church that deal with the individual will contrive that these decrees shall not practically act as binding upon the conscience of every individual ; in a word, what systematic connivance will be practised within the communion at the non-reception of the decrees—with all this we have properly nothing to do. It is enough for us that this will be the Council's statement of truth, promulgated by the full and integral representative Church as true, and being, by the very rationale of Infallibility, absolutely true.

What, then, are the doctrines which the Roman Church will thus incorporate into her teaching, will shape into formulæ, and promulgate with the whole weight of her own responsibility at the Council? Those which bear upon the great questions of the relation of Church and State, and with which we are concerned on the present occasion, are principally two —one of which affects the use and design of civil or temporal power ; the other, the proper holder of that power —whether the Church can, by the rule of Scripture, claim any right to the possession and exercise of it.

With respect to the first of these two doctrines— the Council in ratifying the Syllabus, will assert the right of the temporal or civil power to punish on account of religious belief, or to use force in religion. The Syllabus, by the condemnation of the opposite theses,[1] says, "Ecclesia vim inferendi potestatem habet: ecclesiæ jus competit violatores legum suarum pœnis temporalibus coercendi." Again: "expedit religionem Catholicam haberi tanquam unicam Status religionem, cæteris quibuscunque cultibus exclusis," which implies that such civil exclusion is in itself right. We confine ourselves here, then, to the assertion made about temporal or civil power, that it has a right to punish and to use force in matters of religion; in a word, the assertion of the right of persecution. For when we speak, in religious or philosophical discussion, of the right of persecution, we do not necessarily involve in the fact any outrages, positive cruelties, or barbarities; but only imply, as essential to it, the application of force.

How, then, are we to regard the formal assertion of this principle by the Roman Church? One or two observations will be necessary to show.

Upon the general subject, then, of the right to use force and to punish for religion, the historical language that we use is apt to hide the real moral point involved in it, *i.e.*, to cover from our view the fact that the real question at bottom involved in it is strictly a moral question. We say that mankind has advanced too far to use force in religion; we see the expediency and utility of this forbearance for society; we see that as a fashion of thought the idea of the right of force in religion has amongst ourselves passed away, though

[1] See Note at the end of the Volume.

two centuries ago good and holy men even among ourselves held it. That is to say, we philosophise on the subject. But besides this historical language, and this utilitarian language, and this philosophical language, there is a moral language that we must use on this question.

The morality, then, of this question, is inherent in the very fact that Church and State are two distinct societies; that these societies have two distinct scopes and ends; that with their respective ends what they regard respectively as crimes also differ; and that, therefore, to use the weapons of one of those societies against a sin or error in the other society, is a total irrelevancy and misapplication. The Church is a spiritual society, to educate us by revealed doctrine for an eternal existence: the State is a temporal society, to preserve order and peace in the world, and to maintain human life under its proper visible conditions. If, then, I am guilty of spiritual error, no good conduct in the State gives me any claim on the Church. If, on the other hand, I am respectable in the State, I am not punishable by the State for any spiritual error. Are men pursuing their proper avocations, as peaceable citizens; are they irreproachable members of civil society, living in accord with its plain ends; in that case, to drag them before a court, to throw them into a prison, or to inflict a penalty on them, on account of some supposed error in the spiritual society, is as irrelevant, and speaking essentially, as grotesque, as would be the infliction *vice versa* of spiritual censures upon material faults, upon errors of political economy, of invention, of art, or of military strategics. It is only custom which could make people not see that it was as absurd to imprison a heresy as to strike a bad piece of mechanism with an anathema. And from this utter irrelevancy there springs the plain immorality of the act; the inappropriateness of the punishment constitutes its injustice. For cannot the punished man say—you punish me as civil ruler, but in what, as representative of civil society, have I offended you? I have done you no wrong in that capacity; I have been living peaceably and honestly, and in conformity with all the claims of the visible community. To such a complaint there is no answer; and, therefore, when society decides against civil punishments for religious errors, that decision is not a mere judgment of expediency, it is not the mere voice of material progress; but it is a moral judgment upon a question of right or wrong, which has been evoked out of the reason and conscience of mankind, upon the plain state of the case, when once that state of the case was cleared up; when once the inherent distinction of the civil and spiritual bodies had been extricated from the confusion which had identified them.

Mere historical language, then, or mere utilitarian language, or mere philosophical language, does not adequately represent that which is in reality a moral position, compelled by the moral sense on this subject. It is perfectly true that good and holy men in former times have upheld the doctrine of persecution, or the application of force in religion; and some might be disposed to argue from this fact against the existence of any solid rule or law of morals on this subject. But that would be a blind and mistaken inference. For does not this difficulty of the good acting wrongly apply to any case whatever in which the rightness of any particular conduct follows upon a certain state of facts, while, at the same time, that state of facts may not be apprehended or perceived at all by the individual, or, so dimly, as practically to amount to an ignorance of them. In any case like this, if a good man does not see the facts, he will not of course see the moral inference from them; and he may act wrongly; but that does not show that the moral inference is uncertain, but only that he did not see the premiss of fact from which the moral inference is drawn. An intrinsic and eternal obligation in morals does not require that the basis of facts upon which it arises should be always seen; but only that it should directly flow from those facts when they are seen— that *then* a certain course would be always the right one. This is the state of the case, then, with regard to the morality of not applying force or the civil sword in religion. This is an intrinsic moral truth upon the true state of facts being perceived, that the Church and State are distinct societies, with distinct scopes and ends. But that it is this, does not at all imply that that state of the case was always seen. On the contrary, it is only comparatively recently that it was distinctly seen or apprehended. For many ages Church and State were practically one body in people's minds in this sense, that sins against the one ranked also as sins against the other ; the membership of the two bodies coincided ; the two bodies were not distinguished ; their provinces and scopes were not. Under such circumstances it looked the natural thing to men, if they had power in their hands, to use it for anything that seemed generally a good object to them ; and if it was a good thing to put down heresy by it, they thought they ought to do so. A whole revolution of the status of the world was necessary, a whole train of historical events was necessary, in order to untie in people's minds the two societies that had been confused together, and to make the disclosure of the real state of the case as regards Church and State ; and Christianity itself brought about this revolution and this new set of events, because Christianity engendered such strength of conviction in people's minds, whether correct or erroneous in its subject, that sects when they arose would not be put down by force ; they stood, therefore, as insulations and incongruities—in the State, but not in the Church, obtruding in the very eyes of everybody the visible fact of the distinction of the two. But when once the two bodies were seen as distinct, then the scopes of the two ceased to be confounded, and the moral sense of society on this question, even though late, was drawn fully out. It was evident that the arms of the visible order were appropriate to the defence of the visible order ; and that to use them for the ends of the spiritual order was a plain misapplication of them. The conscience of the community saw the impropriety of the civil power using its punishments and its penalties for a purpose wholly alien from its own scope. But the moral sense which was just awakened had been inherent in society all along, and only waited for the true disclosure of the facts to draw this conclusion from them; which indeed arose of itself, as soon as ever the scope of the civil power was extricated from the vague confusion in which it had lain, and eliminated from the double and complex aim of the union, when the two were confused together. The verdict is recent then, because the true aspect of the facts on which it is founded is recent; but the principle of the verdict is no less an eternal principle of morals, because it is the principle that you have no right to punish a man in the sphere in which he does not offend, and for a sin which does not come under your cognisance. This principle was as true and as inherent in the mind in the Middle Ages as it is now, but the facts upon which this particular application of it arose were not properly understood. It waited for that light; but that given, that sense of justice forthwith arose which said, You have no right to apply the weapon of one order to the sins against another order; the weapons of the temporal world to the errors of the spiritual.

In this, then, lies the critical character of the doctrine of persecution, or the right of using force against errors in religion, promulgated in the Syllabus, and to be confirmed by the Council, viz., that such a doctrine comes in most direct collision, not only with the sense of expediency in society, not only with an intellectual idea in society, but with the plain and downright moral sense of society. We dismiss from our minds any notion of practical consequences in the way of persecution to follow upon this judgment; nothing of that kind is likely to follow. We simply look upon the judgment in its dogmatical aspect; as committing the Roman Church to a false doctrine in morals. Because this is not a question of theology, not a question of ecclesiastical order, but a plain question of morality, upon which the Church of Rome will say one thing, and the whole moral sense of society another. The position may not be immoral in the holders, who may be excused by prejudice and tradition, but it is not the less in itself an immoral position.

It must be observed here, throughout, that what has been spoken of has been a *unity* of Church and State, such a unity as that, what is a sin against the one is a sin against the other too. Such a union of the two as this, must essentially issue in persecution; because, if what is a crime in the eye of the Church is a crime in the eye of the State too, the State must punish that crime, and heresy is such a crime. How can the State avoid punishing the Church's delinquents, if the Church's delinquents are also the State's delinquents? A *contract* between Church and State, such as exists in this country, with special concessions on one side, and special grants on the other, is not chargeable with any such result as this; but from the unity of the two, there does so necessarily flow the consequence of persecution, of civil punishment on religious belief, that we cannot but consider our brethren and fellow-subjects, the Roman Catholic hierarchy in this country, placed in an unfortunate position, in having at this juncture to sigh in their pastorals after the restoration of that unity; to sigh in obedience to the Syllabus; to sigh, that is, for a return of the era of penal laws and disabilities; to sigh for them, that is to say, in Continental States, for here they obviously would not be for their advantage. They repudiate the heathen State, *i.e.*, that which gives equal civil privileges to all communions; they discard the Christian State, *i.e.*, that which confines such privileges to the Church. They stand, indeed, in a somewhat eccentric attitude before this country, in insisting on the moral right of persecution; but they speak at the dictate of a higher power, whose word is law. Such a yearning for unjust and obsolete governments,—governments excusable in the confusion of ideas in former days, but utterly inexcusable in our own; such a longing— especially on the part of the heads of a communion which has so singularly benefited by a free government,—is, we may hope, only a sudden enthusiasm, which will disappear with the stimulus which has communicated it; more especially as such a preference cannot but be a barren and unrepaid attachment, a wasted affection. It is, indeed, the most disinterested of conceivable championships, the championship of the theory of persecution without the advantage of the fact, which is now no longer possible.

From the first consideration of the scope of the temporal power, we now come to the second, of the holder of that power,—that the right of force or the use of the temporal sword, is asserted as inherent in the Church. Upon this point, then, it is pleaded, in extenuation of the approaching Council, that the dogma of the Papal Infallibility erected, will yet not commit the Church to the sphere of that Infallibility, but will leave it, as it has been, an open question in ecclesiastical theology whether that Infallibility extends to the field of worldly power or is limited to spiritual subject-matter; whether it involves a divinely-ordained sovereignty over monarchs and governments, or does not carry this corollary with it. It may be admitted, then, that the dogma of the Papal Infallibility does not of itself impose the sphere of it; although it cannot but be seen that in the eyes of the whole school which maintains that the temporal sovereignty is inseparably connected with the Infallibility, the one dogma includes and takes under its warrant the other truth; and that school is the authorised representative of the Papacy.

But what, after all, does the resort to this distinction obtain for the extenuators of the Council, when the distinction itself, the whole of it, root and branch, is abolished by the articles of the Syllabus? The Syllabus expressly asserts for the Church an inherent temporal power, an inherent right to the use of force: it arms her with the temporal power not as an adventitious appendage, not as the accident of an age, not as an auxiliary instrument which the civil government lends and may take away—that idea of it is utterly condemned—but as a power which springs out of herself, out of the very bosom of the Divine design, and out of the very charter of her foundation and institution as the Church of Christ. " Ecclesia vim inferendi potestatem habet: temporalis potestas non est a civili Imperio concessa, nec revocanda a civili Imperio." But if the Church has an inherent temporal power, and if the whole power of the Church is in the Pope, as by the dogma of Infallibility it is—if he wields the power of the Church, how can the Pope not possess a temporal monarchy, a monarchy extending everywhere where the Church extends? He possesses it by virtue of his very spiritual office as Head of the Church. His Infallibility is *ipso facto* a universal empire.

The student of history may indeed see much that is majestic and magnificent in the development of the temporal power of the Church of Rome; and the first outbreak of the Empire of the Church under Gregory VII., is not only so splendid an historical spectacle, but one which brings so much purity and nobility of character before us, that this claim may be said to have started with an advantage. It is difficult to get at all the motives which animated that wonderful, and we may almost say, mysterious man; but amidst a large mass of aims connected with the political greatness of the priesthood, there certainly breaks out from him a spirit very distinct from that of the mere advancement of his order. There is the revelation of a great moral hatred, a hatred of all the visible power of the world regarded as a vast selfish manifestation and embodiment of evil. The spectacle of triumphant evil and of the world's corruption, has acted upon some remarkable minds like the perpetual presence of some hateful apparition, penetrating them with disgust, depressing them with gloom, or goading them to retaliation. They are ever in imaginary contest with that foe—that hostile impersonation—challenged by his success, and disquieted by his satisfaction. Such minds have embraced the appalling vision of the world's evil with the keenness and illumination of inspired prophets; but the malignity of it has fastened on them, sometimes to solemnise and fortify, and sometimes only to embitter and exasperate them. And hence the most discordantly opposite characters, that look as if no division could bring them under a common head, have yet exhibited a common element in this inspiration of a great hatred; it is the one bond which unites the stern judge with the satirist, who laughs at everything: the great religious poet of the Middle Ages with him who lies under the arches of St. Patrick, in that last home, " ubi sæva indignatio ulterius cor lacerare nequit."

When men of action, then, are animated by this great hatred, when they feel themselves in passionate hostility to this great evil manifestation, this gigantic spectacle of injustice and corruption, they express it *by* action, by revolutionary projects for demolishing or changing institutions. It is impossible not to see that Gregory VII. looked upon the whole government of the world of his day, as a selfish conspiracy for the promotion of oppression and rapine. He gives no credit to kings or emperors for any other motive; and certainly the facts of the case were such that the mistake, if it were one, admits of some excuse. He goes back to the originals of kingdoms. Who is the founder of one of these earthly governments? Some sanguinary adventurer, whose usurpation succeeded. "Who is ignorant," he says, "that our existing dynasties all derive their origin from such men, from the proud and the impious, from perjurers, murderers, and robbers, from men stained with every crime that can debase human nature; and whose blind cupidity and intolerable insolence inspired them with the only motive they ever had in governing, viz., a tyrannical wish to domineer over their fellow-creatures?" And he calls upon us to behold the superstructure which has been raised upon this foundation, and to observe how it fits it. "Look," he says, "at Kings and Emperors; and is it not obvious what their motives are, that they are motives of selfishness and ambition, of worldly glory and vanity? See them elated with pride, seeking their own interests, ruling for themselves and not for their subjects, and only anxious to despotise over their brethren. When they have deluged the earth with blood, they sometimes pretend to express some slight regret for the result; but who believes them? For so long as they gain some extension of their dominions they are indifferent to human life. Will they express their penitence for the miseries they have caused by abandoning one morsel of rapine? No! But if they act thus, what good Christian has not a much better right to the title of King than they have? for good Christians at any rate rule themselves for God's glory; but these men only oppress and tyrannise over others for their own selfish advantage."

Inspired by disgust and indignation at the governments of his day, and at the whole state of civil society in his day, the great aggression of Gregory VII. upon the kingly power over the world, his attempt to reduce it to a subjection to a higher Sacerdotal Sovereignty, which was to hold it in check and exert a general direction over it—this project of a Universal Empire, of which Rome was to be the seat, was founded not exclusively upon the claims of an order. There was an alliance of a much larger and grander motive, which may indeed justly be charged with utter visionariness, but which still stamps the scheme with an aim with which even we at this era of the world may partly sympathise;—the subjugation of coarse and brute strength to the yoke of a superior power, possessed of larger interests, and a larger scope, and more identifying itself with humanity at large. He was, indeed, one of those men who have a singular power of making themselves see what they wish to see; and as the earthly monarch is in his eyes only the embodiment of insolent force, so the priest is only the personification of benevolent wisdom; "for how," he asks, "can the Holy Pontiffs misgovern, whose motives are above distrust? Do they court glory? does any carnal ambition ever reach their sacred breasts? No! they think only of the things of God; those mild forgiving men, they care not for offences against themselves personally, they overlook them wholly; and offences against God are their only grief.[1]" Alas! the picture wants the verification of history, and the project of this great pontiff has to plead in its excuse, rather the motive of it, than the event.

[1] Epist. l. viii. Ep. 21.

But though the Empire of Justice which Gregory VII. proposed to himself may win our historical sympathies, and though we may acknowledge a broad distinction between a vigorous practical grasp at the reins of earthly government, in an age when government was such a disorderly proceeding, and so entirely fell short of its intended object that the field appeared to be open to a new claimant, and to justify the institution of some general corrective power;— though we see, I say, a distinction between a great aggression in action, in its own age, and under its own circumstances; and the same aggression stiffened into a dogma; still if this aggression is made a dogma of, it does plainly convert the Church into a kingdom of this world. As a suzerainty over the governments of the world, with the right of deposing the heads of those governments if they disobey, what test of an earthly kingdom does the Church not fulfil? Vain it would be to say, that the ultimate penalties of the Church's kingdom being spiritual, the Church's kingdom ultimately depended on moral influence and not on physical force. Every kingdom ultimately depends on moral influence and not on physical force; a king rules a country by his army; but his army collectively is only tied to him by a moral tie: and if it deserts him, he has no remedy. The executive force is the immediate fulcrum of government; but the ultimate one is the hold of the monarch over that force; which hold is only that of good-will, custom, and mutual understanding. Vain, again, would it be to say that the ultimate objects of the Church's kingdom were spiritual and not worldly. The test of an institution or society being a power of this world and of the political order, is not the nature of its ultimate objects, but the nature of the means it uses for gaining those objects. If it uses the regular forces of the world for this purpose—armies, soldiers, and military apparatus, and declares that it does this by a right inherent in itself, it is by its own profession a power or kingdom of this world.

What is the particular time, then, that the Church of Rome has chosen for this great renewal, this solemn republication of her claim to temporal power—her claim to the headship of all the temporal power in the world? The time is when to all appearance every vestige of the fact is going to desert her; when even the last relic of it, in the shape of a small territory, which the recent large absorptions have reduced almost to an English county, is going to be removed; and she is about to become in the eyes of the world one communion among others—a sect among sects. A strange time, indeed, it does appear for the assertion of this particular claim; yet when we compare the act with the situation, we may see that it is not without the promise of an immediate advantage to her. Undoubtedly there is in this remarkable step something of that spirit of longing for what is lost, which is so common a trait of human nature—that desiderium and regret which magnifies the past, even because it is past, and clings to it the more because it can never return. The dream is embraced with more longing than the reality, though the phantom mocks the grasp, according to the poetical description—

"Ter conatus ibi collo dare bracchia circum ;
Ter frustra comprensa manus effugit imago,
Par levibus ventis, volucrique simillima somno."

There may be even something in this act of an inferior and perverse instinct of contradiction, which makes men often just choose what they cannot do, as what they most try to do; that curious ambition to be what one cannot be, or when one cannot be it; which ignores some impassable chasm and imagines that it is close to its object, and that it is accidental that it does not touch it, and that it will do so the next time, when in truth infinity is between. Is it hence, then, that when the temporal power of Rome is over in fact, it just then exists most rigidly and imperiously in speculation; and that the greater intensity of it as a dogma, compensates for the absence of it as a possession?

It is so; and yet with all this, may she not attain an immediate practical advantage by this act? For is not this the act of a dispossessed monarch, who, upon the eve of the crisis, collects all his greatness about him, and prepares to quit his throne with a rigorous statement of his rights first put forth? It is true a statement or protest is, compared with the reality, a poor thing; but after all he lives upon that statement; it is all that he has left, and it does in a sense give him a regal position. So I apprehend in the present case; the Papacy selects this very time for making this great assertion of its temporal power because it is just on the verge of being dispossessed of it; and it is the very eve of the catastrophe which elicits and gives its significance and its expediency to the demonstration. It is a mode of meeting and preparing for actual coming events, which Rome is much too sagacious not to see; the assertion is a mode of meeting deprivation; it is a provision made for her own status and dignity in the new era of denudation of externals on which she is entering. She brings together, at parting with the old era, all her claims on this head; she fortifies and consolidates a doctrinal position; she puts into definite and compact shape her whole theory about herself; she equips herself in the full panoply of her dogma of temporal sovereignty; and to any one who asks, Why do you do this just now, when you are going to lose the fact? she may reply, I do it *because* I am going to lose it. It would be just a day too late, after the setting in of dispossession, to publish from the reduced standing of a mere voluntary communion such a challenge; the act to be done fittingly must be done before, while she has still a temporal crown upon her head. That time is now. And now, accordingly, just before retiring from her temporal position, she promulgates her statement of rights regarding it. That assertion keeps up a connection with it. She gains the effect of an assertion upon her followers; there is a rank contained in that assertion,—the rank of a great claimant of power; there is a sort of continuance of the situation itself, in keeping up a right to it. It is the link with the past. It is true there will be something visionary, we might almost say fanatical in look, in the president of a voluntary religious communion, an ordinary citizen, a subject, perhaps, of the Italian Government, perhaps —for the rumour did obtain—of our own, claiming formally to be the head of all the governments of this world; as a new claim it would be grotesque only; but the claim of the Papacy represents a real history; it has been yielded to, it has been exercised. A claim which is no more than obsolete may be said to be worth something, and to be as such a substantial and valuable property. It represents former possession. Rome issues out of her own gates, taking her history with her; she collects her prestige, she gathers up the past, she calls in all the antecedents of her temporal greatness; she stereotypes memory in decrees; she condenses history into dogma; she surrounds herself symbolically with all the insignia of her secular glory; the archives are exhibited, the rolls are displayed, the memorials of her triumphs and successes come in procession before us; great wars and great diplomacies, great alliances, great battles, are all seen by reflection in this list of dry decrees, which embalms the dignity of the past; a thousand banners and escutcheons are hid in one of these sentences, which makes the statement of her dominion, in order to serve as a support to her in the loss of the fact.

It is in vain, however—in vain in the long run. The stream of time is too strong for such memories to divert it. The whole weight of facts, the whole weight of truth, is soberly but irresistibly against this claim. This is a point on which Christianity and civilisation, which look suspiciously at each other at times, entirely join hands; they speak one language; they abjure with one mouth force as the property of the Church, and force as applicable to religion at all. The earth must roll back on its axis again before the moral sense of society recants on these questions; nay, the more the world advances and the better civil government becomes, the more clear will be the distinction between the scope of civil government and the scope of the Church. The Gospel cannot recant and retract one of its laws. Although an immediate advantage, then, may be gained by an act of defiance which revives and casts in the teeth of the whole world every pretension to temporal power ever made, is not the Church of Rome storing up difficulties for the future by it? Will not such a violent and forced transplantation from a past era make a very awkward and unmanageable insulation in the present, and these dogmas become a millstone about her neck? What does the Council bequeath, then, to the Church by this act, but a tremendous difficulty—the difficulty of resisting the double law of the Gospel and of civilisation,—a rock, to strike against which is to jar her whole fabric? In what light can such an opposition to well-ascertained principles appear, but as a fanatical development of the Papacy, surviving its wisdom, and trusting itself blindly to the arms of a single close corporation, as its guide and director. People will look for the old sagacity of the head of Christendom, and see only an enthusiast, at cross purposes with society. The Papacy is indeed in a dilemma in the matter of her own defence. It needs an organised phalanx for its support, and this powerful corporation supplies that need; but if it has the benefit of this close corporation, it must have the disadvantage of it too. For close corporations are proverbially inaccessible to new ideas, and blind to new facts; they are averse to any enlargement of mind from without, and their natural tendency is to be the whole world to themselves. Such a guide must be, with ever so much strength, a dangerous one; and indeed it is evident that the action of the Papacy was much freer and more natural in the Middle Ages than it is now. Then it was seized hold of by the different currents of the Church, just as a government is now in popular states, and it had a free life in the open air of the Church. Now it is an immured institution, living in walls, and worked by a close corporation. This is an artificial system, and a morbid system; when a tremendous strain is thrown upon the centre to work the whole, without the supply of blood from the extremities. This corporation has one recipe against all difficulties—organisation; but organisation cannot do everything; organisation cannot stop the light which the progress of the world has thrown, and must further throw, upon the respective ends of Church and State. Those who are on the side of Rome, then, in her controversy with the infidel, those among us even who approximate critically to her distinctive theology, will not be able to follow her into her moral code. In one of these dogmas her Infallibility splits upon a rock of morals; in the other it splits upon the rock of Scripture. Her Infallibility is risked by such an encounter with definite and plain truths. Civil justice and the rights of conscience belong so much to the morality of society now, that they must falsify any moral creed opposed to them.

Thus do the human incrustations upon, and the human props to, Christianity, disappear at the ordained time, and leave Christianity to itself. We live amid closing histories, and amid falling institutions; there is an axe laid at the root of many trees; foundations of fabrics have been long giving way, and the visible tottering commences. "The earth quakes and the heavens do tremble." The sounds of great downfalls and great disruptions come from different quarters; old combinations start asunder; a great crash is heard, and it is some vast mass that has just broken off from the rock, and gone down into the chasm below. A great volume of time is now shutting, the roll is folded up for the registry, and we must open another. Never again—never, though ages pass away—never any more under the heavens shall be seen forms and fabrics, and structures, and combinations that we have seen. They have taken their place among departed shapes and organisms deposited in that vast mausoleum which receives sooner or later all human creations. The mould in which they were made is broken, and their successors will be casts from a new mould. The world is evidently at the end of one era, and is entering upon another; but there will remain the Christian Creed and the Christian Church, to enlighten ignorance, to fight with sin, and to conduct men to eternity.

THE PHARISEES.

Matthew v. 20.

"*For I say unto you, that except your righteousness shall exceed the righteousness of the scribes and Pharisees, ye shall in no case enter into the kingdom of heaven.*"

THERE is a fundamental difference between the religious and historical standards of character. To an historian a man appears only as a collection of different qualities: he has good habits, he has bad habits; he is virtuous here, he is vicious there. This is the man's historical character; he has presented himself as this mixture to the world; and the historian has only to do with character as a phenomenon, or collection of facts. Its moral unity is nothing to him. Is this man a good or bad man? He does not trouble himself with that question. On the other hand, religion is not content with a collection of qualities, but seeks the moral unity of the being. Religion seeks a good being as distinguished from a bad being.

When we are engaged, then, in the search after true goodness, particular virtues fail as a test. They are like mountain paths, which are very clear and well marked for a certain way, and then suddenly stop. They do not give the clue to this unity. These are what we call natural virtues. They are beautiful, they are fascinating. Yet how deep is the treachery of nature; as we find when we come across some obstinate lump of evil that will not give way. It is a disappointment we cannot help—so naturally do we expect a moral unity in the being where we see so much that is beautiful—thinking that it must go on to a whole; but it does not; it stops short; it is a fragment; something evil succeeds, and breaks up the concord of the character; not mere imperfection, but evil.

Again, imitation, as well as nature, is a source of particular virtues;—the virtues of a class, the virtues of an age. This is different from the sacred principle of example, which implies selection, and extraction out of the general mass of human conduct; imitation takes society as a whole, and goes along with it. These virtues, then, are too compulsory to test the man; society imposes them; he must adopt its standard if he wants to be at peace with it. Instances might be given of virtues which are so absolutely necessary in particular classes, that the individual has hardly any option in the matter.

But again, besides the virtues of insensible and unconscious, there are those of systematic imitation; when men who possess power of will and perseverance, as well as insight into the structure of society, see the great importance of certain virtues, their pre-eminent public utility, their just rank, and deservedly high estimation; when they set them up as a standard in their own minds, and cultivate them; but do so at the same time upon a basis of secondary motives. These virtues, then, are real virtues in this sense, that they are real habits, that they are got possession of as modes of action. But are they tests of the goodness of the man? It is of the very structure of morality that it demands a motive as well as acts. Let us take a person practising a set of virtues, such as justice, industry, public spirit, benevolence, and the like, upon a ground connected with the life of the soul—*i.e.*, simply because it is right—his practice is immediately invested with the unearthly greatness of its motive; it is founded upon a basis of awe and mystery, upon the instincts of the soul, its presages, its prophecies, its sense of trial and of a destination for future worlds of existence. But let us take a person practising such virtues because they are popular, because the age requires them, because they are part of the machinery of success in the world, and though the virtues themselves are the same, it is evident that the possessor of them is a very different person from the other. Appeals from such a quarter as the prospects of the soul, are like shadows beckoning to us from a distance; they are wanting in tangible force as addresses to the spring of action within us, unless they are supplemented by an extraordinary strength of conscience. But any motives connected with this world wrap the man so completely round, they seize hold of him with such a firm grasp, they are so thoroughly entered into, and all their strength sucked out by him, that nothing is wanting to their force and power as motives; which motives, therefore, in reality make the virtues which they so immensely facilitate, and are almost the very

The Pharisees. 31

substance of them—*e.g.* revenge might make an act of marvellous courage no difficulty at all to a man. And when self-interest is embraced as a strong passion by the mind, it has a like facilitating consequence as regards the possession of various virtues. A man who has his own interest strongly before him can make vindictive and malicious feelings give way to it; that is to say, he can acquire with facility a habit of forgiveness. The same motive can give him gravity and application, and can preserve him from many frivolities, weaknesses, and caprices. One great vice produces many virtues. It attains successes which are missed by the frail and imperfect good who have not strength to form these habits or avoid these infirmities, simply because their high motives are weak and fluctuating; the lower motives are strong and steady. Society is thus able to produce men who are fabrics of virtues, who do not, like the volatile, leave their virtues to chance, but adopt them upon a system; but who at the same time may be said to possess the loan of them, rather than the fee-simple of them—who have the *use* of them, a fructifying use, without a true property in them. They are outside of him. The outward possessor is not their moral possessor. These fabrics include, when we inspect them, all those virtues which are consistent with a certain aim in life, and exclude those which are inconsistent with it. Just so much in quantity and kind as coincides with this scope is admitted; what is in disagreement with it is excluded. They are, to borrow an expression from the poetry of architecture, virtues in service;

they work within a strict inclosure, which, whatever apparent freedom they may have, really bounds their action; they are imprisoned within the outline of an original plan. I use the term virtue of course here in the sense in which it is often used, which is exclusive of the motive, and only denotes certain lines of action.

Particular virtues then, whether they are natural virtues, or virtues of imitation, do not make the being good. There must be some general virtue underneath all these, which consecrates and roots in him the particular ones, and makes them his moral property. Aristotle's general virtue then holds good as a safeguard against the crudity and wildness of more natural goodness, but fails as a security against subtle egotism and selfishness. It secures discipline of some sort; but there may be plenty of discipline upon a corrupt basis. It does not command the motives. The Gospel, however, was a republication of the law of nature, as in other respects, so in this that we are speaking of— I mean with respect to the composition and structure of moral goodness—that it consisted of a general virtue as the root of particular virtues; and the Gospel gave a general virtue which commanded the motives,—viz., Love. Love in the Gospel sense is that general virtue which covers the motives; like some essence which we can hardly get at, it is not itself so much as it is the goodness of everything *else* in us; not a virtue so much as a substratum of all virtues; the virtue *of* virtue, the goodness *of* goodness. It is what gives the character of acceptableness to all our actions; on the other hand its absence is that great withdrawal which leaves all action dead and worthless, and the whole man a rotten branch deserted by the sap of the true vine.

With these introductory remarks I come to the subject of the text—viz., the Gospel language relating to the Pharisees. Christ's denunciation of the Pharisees is a part of the language of the Gospels which strikes us as very remarkable. It is language which is altogether tremendous; it arrests us, it astonishes us, it makes us ask the question—What was there in these men which made them deserve this language? Such language, as applied to a class which might be called a religious class, paying such attention to many parts of religious practice, free from sensual vice, very zealous and jealous for the Mosaic law, and the worship of the one true God, was totally new to inspiration. We want an explanation of it. The preceding observations then appear to give some clue to one. This language is part of the judicial language of the first Advent. Christ's first Advent was not indeed a judgment of the world in a final sense, but it was a judgment in this sense, that it laid the *foundations* of the final judgment. He came to lay the foundation of a great separation of the bad from the good, the tares from the wheat, the chaff from the wheat; He came to lay the foundations of a perfectly virtuous society, which, begun here in struggle and imperfection, was to emerge pure and triumphant in another world, and live throughout eternity. It was essential for this purpose that some great decision should be made as to what constituted a good being as distinguished from a bad being; as to what true goodness was. It was essential that a great revelation should be made of human character, a great disclosure of its disguises and pretences; unmasking the evil in it, and extricating and bringing to light the good. But how was this decision which divided good character from bad character to be made? In no other way than by declaring what was the very structure of morality—viz., the one just mentioned, that particular virtues are nothing without the general ones; that is to say, by a republication of this great truth of nature in a final and improved form. By this criterion then, Christ made that decision, distinguishing between good and bad, which he came at His first Advent to make,—that great preliminary judgment. There is a point in the block of stone which, being struck, the mass parts asunder in its proper and natural sections. Particular virtues never would give the key to this division; but, struck upon one fundamental virtue, the whole block of humanity fell asunder in its true divisions, and there was a judgment.

The Pharisees then were the sample of mankind which came before Him for the application of this criterion, and at the same time the great example for the promulgation of it. The Pharisees were not mere formalists, mere ceremonialists. Our Lord did not deny them activity; we know that they worked; that they worked in public, in the thoroughfares and in the marketplaces; that they worked hard for the spread of their own religion; that they compassed heaven and earth to make one proselyte; we know that they had a fiery courage of their own, and that they headed mobs against the Roman Governor. But their activity had a selfish root, and a selfish scope, while at the same time they disguised this motive from themselves, and this constituted their hypocrisy. They were that combination of earnestness and ambition, in which earnestness, by an assimilative process, *turns* into ambition, and is the feeder of the great passion. Religion is so much a part of our nature that even the pride of man cannot culminate to the full without it. Religion undoubtedly makes him a greater being; if, then, he grasps like a robber at the prize, and takes a short cut to the end without the humbling means, he does become the prouder for it. And then in *its* turn, religion grovels in the dust. In the Pharisees it allied itself with the pride of life, in its most childish and empty forms,—it coveted state and precedence, and became a mockery and the very slave of earth. The Gospel then was an active religion, and Pharisaism was an active religion too; particular virtues were common to both; but the Gospel was an active religion founded upon love, and Pharisaism was an active religion founded upon egotism. "Verily, I say unto you, they have their reward." Upon this one fundamental point then mankind divided into two parts; the great block split asunder, and our Lord judicially *declared and announced* this division—the division of mankind upon this law and by this criterion.

But again, Pharisaism was a *new* evil character in the world; not that the elements of it had not existed before, for it is part of human nature; but as a fully developed character and form of evil it was new. The prophets attacked gross vices, shameless sensuality, robbery, avarice, open rapacity, crying tyranny and oppression, insolent injustice and violation of common rights, the flagrant abuses and corruptions of society. "Thy princes," they said to Jerusalem, "are rebellious and companions of thieves; they declare their sin; they hide it not; run ye to and fro through the streets, and see now and know, and seek in the broad places thereof if ye can find a man, if there be any that executeth judgment; every one loveth gifts and followeth after rewards; they have altogether broken the yoke and burst the bonds." In a word, they attacked open sin. Old Jewish sin was heathen sin— it was open. The heathen defied the law within him. There was no disguise in Paganism. The *gloriæ cupiditas* was brandished aloft; the conquerors said they wanted to conquer the world; the covetous said they wanted to be rich; as Cicero said of Crassus, he would jump in the forum—*saltaret in foro*—if any new device for making money occurred to him; neither said that they wanted, the one power and the other wealth, for the sake of doing good. The old heathen spirit boldly pursued appetite; it said, "Life is short, we know not where we are going; and while we live let us live; let us live gloriously, or luxuriously, or sensually, or pompously, as our taste happens to be."

Now we cannot say that because a new evil character rose up in the world, the old has disappeared. There are no extinct species in the world of evil; but Pharisaism was not the less a new form of evil in the world, which did not exist to attract attention in the days of the prophets. It was a new development of evil in the world when a class, socially and religiously respectable, was discovered to be corrupt at the root. Evil which produced evil, which issued in disorder and crime, was an old fact; but evil which was the parent of outward discipline and goodness was new. It was new that man could work his own will and obtain his own ends by this medium; and that that which once required vices could now be done by virtues. This was a great discovery; it was a great improvement, so to call it, in the science of evil; it was a new method, analogous to new methods in philosophy, new combinations in physics, mechanics, or art, which operate like successful surprises in effecting their object. It was a new stroke of policy in evil, like a new principle in trade or economical science. It was a new revelation of the power and character of evil that it was not confined to its simple and primitive ways—its direct resistances to conscience; but that it had at its disposal a very subtle and intricate machinery for attaining what the simple methods could not reach. It was a revelation of human nature that it *contained* all this machinery, this duplicity of action, and working of wheel within wheel. And it was fit,—there was a special aptness in the task, that He "who knew what was in man," should summarily and decisively arraign this new form of evil upon its appearance in the world; that He should at once stamp upon it that ineffaceable stigma which it has never been able to erase. He did this in His denunciation of Pharisaism. He disclosed the enormous elasticity of evil, the secret of its self-accommodating nature, its fertility, its flexibility, its capacity for acting under disguises. And He who saw the imposture and exposed it, knew that it must be exposed in no doubtful terms; and that less severity would not have answered His purpose, and left the mark which He designed.

For, indeed, not only was this a new form of evil, but it was a worse type than the old and known ones. It matters not, indeed, if the will is wholly depraved, whether it be an open rebel or a cunning one; and the rich man in the parable who said straightforwardly to his own soul—Henceforth do nothing but please thyself, was reprobated as much as the Pharisee. But when the will is not radically bad, it is evident that, in the Gospel estimate, the evil which is the excess of appetite and passion is not so bad as the evil which corrupts virtue. The Gospel is tender to faults of mere weakness and impulse; it watches over the outbursts of a vehement and passionate nature, to see if, when the storm is past, it cannot elicit the element of good which lies underneath; it breathes the purest compassion for the victim of impulse, it regards him as the future penitent, and its hopeful eye is quick to catch the first symptoms of a better mind. But while this is its temper toward natural frailty, the Gospel casts an obdurate and inflexible look upon false goodness; and for this very reason, that false goodness is in the very nature of the case an unrepentant type of evil. For why should a man repent of his goodness? He may well repent indeed of its falsehood; but unhappily the falsehood of it is just the thing he does not see, and which he cannot see by the very law of his character. The Pharisee did not know he *was* a Pharisee; if he had known it, he would not have been a Pharisee. The victim of passion then may be converted, the gay, the thoughtless, or the ambitious; he whom human glory has intoxicated, he whom the show of life has ensnared, he whom the pleasures of sense have captivated—they may be converted, any one of these—but who is to convert the hypocrite? He does not know he is a hypocrite; he cannot upon the very basis of his character; he *must* think himself sincere; and the more he is in the shackles of his own character, *i.e.*, the greater hypocrite he is, the more sincere he must think himself. A hypocrite in the vulgar sense knows that he is one, because he deceives another; but the Scripture hypocrite is the *deceived* too; and the deceived cannot possibly know that he is *deceived;* if he did, he would not be deceived. An impenetrable wall hides him from himself, and he is safe from his own scrutiny. "Evil," as has been said, "ventures not to be itself; it is seized with a restless flight from itself, and conceals itself behind any appearance of good."

Hence, then, that great and conspicuous point of view in which the Pharisee always figures in the Gospel—viz. as incapable of repentance. Self-knowledge is the first condition of repentance, and he did not possess self-knowledge; and therefore it was said to him: "The publicans and the harlots go into the kingdom of God before you;" because the publicans and the harlots knew their guilt, and he did not. He had degraded conscience below the place which the heathen gave it. The heathen, at anyrate, allowed it to protest. There is, indeed, nothing in all history more remarkable than the wild and fitful voice of the heathen conscience, which would suddenly wake up out of its trance to pierce heaven with its cries, invoking divine vengeance upon some crime. The heathen conscience was an accuser, a tormentor; it brooded over men; it stung them; it haunted them in their dreams; they started out of their sleep with horror in their countenances, wanting to fly from it, and not knowing where to fly; while the more they fled away from it the more its arrows pursued them, wandering over the wide earth, and seeking rest in vain. Or if they tried to drown its voice in excitement or passion, it still watched its moment, and would be heard, poisoning their revelry, and awakening them to misery and despair. Compare with this wild, this dreadful, but still this great visitant from another world, the Pharisaic conscience—pacified, domesticated, brought into harness—a *tame* conscience, converted into a manageable and applauding companion, vulgarised, humiliated, and chained; with a potent sway over mint, anise, and cummin, but no power over the heart—and what do we see but a dethroned conscience deserted by every vestige of rank and majesty. Our Lord treated the Pharisees then with the coldness due to those who were without the element of repentance—"How *can* ye, being evil, speak good things?" How can the bad be good? and with the holy sarcasm that they that were whole needed not a physician, He left them to themselves.

The Pharisees.

We observe, therefore, further, and the fact is remarkable, that not only did our Lord denounce the Pharisees, but that they were the only *class* which He did denounce. He condemned all sin, indeed. He sentenced by implication, in each precept to purity, to temperance, to charity, to humility, every impure man, every drunkard and glutton, every malignant man, and every proud man ; but looking on His attitude toward Jewish society, and the different portions and sections of it, we find that when He came to actual classes of men in it, the Pharisees were the only *class* which He cared or thought it appertaining to His work and mission publicly to expose. He singled *them* out of the whole mixed mass of Jewish society for this purpose. Why did He do this? Why did He thus confine to one channel the great current of His condemnation? Was there any want of vice in the Jewish community? Was there any want of variety of vice?—None ; there was plenty of it ; plenty of all kinds of it. There was avarice, exaction, luxury ; there were the pride and pomp of life ; there was sedition, violence, rebellion, murder. All these vices of the individual and of the nation come out in the very disclosures of the Gospels themselves. But all *this* vice had been condemned before ; the page of prophecy is one continuous reprobation of such vice as this. The Divine censure then had done its work with respect to this whole form of sin. But there was a new sin in the world which no prophets had rebuked, because it was not a fact of their days. It was the child of a later age, when the opening consciousness of nature revealed the stringency of the law within; and, as it did so, suggested the exchange of open resistance to it for evasion; when the evil nature awakened to the subtlety of its own interior, and grasped the new art of retaining motives and yet producing virtues.

The Prophet, then, who went before our Lord, even His Forerunner that ushered Him in, might denounce old sin, but it belonged to Him especially to smite the new evil character. John the Baptist rebuked the audacious licentiousness of king and noble; but He Himself turned from the gross spectacle without a word. He would not look at it. He averted His eyes from the undisguised scene. Others had dealt with it. He passed by the crowd with its low vice; He passed by the Court of Herod with its splendid and luxurious vice; He looked apart from the wretched victims of open sin to strike with His anathema those who made a gain of their virtues; He turned away from the thoughtless passion of the dissolute to judge the self-discipline of the vile. Once only did he send a message to Herod, and then it was not to rebuke that proud and vicious prince as a murderer and a sensualist. He addressed him by an epithet which expressed a part of the monarch's character, which he possessed in common with much more decorous and reputable men:—" Go ye and tell that Fox: Behold I cast out devils, and I do cures to-day and to-morrow, and the third day I shall be perfected."

And this consideration may contribute to explain Christ's conduct to the woman taken in adultery. Stung by His severity toward their own form of good-

The Pharisees. 43

ness as contrasted with His compassionate tone toward sinners, the Pharisees had contrived this dilemma for Him, and stood round in triumph, not expecting that He would take so bold a way of extricating Himself from it as He actually did take. Yet His refusal to condemn the sinner here was only in keeping with the whole tone of His judicial mission : " You bring this woman to me to condemn," He appears to say ; " but the condemnation of such as her is not my office ; the Law and the Prophets have condemned such vice as hers already. As Judge I have another office. You are the criminals for whom my court is instituted ; I sentence you ; but to this poor sinner I stand in no special relation of judge ; my special work to her is one of pardon." He would not waste, in condemning wretched confessed crime, that judicial mission which was to unmask false goodness.

After this general review, however, of the character of the Pharisee, it still remains to ask whether the character was confined to its own day, or whether it is not in its essence a character of all ages. The great attention which is drawn to it in the Gospels would lead one to suppose that it is ; as otherwise it would not have been so much brought forward. For why should we at this day, *e.g.*, be reading so much about the Pharisees if they were really only a curious sect in Judea two thousand years ago ?

Can we imagine anything more irrelevant as a lesson to the present day than the reproof of—if they were no more than this—a quaint school of religionists, who paid minute attention to ordinances in connection with certain herbs, and prayed conspicuously in market-places? It cannot be said that these are our perils. But indeed it is sufficiently clear that these are not the substance of the character.

It is true the special virtues of the Pharisee were virtues of his own age, and the popular and creditable virtues of one age will differ from those of another; those of an earlier from those of a later. These credentials to public favour may alter. But look at the character in its essence, only changing its dress, its class of particular virtues, according to circumstances, and taking off one and putting on another as the public standard shifts; thus cleared of its accidents, look at it; is there anything old about it? It is new; it is fresh; it is modern; it is living; it is old in the sense of human nature being old, but in no other. It is a type of evil indeed much more likely to increase than decay—to increase as the standard of advancing society throws the corrupt principle in man more upon policy, rather than open heathen resistance. Formality and routine are not essential to the Pharisee; he feeds his character upon ancient disciplinarian virtues if he has nothing else to feed it upon; but he flourishes in reality quite as much upon utilitarian and active virtues, if they are uppermost. He can assume the new virtues upon the same terms upon which he assumed the old ones. The freedom, the flexibility, the play of a modern standard are mastered by the character exactly in the same way in which the rigour and formality of an old standard were mastered.

The condemnation of the Pharisee is not the condemnation then of an antiquated character; it looked forward to futurity; it was specially adapted to meet the sin of a more advanced and a more refined and civilised state of humanity, when gross crime is more and more discarded as a mischief to society, and when the minds which go parallel with the times are tempted more and more into a specious development, into adopting, *e.g.*, the virtues of the age with the taint of the motive of the individual. That this must be more and more the moral peril of civilisation, cannot but be obvious to any one who examines what civilisation is.

But this is Pharisaism. The condemnation of it then was prophetic; it was a lesson provided for the world's progress. A civilised world wanted it because it is the very nature of civilisation to amplify the body of public virtues without guarding in the least the motive to them. A Christian world wanted it because it is the law of goodness to produce hypocrisy; it creates it as naturally as the substance creates the shadow; as the standard of goodness rises the standard of profession must rise too.

Every particular age is indeed apt to suppose that its own virtues are of such peculiar excellence that they cannot but guarantee their motive. So the Jew argued in the case of his favourite—the Pharisee. How could there be anything amiss with the motive, when there was so much zeal? And so any one might say of the virtues of an advanced age,—How can such candour, such moderation, such benevolent activity, fail in motive? But the excellence of the virtues has nothing whatever to do with the motive of the individual; *they* are admirable—beyond commendation; but what is his relation to them? In what mode does he possess them?

Nothing indeed can show more clearly that the superiority of the virtues is no credential to the motive, than the very Pharisaic age itself. The great yearning of prophecy was the total destruction of idolatry; the prophets did not see this in their days, and were in perpetual war with a lapsing and idol-loving nation. This was their great crux; and their great longing was the worship of one God. Well then, years roll on, and this great desideratum of law and prophets is actually accomplished: the Jewish nation does wholly discard idolatry; and what is the result? The very age of true worship was that which saw the consummating act of national apostasy; and the rejected Jew, upon whose forehead the mark of Cain was fixed, was not an idolater, but a believer in the one God. Imagine, if we can make the supposition, that one of the ancient prophets who had testified against the idolatry of his own age, and had exulted in the return of Jerusalem to the worship of one God, as the crowning vision of prophecy;—imagine him *seeing* Jerusalem and the Jewish people, when his own vision was fulfilled. The Pharisees were the very heads and leaders of the nation in the maintenance of this all-important article of faith; the most jealous of the least apparent infringement of it; the most vehement in the hatred of images; even the Roman eagle was an abomination to them; they trembled for the temple and the holy place on its approach; they rose up for the insulted dignity of heaven, and headed the popular outbreak upon the sight of it. When idolatry then was more than ever flourishing in the world, and when even a living Roman emperor was a god, the Pharisee seemed to be the very person whom the prophets longed for, and on whom they would have fixed as their very ideal of one of the people of God. The prophet lifting up his voice against the crying abuse of his age, would naturally expect that when that abuse was removed, everything, so to speak, would be right. But what would he have said when he saw a Pharisee? Imagine him coming into the temple when the Pharisee worshipped and made that prayer—"My God, I thank thee that I am not as other men are." Was this then the long expected fruit of a true monotheistic creed? He follows him into the market-place: he follows him into the feast; we know what he sees there. What an issue of glorious anticipations! Can we conceive a more utter disappointment, than when he saw in the monotheistic Pharisee the same identical Jew whom he had denounced as an idolater?

The truth is, and this is the explanation of these and such like facts, the real virtues of one age become the spurious ones of the next. When, in the progress of the human race, any new ground is gained, whether in truth or morals, the original gainers of that ground are great moral minds; they are minds which were penetrated by true perceptions and by an inward sacred light, and they fought with the society of their day for the reception of that light; they therefore stand high in the scale of goodness. But it is totally different when the new ground being once made, a succeeding generation has to use it. The use of it then is no guarantee of moral rank. There is a starting power in true goodness, by a struggle, to get itself accepted as a standard,—accepted even by the very society which is in heart opposed to it. This is that peculiar homage which is paid to goodness, that it extorts a public support even from those who individually reject it. Otherwise there never would be any rise in the standard of society at all, which is in heart always at the time hostile to it; but this principle provides one. The new virtues then are started; they are erected as a standard; they are established, received, and taken into the system. But *then* inferior men can practise them; and more than this, selfish men can practise them. The selfish principle does not require vice as its instrument; so long as it can get behind the last erected class of virtues, can command the situation, and dictate the motive, it is enough. It retreats then behind the last ground gained, whether of truth or morals, and uses the latest virtues as its fulcrum and leverage. A standard once raised by the convulsive efforts of a fervent minority, a mass of lower character is equal to the adoption of it; but the originators of the standard are separated by an immeasureable interval from their successors. The belief of the Pharisees, the religious practice of the Pharisees, was an improvement upon the life of the sensual and idolatrous Jews whom the prophets denounced. But those who used both the doctrinal and moral improvements as the fulcrum of a selfish power and earthly rank, were the same men, after all, as their fathers, only accommodated to a new age, though this indeed was just what they denied. They said, on the contrary, *we* build the prophets' sepulchres, whereas our *fathers* killed them; and exposed themselves to our Lord's irony, that the builder of the sepulchre was a very fitting successor of the killer.

How, in the highest sense, natural then is this whole language of the Gospels, though it has recently been made a Scriptural difficulty—most gratuitously. For is there any language, I do not say in the Bible, but in any book that was ever written in this world, with which human nature—on the good side—more sympathises than with this? Is there a single vein of any moralist, of any dramatist, of any one exponent of human character, that ever wrote, with which it feels itself more at one? It could not perhaps have trusted itself to such a condemnation of character, it could not have resisted the apparent weight of outsides, which is often great, without this aid; but the plain outspoken decision of the Gospel has backed up the sense of truth in Nature,—has enabled it to speak out when it might have been mute. The high judicial voice of Him who knew what was in man, has founded a great human judgment; and this type of evil has never recovered from its exposure in the Gospel; the honesty in man's nature is armed against it, and keeps up a witness against it.

Such was the judgment of the first Advent—not the final, but the prophetic judgment of Christ. It lays the foundation of the kingdom of God, of that virtuous society which is to last for ever in another world; it lays it deep—deeper than in the virtues of classes, than in the virtues of ages. These virtues, which depend upon motives beginning and ending with this visible system, are not the immortal part of virtue; these are not the soul or substance of it; these are but the husks and coats, the outer surrounding and integuments of that inner goodness which is the property of the individual being alone. There emerge, in all generations and in all ages, out of the mass which is formed and moulded by the outer world, with all its virtues and its motives, men whose character springs out of some fountain within; out of a hope, a faith of some kind, which does not belong to them as mere members of human society, but which they find implanted within them. The virtue which springs out of this root is hardy; not like the goodness which feeds upon mundane motives, and is weak and sickly in proportion to the pampering nature of its nourishment; this virtue is strong, and this virtue will found the future society. If this world did not contain now the elements of a perfectly virtuous society, how could we possibly believe that there would be such a society? The very idea of it would be a fiction and a dream. But these individual characters are the elements of it. If it be asked indeed, what is it which supplies these individual characters—from what great deep arise these lesser fountains—that is a question beyond us. The foundations of character as of other things are hid from us. The wind bloweth where it listeth, and thou hearest the sound thereof, but canst not tell whence it cometh. We know as a fact, however, that these characters do rise up; that a good society is forming in the world; that there are the rudiments here of the kingdom of God. Our Lord at His Advent separated these virtuous manifestations from those of a mundane foundation. This virtue, therefore, will live, and live for ever. So do we see a vigorous blade spring out of its seed;—the dead and rotten parts fall off on all sides of it; it shoots up; it pushes its way higher; it emerges; it rises to the top; it cuts the upper air and exults in the light of day.

ETERNAL LIFE.

ROMANS VIII. 24.

"*For we are saved by hope: but hope that is seen is not hope: for what a man seeth, why doth he yet hope for.*"

ONE of the most remarkable combinations which this age has produced, is an Atheism which professes a sublime morality. We have been accustomed to connect Atheism with immorality and licentiousness; but here the coalition is in theory dissolved. The ethics indeed are simply borrowed from Christianity; and it is always easy for the originator of a new philosophy to plaster any amount of high morals upon it, which he finds ready made for him. He can endow his philosophy with all the virtues under the sun, just as a writer of fiction can make the characters that represent his favourite school as good as he pleases. Nothing whatever is proved as to what Atheism naturally bears as a root and principle. We can conceive indeed — though the experiment has never been tried—a civil community of Atheists; for men do not value this life the less because they do not believe in another, and the instinct of self preservation penetrating the body would dictate the coercion of crime. But whatever was done with *crime*, the absence of the powerful motives of religious fear and hope must give an advantage to *vice*; and as for the highest moral spirit—this is really but one with the religious; and Atheism is wanting in the very ideas which are essential to this—the ideas of sin; of repentance; of humility which requires the transference of the source of good out of ourselves; of sanctity and awe which point to a Higher Being. And for morality again you must have affections, and for affections you must have beings, and Atheism does not provide beings. The beings it provides are not substances and spirits. Can you love phenomena? Nature is moved indeed, and a spirit half volatile and half melancholy breathes in light classic poetry toward all vanishing being even upon the sympathetic ground of a common transciency; but love by its very law tends toward a substance; it wants the solemnity of eternal being; it wants a beyond, and no being that is without this beyond can duly answer to it as an object. Atheistic morals, therefore, must always be stunted morals.

It is, however, this combination in the Comtist philosophy, which has given it the position it has got; because a great number of people in every age, whether they do or do not express the want accurately to themselves, *do* want morality without religion. It is a great desideratum. There is this great distinction between the two things; the moral notion is an actual *fact* of our nature, almost like a physical fact; it is plain and palpable; everybody praises and blames with reference to it; it is a part of the very world in which we are. But religion is not a fact but a vision; though a vision of which reason augurs the fulfilment. There are then always numbers who accept the fact but not the vision; nay, who would fain develop the fact and carry it into high forms of life, for moral goodness is an actual sensation which they enjoy and need; but who still cannot accept conceptions which take them so much out of this world, as those of religion do.

This then has been the great exploit of the new philosophy. People cast aside its frivolities and affectations, its ceremonial, its rites, its commemorations, its scholasticism and its pedantry—they passed over all its fantastic rules and particularities, to seize what was really the kernel of it, what was really powerful in it, what was to the point—viz., morality without religion. Atheism had lain under the stigma of licentiousness, but now that it had freed itself from this connection, and become moral, it gave the morality which was wanted,—free from the encumbrance and the tie of obnoxious ideas. This was the combination then in the system which took hold of men. It was caught at because there was a want felt for it; though the influence of the new type was not nearly so large in the shape of actual discipleship as it was in its oblique effects, or in certain modifications of religious ideas in numbers of ordinary believers. It is one of the remarkable concomitants of the erection of any great infidel position, that it issues in numberless shades and gradations of unbelief in Christians. Does a great theory come out which rejects any world but this one;

—the invisible world begins to present itself as a vanishing point to numbers of minds; they shrink from any truths which are specially connected with it; they feel a kind of awkwardness, an uncomfortableness, a shyness in their presence: an offence and stumbling-block lurks in any conception which is not part of this conscious life; religion is glorious and grand, but has not even religion itself after all a very good fulfilment here? They prefer the outer erections which have grown around a doctrine to the doctrine itself, which is a troublesome visitor if it ever comes into their minds and demands to be treated as an inward truth; in that capacity it receives a very frigid welcome. They will aid actively any machinery for setting in motion the high morals of Christianity; but activity is not the Gospel's sole test. It requires faith too. It speaks of much work, and work which we know was not mere formal and ceremonial, but real work,—active strong work,—as dross; as dead works which had physical vivacity but not the breath of heaven in them. Activity is naturally at first sight our one test of faith—what else should it spring from, we say: and yet experience corrects this natural assumption; for active men can be active almost about anything, and amongst other things about a religion in which they do not believe. They can throw themselves into public machinery, and the bustle of crowds, when if two were left together to make their confession of faith to each other they would feel awkward. But there is something flat, after all, in the activities of men, who *accommodate* themselves to the Gospel;

whereas, take but a fragment of true action, anywhere, in one who *believes* in it, and it captivates us; this has soul; it is tested by the interest with which we cherish the image of it; whereas there is nothing which so little interests us as soulless earnestness, ardour without faith.

But though this philosophy has one strong powerful idea in it, when we come to its argument we are struck with the very little there is which has any direct weight or force against the Christian position; while in morals, the only discovery which it has made in pretended advance of Christianity is so absurd and fantastic that it would have been much to the credit of the system to have kept it back. It has undoubtedly struck a great blow; it has produced an extraordinary reaction in many quarters against the solemn verdict of the collective reason of mankind for the existence of a God and a Future State; though rebounds against the established positions of human reason are by no means not to be expected at times—they take place even in politics and science. But how has this reaction arisen? From any rational argument? No. It has arisen from the fact that in a vast number of minds a future state, is an idea rather than a belief. A future state is like the future of this life, an image or picture in the mind, though there is this great difference in the two pictorial futures, that I believe mechanically in the one, but as for the other —. I can raise the *idea* perfectly easily, there is no resistance, it comes at my summons: but will the idea ever be a reality? Well, enlightened reason says that it will, and produces a *belief*; still multitudes hold it as a mere idea or picture; the reasons for the truth, which are founded in our spiritual nature, not being realised. Consequently the idea, not being backed by its reasons, is held upon such a tenure, that at any moment the discovery may be made to such minds that the idea in their case is no more than an idea—a picture. Suppose then a great infidel philosopher to spring up, a man armed with all the powers of argument and language; he suddenly turns round upon all these persons, and looks them in the face with the question—Do you really believe in this idea? Examine it, he says, is it not a mere idea? a mere image that you have raised, or that has been raised for you? Where is this heaven that you talk about? Is it above your head? is it beneath your feet? Do you seriously think that if you were to go millions of miles in any quarter of the compass you would find it? Is it anywhere in all space? and if not, *what* is its *where?* Is there another world besides the whole world? When thus suddenly challenged, then, what can such minds do? The secret is out, and the disclosure is made to them that the idea *in them* is only an idea. The world to come disappears in a moment like a phantom; the reign of the apparition is over, and a dream is dispelled. It is the unbelieving counterpart of conversion; a man awakens in conversion to the reality of the invisible world; here he awakens to the nonentity of it.

But while this great concussion has been produced by the force of mere impression and by a sudden shock, there is not one argumentative blow struck by this philosophy against Christianity. Its ground is that

Religion has not scientific evidence; and with that as an argument it begins and ends. But who ever said that religion *had* scientific evidence? Scripture indeed, if we did say so, would be the first to rebuke us; it rests the very excellence of the temper which accepts religion upon its being a temper which does not require sight; sight meaning either physical or demonstrative certainty. "We are saved by hope," says St. Paul, "but hope that is seen is not hope." This is the great contrast which runs through the New Testament. Indeed, scientific proof is just what, in the very nature of the case, religion does not admit of. What we mean by scientific proof is the verification by event or experiment of some calculation or reasoning, or interpretation of facts which has pointed to some particular conclusion, but not as yet actually reached it. Before this verification there is a direction in which things plainly go, a disposition of facts our way, but there is only probability; after, and by this verification, there is certainty. In practical life, *e.g.*, when we argue from circumstances that something has taken place or will take place, the event is the test of the truth of our reasoning, or the scientific evidence of it. And in physical science experiment is the scientific proof. To have scientific proof then of a future state, is to have found out, by having died and actually passed into that state, and felt yourself in it, that the reasoning on which you had previously in life expected and looked forward to that state, was correct reasoning, and that you had made a true prophecy. But this proof, in the nature of the case, we cannot have now.

The Comtist argument, therefore, begins and ends with something which is altogether irrelevant as regards the Christian evidence, and which does not even come into contact with it. There is, however, an assumption lying hid under this charge—that religion has not scientific evidence—viz., that no evidence which is not scientific is of any value; which undoubtedly *has* a strong bearing upon the Christian evidence. And therefore the scientific evidence of religion not being the question, what we do join issue upon is the nature of the evidence which is *not* scientific—the nature of the evidence which precedes and as yet awaits verification. Is all evidence in this previous stage valueless? Let us see.

What then is, in the reason of the case, the very nature and scope of all probable evidence? Is it not to direct our persuasion and belief toward some end which is not yet ascertained, and which therefore we do not actually know. Indeed, had we to wait for the verification of the evidence before we used it, we should be in the most extraordinary dilemma; because we should have to wait till an event had happened before we could calculate on its happening, and depend on certainty as a preliminary stage of probability. The only likely future would be an ascertained past; we could only foresee what *had* occurred, and only look forward correctly by looking backwards. We should have no prospective evidence, but what was subsequent to knowledge. Probable reasoning, therefore, is in its own nature unverified reasoning; it *ipso facto* wants the fulfilment of experiment; it is therefore unscientific evidence: and yet it is capable of producing rational belief. Every fresh concurrence of circumstances is a ground upon which we reason, and upon which we predict, infer, conclude something which is not mathematically contained in those circumstances, but to which they point. This ever new, fresh, living, ceaseless flow of interpretation and construction, which almost makes up life, is not knowledge, because its very nature is to be a substitute for knowledge; we reason toward a thing *because* we do not know it; and yet it is not blind guess-work: there is evidence in it: it produces belief. Those who will not recognise evidence apart from knowledge, who will not see reason as belief only, who reduce all that is not certainty to pure ignorance, and divide the realm of mind into demonstration and darkness, must have expunged from their understandings the obligation to attend to facts. There is something between certainty and nothing,—what we call belief; which has more or less of the effect of knowledge, and yet is separated by a whole chasm from it. This intermediate state of mind may be a stumbling-block to a philosopher who argues from the abstraction, or *word* knowledge, that there must be either wholly knowledge or wholly not knowledge; and it may look like a contradiction to him to know or not to know at once; but it is our reason in actual operation,—in practice.

The evidence, then—to take that branch of religious doctrine—for a future state is of this kind; that is to say, like all other probable evidence, it awaits verification; but yet, prior to verification, it is evidence.

It is, like all other probable reasoning, an interpretation of facts, only facts of inward consciousness instead of facts of outward life. It would be absurd to say that the inward world of our minds, with all its remarkable contents, cannot be reasoned from because it is inward and not outward; because it is not gained by the senses but by reflection. We observe then, first, what the facts *are* about ourselves—viz., to begin with, that our bodies are not *we*,—not our proper persons; indeed, to say that they were would be to say that one thing was another thing: next, that we have a moral nature; and so on—and then from these facts we draw the argument we do; we interpret them; we say in what direction they point—viz., to our immortality. Nor does it make any difference if you call these facts impressions. Impressions are facts; that we seem to ourselves to see such facts about ourselves is a fact. I reason then upon these facts, as I should upon facts of natural history.

It is in philosophy, then, as it is in the world;— the most visibly flourishing and busy department, that which can boast the newest discoveries, shoves the others out of sight, and the great prosperity of the Inductive Sciences has had the effect of driving into the background this whole inward ground of reason for a future life, under the name of metaphysics; which is regarded as an old obsolete species of reasoning, curious as a sample of former workings of the human mind, but still a mere quaint technical structure of abstractions, a kind of legal fiction, a reasoning *sui generis*, different from all other kinds of reasoning, and applied to the soul and nothing else : and called metaphysics to distinguish it from anything which has to do with reality and truth. But, in truth, in this inward ground of reason for a future life we are using no separate or isolated species of reasoning at all; we are simply, as we do in ordinary life or in nature, interpreting facts; I should rather say, *fact;* interpreting the one great fact that we are what we are. The argument for the continuance of the soul's existence may be expanded indefinitely, and the chain of reasoning lengthened out and boundlessly illustrated by analogies, but the substance of it is contained in the one fact that we are ourselves. This one fact links us with immortality. Nor have I anything to do here with the question, how came I to be what I am ?—the question of my physical genealogy as a human being. How I come to be what I am I know not. I have not the least idea of the mode of my original, and if I should investigate it for ages I should find myself looking at a dead wall. But, whatever that be, the fact of my consciousness remains the same; this is an actual existing present fact and premiss, which is not affected in the smallest degree by these curious researches backward : I am what I am : and that I am what I am is the argument for my immortality.

There is one great distinction, indeed, between the current probabilities of life and the expectation of a future state. The probabilities of life pass in rapid succession into their state of either verification or falsification ; they do not for the most part keep us long waiting ; when it is evening, we say it will be fair weather, for the sky is red; and in the morning, we say it will be foul weather for the sky is red and lowering; the morning soon fulfils or refutes the presage of the evening, and the evening soon fulfils or refutes the prognostic of the morning. It is the same with respect to the transactions of life. Every day and hour brings its collocation of facts, from which we infer something, and the next day or hour brings the event which decides whether that inference was right. The decision at any rate comes some time, it may be months or years. The same scene of action which brought the rational expectation brings also the event which tests and verifies the correctness of it. But the great prophecy of reason has not yet received its verification. A future life is not proved by experiment. Generation after generation have gone to their graves, looking for the morning of the resurrection; the travellers have all gone with their faces set eastward, and their eyes turned to that eternal shore upon which the voyage of life will land them. But from that shore there is no return; none come back to tell us the result of the journey; there is no report, no communication made from the world they have arrived at. No voice reaches us from all the myriads of the dead, to announce that the expectation is fulfilled, and that experiment has ratified the argument for immortality. Between us and them there is a great gulf fixed, which all indeed do cross that go *from hence*, but which none can pass that would come from thence. The fact of a life to come still holds back, and remains in reserve. Thus, while a quick current of verifications passes by us on the physical side, on our spiritual side there stands motionless one great unverified prophecy from birth to death; it spans in one arch the whole of life, and one pier rests on the eternal shore. On one side of our road the objects move with rapidity past us, on the other all stands still. All points in one direction; but the great interpretation, the marvellous anticipation, still awaits the crown of experiment. Even the historical evidence, however strong, of a Resurrection which has taken place, comes, in its bearing upon our own faith, under this law.

It will be said, then, that this is an extraordinary stretch of the principle of probable evidence; to call upon us to trust it without its test; that is, it will be said, to trust in a shadow; to act for a whole life upon an expectation which will never be experimentally decided here; to go on to the last upon an unfinished argument, which breaks off in the middle. But we do take this unverified evidence in this world, in every department. As practical men, as scientific men, we trust it—to what degree depends upon the degree of the evidence. If facts look very strongly one way, we believe that look—*before* it is verified—*till* it is falsified. And if this look holds good for a day, it holds good for a life; it is valid till it is disproved: even if we carry it away with us at the last, an unfulfilled forecast. It leaves this world with all the strength and force that it ever had. This is a development indeed, an expansion, but not a strain of the principle of probable evidence. There comes a point in the course of every great principle, when it takes a leap; when it passes from a confined mode of application, in which it is connected with certain particulars, and people think it can only act in that circumscribed connection, into a large and full action. This is often seen in mechanics. Then, when it has taken this stride, it looks to many who have only seen it with its old particulars, and only know it in its old shape, as if it would break down, as if it would not bear the strain upon it. But it can; and what looks like a strain upon it is only the full development and pure application of the principle. It acts with a plenitude with which it did not act before. In general probable evidence acts within limited ranges, and with a succession of short prospects; but in the religious application, the principle all at once lengthens its range and bridges over a life; it summons man to wait, and gird himself to a long trial, before the final experiment; to a lifelong repose in an expectation; to an argument which never concludes; and to an act of interpretation which never stops. But is the interpretation a blind guess in consequence? No more than any other construction of facts, which may be the most convincing. Even in physical and scientific discoveries, how long has the stage of probability often staid? How long has the test of experimental success been postponed? But in these cases had that evidence which preceded that verification no weight? It produced often, even before it had that coping-stone, thorough conviction. The philosopher felt practically certain of his conclusion; he knew he could not be far wrong.

I am aware I shall be met with the distinction
F

that in practical life probable evidence only raises a provisionary belief; that being obliged to act some way or other, we act upon the best evidence there is, but that it is only tentative action; not, so to speak, action of certainty. Upon all physical subject matter, it will be said the law of belief is that it never exceeds the evidence upon which it rests, but keeps exact pace with it, and this law issues not in a complete conviction, but in, at the least, a favourable conjecture: whereas in our use of probable evidence in religion, our belief exceeds the premiss, and upon a ground of probability we raise acts of certainty; we found religious language; we found prayer, praise,—public and private; churches, institutions, rites, and ceremonies, orders of ministry, preaching, sacraments, and the Catholic Church. How can you raise this whole fabric, it will be said, upon a probability? Supposing the correctness of your principles had been verified by the most stringent test of experiment, and it were strictly scientific evidence that you had got, what more could you do than what you have done now? You would only then pray, build churches, practise rites of worship. What greater acts of certainty will you do in heaven? Previous, then, to the test of experiment, and while your evidence is in the antecedent and unverified stage, to do all this is plainly to exceed your premisses; while at the same time every step that you *do* advance beyond them is without a ground to rest on.

So does rigid science sometimes talk: but I apprehend it would be very difficult to show that practical certainty was never founded upon a premiss of probability. It would, *e.g.*, be an extraordinary assertion to make, that there were no historical questions which were fully decided. But what is the kind of evidence by which these questions are decided? It is what we call circumstantial evidence; that is, when there is a certain quantity of coincidence in the facts of the case, which is only explained by one particular hypothesis, which is therefore adopted as the true conclusion. But such evidence as this in the nature of the case wants the final verification; because there is in every instance an abstract possibility of a solution by some other explanation different from this one. These questions then are decided upon evidence of which no ultimate test can be got; and yet are not many practically completely decided? Or what are we to say to the judgments of our criminal courts? We take away a man's life—upon what evidence? Circumstantial: it wants then the final verification: it is therefore unscientific; it can therefore, upon this theory of evidence, only justify tentative acts. But it would be very difficult to say that to deprive a man of life was a tentative act: it is certainly a final act as relates to the individual; it supposes and can only be justified by complete practical certainty in the jury or representative of society. Every single verdict in our courts of justice upon circumstantial evidence is a conclusion which theoretically exceeds the evidence; some other supposition is in the abstract possible, as an explanation of the facts; they are therefore unscientific, untested conclusions; and yet it would be absurd to deny that in multitudes of cases no one has the slightest doubt about them. It would be endless to pursue this subject through all the instances. Does the most certain evidence from testimony correspond to the test of science, and not want the final verification? Even in science itself is there not often a certainty which precedes the scientific; the natural philosopher is practically assured from the concurrence of data before him, of a result, before the ultimate test is got? Whatever may be urged then in the abstract against the excess of belief over evidence, as a matter of fact life and history are full of undoubted conclusions based upon this excess. How can history justify its assertions, how can society explain its acts, except upon the principle of this advance? Do we then in religion advance upon our evidence? Do we found prayer, worship, institutions, upon premisses which yet await final verification? We do no more than what the world itself does; *it* advances upon its premisses. Religion and the world both do the same thing; they look at reason as it exists in fact, and not as it exists in abstract conception. It is the same trial of evidence which both use; only it is called good evidence when it serves society, and no evidence when it serves religion. In matter of fact there is such a thing as reasonable certainty which is not scientific certainty. There can be evidence which even in the stage of probability cannot practically be distinguished from certain. And this may meet the objection of those who would not regard probability as adequately expressing the proof of immortality, which they would call an intuitive conviction. Under probability all evidence comes which is short of demonstration, and which is capable of being strengthened by verification, as this intuitive conviction, however strong, must be.

What then, if the great prophecy of Reason has not yet received its verification; if the interpretation of the facts of mind wants as yet the final touchstone of experiment; a future state has still been incorporated in our reason. The mind of man looking into itself, has gone from that investigation with a certainty of its destiny as the result. This translation to a higher state has entered into his very idea of humanity, and become part of the very portrait of man to himself: take this destiny away from him, and he becomes at once another being to himself. What name, therefore, are we to give this bold reaction against the belief in a future state, but an apostasy from reason. It is the abandonment of the great prediction of reason, of the great verdict and conclusion of reason upon the facts of consciousness. It is the recantation, the retraction of the great hope of humanity, which reason has built upon the premiss of humanity. Suppose for a moment that this exception to human belief were the rule, *i.e.*, suppose the whole of humanity without this anticipation in it, untenanted by this prospect,—what an appalling abortion, what an entombment of mind, should we have! What a terrible extinction of the lamp of truth! What a spectacle of a blind immured reason! What a spectacle of death! When reason itself has opened a view into immortality, to put up contentedly with annihilation,— what a dreadful stupefaction of the human spirit! This horrible materialist indifference to the extinction of our being, this taking up with it as the natural end of man, What are we to call it? It is the lapse of human nature. It is a fall. This low apathetic insensibility to the continuance of his being, is the recurrence to an animal nature. The race continues indeed: and what is that to me, if I perish? And if to-morrow I am not, what am I to-day.

It is indeed true that this philosophy which shuts man up in life, and makes him a being coinciding with this life, does reflect and carry out Nature in a certain part of her;—that it can extract a sort of authorisation from her, viewed partially; and appeal to a sense in which it represents nature. I will explain.

Nature does undoubtedly in a sense make life an enclosure. There is a peculiar machinery in her by which we are guarded against the naked effect of the perpetual foresight of death. This world must be kept going, and it is necessary for its being kept going, that man should be provided with a shield of instinct, to modify this prescience of reason; otherwise, were there no barrier against the full piercing force of rational foresight, the approach of death would paralyse him, would benumb his faculties and crush his energies. He would be prostrated; he could not possibly keep up his interest in this world and its affairs, especially as he advanced in the journey of life. But it is essential, for the very working of the system, that man should be able to keep up his interest in it, and devote his attention to it. There is therefore a secret machinery in nature which makes him able to do so, by interposing an instinctive enclosure in the very sense of life. He is mechanically, as it were, disabled from realising the prospect of an end in all its keenness; and life includes and bounds him, resisting even in idea any contradiction to itself. The effect of this secret contrivance in the structure of our minds is to station us in the present. I do not refer here to the power which mere sensual pleasure has of engulphing us in the vulgar sensation of physical life, but to a much finer and more subtle power appended to life itself, whereby, as long as it lasts, it grasps hold of us, and encircles us; being up to the last a future and a prospect, as well as a present. So successful indeed is the art of nature, that even when under some agony of mind, and extreme disgust with life, men try to realise the end of it, as a consolation to benumb the pain of the present moment, they find that they cannot by all their efforts do it; they may say—Oh mihi tum quam mollita ossa quiescant; but life is life still, and they cannot extricate themselves from its embraces. Nature provides with a marvellous cunning for her own conservation, and contrives that her structure should never at any moment fail; but that, when pure reason would appal and prostrate, then should be introduced a special instinct to counteract it. Meantime the foresight of reason is not deadened, but only softened; there is an interim provided during which the religious view of death can work in the mind calmly, without being forced and extorted by its naked approach.

The mechanism in nature then which was primarily designed for good, man can use for evil; he can apply what was only intended as a mitigation to stupefy and harden; he can abandon himself to those instincts, and if he does he can succeed in drugging the prescience of reason, in relieving himself from the sense of futurity and obtaining a complete absorption in this life. He does not then stand in need of religious hope; he can do without it; life is his whole; life is made perpetual by the view of its end being cut off. Yielding himself up to this management of nature, he grows and expands as a member of this world; he pursues success, and does not feel its transciency, because life is boundless to him till it closes, and endless till it ends; it is an imaginary immortality which encloses him in sevenfold security, even while he stands upon its very last edge. Death does not affect his situation in the least to himself; it is a word to him; he knows the word, but the meaning is hidden from him; so thick a veil of physical instinct wraps him round, and intercepts the rational foresight. And lastly, imagination completes the work of enclosure by creating a future life which is only the reflection of the present. Even the heathen poet saw that the common mind did not really apprehend and embrace what was so contrary to experience as an end, —a total termination of connection with this world; he saw that it only realised things going on, and not their stopping; and that the end which it did embrace was a counterfeit;—non sincerum sonat; that it was the idea of an end which was not an end,—of a life which still somehow continued as a reflection of itself.

The evening light reveals the real landscape, though it may reveal it dimly; while the mirror in the full blaze of light only shows us a reflection of ourselves, and the scene in which we are. The modest light of faith discloses a real future life. But there is a deceptive future life, which is only a man throwing forward into the darkness of futurity an image of himself here, with his reputation, his credit, his success, his position, the tokens of his favour and the symbols of his pride; a mock eternity, which is only the reflection in the mirror—only life after it is over made to go on again.

The philosophy then before us may call itself, in a sense, a copy of nature. That is to say, it raises itself upon these instincts in nature. It takes the enclosure which natural instinct makes of life, and which man uses practically to imbed himself in life, wrapping even futurity in it; and it converts it into the formal doctrine of a termination of existence and subjective immortality. It might be thought beforehand, how can the instinct of self-preservation allow a man to accept the doctrine of his own annihilation? How can he go on with such an end facing him? We leave off saying that he ought not, that he *can* is the difficulty. But nature, we have seen, solves the riddle. Comtism, however, represents a part of nature only, and a lower part; it falsifies and misrepresents the whole. It reflects the self-preservation and instincts of the system, and contradicts the reason of the individual. The prescient reason is at war with these physical instincts: it is sensible to the shock of the idea of annihilation, and resists it with its whole force as dreadful.

If, from the Comtist argument against Christianity, which is simply a tacit ignoring of probable evidence, we turn to the *moral* improvement and advance upon Christianity, we shall see that there too there is a conspicuous failure. Its argument, as we have seen, is a pure assumption; its moral improvement is a literal blunder and misapprehension. The Gospel says —Love thy neighbour as thyself; the new precept is, Love thy neighbour and not thyself—or Altruism, as it is called. Infidelity refines upon the religious moral standard, and gives itself credit for a higher moral sense. But the new precept is a simple mistake of one thing for another. One mode of self-love is a wrong relation to others,—a man pursuing his own advantage at the expense of others; another is the pure relation of a man to himself. By virtue of this relation he necessarily wishes his own good; the wish is included in his conscious existence, and is no more selfish in him than it is selfish in him to *be* himself. But the Comtist confounds these two acts, and takes the term selfish from its true application to a man's wrong relationship to others, to apply it to his naked relationship to himself. To take from under man, however, this fundamental relationship to himself, is not to raise him to a higher pinnacle of purity, but rather to fling human nature down a precipice and shatter it into fragments.

But this new precept is specially applied to a future state as a motive of action. What are you pursuing,

he says, in your look thither but your own advantage?
—there is nothing sublime in this motive.

Those, then, who thus degrade under the name
of selfishness, all those solemn feelings and profound
wishes that a man has respecting himself and what he
is to be, are arguing from a word. It relates to self,
they say, and is therefore selfish. But,—we would
ask of one who thus reasons,—when you come
to the *actual* in man, can you deny that there is
something excellent and lofty in his pursuing the good
of a distant and supernatural sphere, from which he is
divided by a whole gulf of being? Can you help yourself recognising a nobility in this reaching forward toward the happiness of an unseen world at the sacrifice
of the present, though it *is* his own happiness that he
aims at? Is it not something which you cannot help
morally admiring, though it is for himself that he
wishes? And if so, is not your argument from self
gone? You have been reasoning from a word, but
when it comes to the reality, your moral sense will not
allow you practically to call such a man a selfish man.
You confess that under certain circumstances there is
something high in the pursuit of one's own good; and
what is real, what is fact, shoves aside what is verbal
and abstract. It must be observed that even with
respect to this world, the power of acting for a distant
object, of realising distant good, and reaching forward
to it over an intervening period of labour, has something moral in it. The will acts freely when the
object is remote, not by compulsion; and therefore
the inward energy of the man is more tested, and a

higher act of self-exertion is produced. The stimulus of immediate reward, or of immediate necessity, is a slavish motive to action; it acts as a constraining force from without, and the will plays a servile part in acting upon it. But the distance of an end raises the rank of the labour undergone for it. And though in mixed human character a part òf conduct, moral in itself, may have its morality reversed, by its being made subordinate to, and the instrument of, an immoral and vile part of the man which is nearer to himself, such an objection cannot apply to the pursuit of a distant supernatural good. In the case of such an aim, at the cost of present prizes, an admiration of it is an instinctive emotion which you cannot repress, it rises up in you before any philosophical doubt can intercept it. The facts of our nature disprove the argument from words; when we look at the actual thing in human conduct, it captivates us. Dismiss words then. This respect to self and its ultimate good pertains to the very nobility of man's nature; without which all the moral solidity of his character would evaporate, nature would be unmoored and drift away from its anchorage.

For it is forgotten, in this charge of self-interestedness against the motive of a future life, that this motive is not only a desire for our happiness, but a desire at the same time for our own higher goodness. The two wishes are essentially bound up together in the Christian doctrine of a future state, as not only a continuation of existence, not only an improvement in the circumstances of existence, but as an ascent of existence. In the Christian doctrine of a future state we have this remarkable conjunction, that the real belief in the doctrine goes together with, and is fastened to the moral sublimity of the state. In the Pagan doctrine both of these were absent; the life itself was poor, shadowy, and sepulchral, on the one hand; and the belief in it was feeble and volatile on the other; in the Christian doctrine both are present together, the glorious nature of life itself, and the reality of the belief in it. The reason is that no ground lays firm hold on our minds for a continuation of existence at all, except such a ground as makes that continuation an ascent. The prolongation of it, and the rise in the scale of it, go together; because the true belief is, in its very nature, an aspiration, and not a mere level expectation of the mind; and therefore, while a low eternity obtained no credit, the Gospel doctrine inspired a strong conviction, because it dared to introduce the element of glory into the destiny of man.

The Christian confessor and martyr, then, who gave up this world to obtain the glory of the next, was, according to the new philosophers, selfish; he aimed at his own gratification : " he should have learnt," say they " from another school, the true spirit of self-abandonment. Behold the genuine confessor, the authentic martyr; we keep the good of this solid material world indeed, but all our interest in heaven we unreservedly surrender : we give it up without a murmur: ours is the very romance of self-sacrifice which has left the Gospel standard far behind ;—the last discovery of moral progress." This may be said, but who, except a disciple of this new law, could ever suppose that self-interestedness showed itself in pursuing the distant vision, and self-abandoning generosity in grasping the present fact; who else could really think that future state, which was itself moral, immoral as a motive and object.

But, in the next place, there is an error at the very root of the description of the desire for immortality given by this school; it is represented as being a different affection altogether from what it really is, in being represented as a desire for one's-self only. This is a false description of it, as we should say of any physical instinct which was wrongly described in a book of natural philosophy. The two desires, for one's own and others' immortality, are in fact bound up with each other, in one affection, and make but one affection between them. This affection is essentially not a lonely one; no human being ever desired a future life for himself alone; he wants it for all for whom he entertains an affection here, all the good whom he has known, or whom he has only heard of.

Let us see then. This philosophy allows us and exhorts us to take pleasure in a subjective immortality — which is practically posthumous reputation. But how does the morality of posthumous reputation, as a motive, stand? It might be said, indeed—a man in contemplating his own greatness after death, contemplates a fact, in which, when it comes, he will have no interest whatever; because he will not be alive to take pleasure in it; the opinion about him will exist in the minds of others, but will his dead body know it? One who did not examine, then, might say, there is nothing self-interested in the desire for posthumous glory; whereas he will be interested in future happiness when he has it; and therefore *that* desire is a self-interested one. But this would be a most deceptive comparison. Is a man, because he will have no interest in posthumous fame, *when it comes*, therefore free from any motive of self-interestedness *now* in desiring it? No: the future fact which he puts before him acts by enhancing his own present existence, and magnifying himself to himself *at the moment;* he regards himself as filling so much of the world's space; and though part of this space is beyond the confines of his own life; still that he *will* fill so much space in the future raises his own estimate of himself *now*. The motive of posthumous greatness has thus its secret root in the present; the greatness flows backward from a fictitious and delusive seat in the future, to its real home in present life and consciousness. The current, which appears to flow onward and forward into posterity, is returning all the time by a side channel to the living man, and is reabsorbed in the fountain-head of present self. The future prospect is a present exaltation.

Compare then, as a moral motive, the regard to this subjective immortality which this school sanctions, with the affection connected with a real immortality, which this school condemns. The motive of a posthumous reputation is like any other motive of self-interest; a good man may have it, because he is not denied the satisfaction of it, and a bad man may have it, and the most selfish egotism be the sole inspiration of the wish, because the wish centres upon the individual, the man's self. It is therefore a neutral motive. But the motive of a real immortality, as just described, cannot be defined so coldly; it demands a higher term, because it works essentially by the law of love. The Christian hope of immortality cannot be an egotistic hope, because the affection does not centre upon an individual; it is in its very essence social; love enters into its very composition, and it looks forward to a communion of good as its very end and goal. Every one indeed can test the scope of this affection; and even the deaths we read of, or those which only imagination pictures, bear witness to the same. When anything beautiful in human character takes its departure from the world, what is the first ejaculation of the human heart, but one for its immortality. Can it perish—the priceless treasure of this personal life. The survivor says no: such being must go on being. He pursues the sacred form through unimaginable worlds—even the bodily form; for even the body is spiritual so far as it is a manifestation of the personal being; and he feels that, though carried away and shrouded in the mist which encircles human existence, it is safe somewhere. Being therefore would find out being, the one left, the one gone, drawn toward it by the current which penetrates all the spiritual creation, and the desire of immortality is as much for another as for ourself. It is not a selfish instinct, it is not a neutral one, it is a moral and generous one. The individual desires the immortality, the perpetuation, the regeneration, the ascent and the glory of that human society with which he finds himself connected now, and aspires after membership with the great community in its state of exaltation. Christianity knows nothing of a hope of immortality for the individual alone, but only of a glorious hope for the individual in the Body, in the eternal society of the church triumphant.

THE REVERSAL OF HUMAN JUDGMENT.

MATTHEW XIX. 30.

"*Many that are first shall be last; and the last shall be first.*"

PERHAPS there is hardly any person of reflection to whom the thought has not occurred at times, of the final judgment turning out to be a great subversion of human estimates of men. Society forms its opinions of men, and places some on a high pinnacle; they are favourites with it, religious and moral favourites. Such judgments are a necessary and proper part of the present state of things; they are so, quite independently of the question whether they are true or not; it is proper that there should be this sort of expression of the voice of the day; the world is not nothing, because it is transient; it must judge and speak upon such evidence as it has, and is capable of seeing. Therefore those characters of men are by all means to be respected by us, as members of this world; they have their place, they are part of the system. But does the idea strike us of some enormous subversion of human judgments in the next world; some vast rectification to realise which now, even if we could, would not be good for us? Such an idea would not be without support from some of those characteristic prophetic sayings of our Lord, which, like the slanting strokes of the sun's rays across the clouds, throw forward a track of mysterious light athwart the darkness of the future. Such is that saying in which a shadow of the Eternal Judgment seems to come over us—"Many that are first shall be last; and the last shall be first." It is impossible to read this saying without an understanding that it was intended to throw an element of wholesome scepticism into the present estimate of human character, and to check the idolatry of the human heart which lifts up its favourites with as much of self-complacency as of enthusiasm, and in its worship of others flatters itself.

Indeed, this language of Scripture, which speaks of the subversion of human judgments in another world, comes in connection with another language with which it most remarkably fits in, language which speaks very decidedly of a great deception of human judgments in this world. It is observable that the Gospel prophecy of the earthly future of Christianity is hardly what we should have expected it beforehand to be; there is a great absence of brightness in it; the sky is overcast with clouds, and birds of evil omen fly to and fro; there is an agitation of the air, as if dark elements were at work in it; or it is as if a fog rose up before our eyes, and treacherous lights were moving to and fro in it, which we could not trust. Prophecy would fain presage auspiciously, but as soon as she casts her eye forward, her note saddens, and the chords issue in melancholy and sinister cadences which depress the hearer's mind. And what is the burden of her strain? It is this. As soon as ever Christianity is cast into the world to begin its history, that moment there begins a great deception. It is a pervading thought in Gospel prophecy—the extraordinary capacity for deceiving and being deceived that would arise under the Gospel; it is spoken of as something peculiar in the world. There are to be false Christs and false prophets, false signs and wonders; many that will come in Christ's name, saying, I am Christ, and deceive many; so that it is the parting admonition of Christ to His disciples—"Take heed, lest any man deceive you"—as if that would be the great danger. And this great quantity of deception was to culminate in that One in whom all power of signs and lying wonders should reside, even that Antichrist, who as God should sit in the temple of God, showing himself that he is God. Thus before the true Christ was known to the world, the prophecy of the false one was implanted deep in the heart of Christianity.

When we come to the explanation of this mass of deception as it applies to the Christian society, and the conduct of Christians, we find that it consists of a great growth of specious and showy effects, which will in fact issue out of Christianity, not implying sterling goodness. Christianity will act as a great excitement to human nature, it will communicate a great impulse, it will move and stir man's feelings and intellect; this impulse will issue in a great variety of high gifts and activities, much zeal and ardour. But this brilliant manifestation will be to a large extent lacking in the substance of the Christian character. It will be a great show. That is to say, there will be underneath it the deceitful human heart—the natura callida, as Thomas à Kempis calls it, quæ se semper pro fine habet. We have even in the early Christian Church that specious display of gifts which put aside as secondary the more solid part of religion, and which St. Paul had so strongly to check. Gospel prophecy goes remarkably in this direction, as to what Christianity would do in the world; that it would not only bring out the truth of human nature, but would, like some powerful alchemy, elicit and extract the falsehood of it; that it would not only develope what was sincere and sterling in man, but what was counterfeit in him too. Not that Christianity favours falsehood, any more than the Law favoured sin because it brought out sin. The Law, as St. Paul says, brought out sin *because* it was spiritual, and forced sin to be sin against light. So in the case of Christianity. If a very high, pure, and heart-searching religion is brought into contact with a corrupt nature, the nature grasps at the greatness of the religion, but will not give up itself; yet to unite the two requires a self-deception the more subtle and potent in proportion to the purity of the religion. And certainly, comparing the hypocrisy of the Christian with that of the old world, we see that the one was a weak production in comparison with the other, which is indeed a very powerful creation; throwing itself into feeling and language with an astonishing freedom and elasticity, and possessing wonderful spring and largeness.

There is, however, one very remarkable utterance of our Lord Himself upon this subject, which deserves special attention. "Many will say to me in that day, Lord, Lord, have we not prophesied in Thy name, and in Thy name cast out devils, and in Thy name done many wonderful works? And then will I profess unto them, I never knew you." Now this is a very remarkable prophecy, for one reason, that in the very first start of Christianity, upon the very threshold of its entrance into the world, it looks *through* its success and universal reception, into an ulterior result of that victory—a counterfeit profession of it. It sees before the first nakedness of its birth is over, a prosperous and flourishing religion, which it is worth while for others to pay homage to, because it reflects credit on its champions. Our Lord anticipates the time when active zeal for Himself will be no guarantee. And we may observe the difference between Christ and human founders. The latter are too glad of any zeal in their favour, to examine very strictly the tone and quality of it. They grasp at it at once; not so our Lord. He does not want it even for Himself, unless it is pure in the individual. But this statement of our Lord's is principally important, as being a prophecy relating to the earthly future of Christianity. It places before us public religious leaders, men of influence in the religious world, who spread and push forward by gifts of eloquence and powers of mind, the truths of His religion, whom yet He will not accept, because of a secret corruptness in the aim and spirit with which they did their work. The prophecy puts before us the fact of a great deal of work being done in the Church, and outwardly good and zealous work, upon the same motive in substance, upon which worldly men do their work in the world; and stamps it as the activity of corrupt nature. The rejection of this class of religious workers is complete, although they have been, as the language itself declares, forward and active for spiritual objects, and not only had them on their lips.

Here then we have a remarkable subversion of human judgments in the next world foretold by our Lord Himself; for those men certainly come forward with established religious characters to which they appeal; they have no doubt of their position in God's kingdom, and they speak with the air of men whose claims have been acquiesced in by others, and by numbers. And thus a false Christian growth is looked to in Gospel prophecy, which will be able to meet even the religious tests of the current day, and sustain its pretensions, but which will not satisfy the tests of the last day.

We are then perhaps at first sight surprised at the sternness of their sentence, and are ready to say with the trembling disciple—"Who then shall be saved?" But when we reflect upon it, we shall see that it is not more than what meets the case; *i.e.*, that we know of sources of error in the estimate of human character which will account for great mistakes being made; which mistakes will have to be rectified.

One source of mistake then is, that while the Gospel keeps to one point in its classification of men, —viz., the motive, by which alone it decides their character, the mass of men in fact find it difficult to do so. They have not that firm hold of the moral idea which prevents them from wandering from it, and being diverted by irrelevant considerations, they think of the spirituality of a man as belonging to the department to which he is attached, the profession he makes, the subject matter he works upon, the habitual language he has to use. The sphere of these men, of whom the estimate was to be finally reversed, was a religious one,— viz., the Church, and this was a remarkable prop to them. Now, with respect to this, it must be observed that the Church is undoubtedly in its design a spiritual society, but it is also a society of this world as well; and it depends upon the inward motive of a man whether it is to him a spiritual society or a worldly one. The Church as soon as ever it is embodied in a visible collection or society of men, who bring into it human nature, with human influences, regards, points of view, estimates, aims, and objects—I say the Church, from the moment it thus embodies itself in a human society, *is* the world. Individual souls in it convert into reality the high professed principles of the Body, but the active stock of motives in it are the motives of human nature. Can the visible Church indeed afford to do without these motives? Of course it cannot. It must do its work by means of these to a great extent, just as the world does its work. Religion itself is beautiful and heavenly, but the machinery for it is very like the machinery for anything else. I speak of the apparatus for conducting and administering the visible system of it. Is not the machinery for all causes and objects much the same, communication with others, management, contrivance, combination, adaptation of means to end? Religion then is itself a painful struggle, but religious machinery provides as pleasant a form of activity as any other machinery possesses; and it calls forth and exercises much the same kind of talents and gifts that the machinery of any other department does, that of a government office, or a public institution, or a large business. The Church as a part of the world must have active-minded persons to conduct its policy and affairs; which persons must, by their very situation, connect themselves with spiritual subjects, as being the subjects of the society; they must express spiritual joys, hopes, and fears, apprehensions, troubles, trials, aims, and wishes. These are topics which belong to the Church as a department. A religious society then, or religious sphere of action, or religious sphere of subjects, is irrelevant as regards the spirituality of the individual person, which is a matter of inward motive.

To take an instance of a motive of this world. Statesmen and leaders of political parties may of course act upon a spiritual motive in their work, and have done so; viz., the single desire to do good in the sphere of God's temporal providence; and the motive of their work may stand on a perfect equality with that of winning souls; nevertheless the world's great men do often act upon a known class of secondary motives. Dismissing then the grosser and coarser class of selfish aims, which conspicuously and glaringly put the religious and secular worker on a level, so far as they adopt them, let us take that absorbing frailty, which sometimes figures as a virtue. You see in the case of a political man all the action of life, all its vital energy gathering round himself, and accumulating into a kind of egotistic capital, which is advancing and growing, as life and action go on—a representation of the man to himself, which goes by the name of greatness or glory; an ever accompanying mirror into which he looks for his stimulus and inspiration. This great abstraction, this reflection and adumbration of himself, as it magnifies, becomes his one measure, it gives the worth to everything he does; whatever swells the bulk of this colossal impersonation is valuable, whatever does not is indifferent to him. It wholly empties and depopulates the simple and pure region of motive, until it stands alone within the man, draining all the freshness of his spirit, and drying up the sap of nature, till he only feels one wish which can speak to him. Everything is grudged which does not feed this fount. Natural interests die, even the impress of personal attachments fades away; whatever is outside the central impulse is in the way; he does not want it, he can do without it; everything else is only instrumental to this one devouring end. If this great phantom which represents himself is growing, all is right; it *must* be growing to the last; it is a duty, the first of duties, the sum of all duty, the final cause of his being, and his conscience is pricked if he misses any opportunity of an accession to this mystic treasury, this chamber of imagery within him. Nor is the fault only one of gigantic minds; we may see that even ordinary men are sometimes taken up with creating a smaller sample of this personification. But what substantial difference is there in this class of motives as they act upon a religious leader, and as they act upon a political leader? The former, if he is of an ambitious mind, has the *same kind of* ambition that the other has; he wants success, and the spread of his own principles and his own following is his success. Is there not as much human glory in the brilliant summit of religious proselytism, as in the triumph of a certain set of political principles? Is it not a temporal, an earthly, and a worldly reward to be called Rabbi, Rabbi? Christ said it was. If then one of the great critics of man could speak of "the muddy source of the lustre of public actions," the scrutiny may be carried as well to a religious as a political sphere. The truth is, wherever there is action, effort, aim at certain objects and ends;—wherever the flame of human energy mounts up; all this may gather either round a centre of pure and unselfish desire, or round a centre of egotism; and no superiority in the subject of the work can prevent the lapse into the inferior motive. In the most different fields of objects this may be the same: it is a quality of the individual. Whatever he does, if there is a degeneracy in the temper of his mind, it all collects and gathers, by a false direction which it receives from the false centre of attraction, *round himself.* The subject or cause which a man takes up makes no difference. The religious leader can feel, alike with the political, and as strongly, this lower source of inspiration; can be accompanied by this idolised representation of self, this mirror in which he sees himself growing and expanding in life's area. Are the keen relish for success, the spirit which kindles at human praise, and the gusts of triumph—the feelings which accompany action upon a theatre, guaranteed no place in a man, by his having religious zeal? These are parts of human nature, and it is not zeal but something else which purifies human nature. So far as religion only supplies a man of keen earthly susceptibilities, and desire of a place in the world, with a subject or an arena, so far that man stands on the same ground with a politician who is stimulated by this aim. They are the same identical type of men in different spheres. There is a conventional difference between them, but there is one moral heading. Both may be doing valuable work, important service in a public sense; but if you do not think the politician a spiritual man because he is a useful man, no more must you think the active man in the religious sphere to be so. Spirituality belongs to the motive.

There is a great common stock of secondary motives then, of lower stimulus and incentive, in the religious and secular worker, which feeds their efforts, keeps them up to the mark, and supplies them with strength and power. But there is this difference between the two, in the action of these motives. Worldly passions tend to be made deeper and keener in those who by their place and profession are obliged to disavow and to disguise them. So in Joshua's punishment of Achan, or in St. Peter's punishment of Ananias and Sapphira, regard doubtless was had to the secrecy of the vice in both cases,—avarice. The avarice was stronger, more corrosive, because it was under disguise; the disguise of a high profession; in the one case of a soldier of God, fighting in a sacred war; in the other case of a convert, just admitted into the kingdom of Heaven upon earth. So in the case of ambition; it is a deeper and stronger vice, as a *concealed* vice; it gains *force* by suppression; that *kind* of suppression which is not a moral conquest of it, but only an outward cover. Thus, in a soldier, or a lawyer, or one who has embarked on any worldly calling, there is less danger in it, for the very reason that it is open and avowed; it is a recognised motive; omnia vitia in aperto leviora, as Seneca says; but when it exists under the special profession of religion, and a religion of humility, and has to be cloaked; not only is there the fault of concealment, but the vice itself is more intense by the concealment. It is a law of our nature that it should be. The passion obliged to act under a disguise, becomes different in its nature from the open one; gains a more morbid strength, and corrupts the character. And thus the ambition of the clerical order has always been attended by peculiarly repulsive features, which have been discriminated by the moral sense of mankind.

It must be observed, however, that the Gospel has, with that penetration which belongs to it, extended the province and field of human pride from direct self, to self, as indirectly touched and affected by the success of party, or school, or cause. We see this extension of the signification of the vice implied in Christ's denunciation of the proselytism of the Pharisees,—that they compassed heaven and earth to make one disciple: because if pride only applied to what exalted a man's self directly or personally, the Pharisee might have replied—"I have no private interest in the propagation of the doctrines of my school; it is no profit to myself personally; I only devote myself to it because the propagation of religious truth, or that which we believe to be such, is a duty, and if we value our own belief we must be animated by the wish to impart it to others. We must be zealous in winning over others to our own sect, provided we believe in the creed and principles of our sect, which we show we do by belonging to it." The Pharisee might have said this; but our Lord saw in the Pharisee an aim which was not selfish in a direct sense; but which still indirectly, and on that account not the less strongly, touched the proud self of the Pharisee. His rebuke recognises and proclaims a relation to truth itself in man, which may be a selfish one. It was a new teaching, a disclosure beneath the surface. Truth is an article of tangible value, it gives conscious rank to its possessors, it gives them the position of success in the highest department—viz., that of the reason and judgment; while to miss getting it is failure in that department. Man can thus fight for truth as a piece of property, not upon a generous principle, but because his idea of truth—the correctness or falsity of that idea—tests his own victory or failure. And his way of fighting for it is spreading it. Its gaining ground, its being embraced by numbers, ratifies his own decision.

Thus a selfish appreciation of truth, and not the motive of charity only, is able to lead to efforts for its propagation; and there is such a thing as corrupt proselytism, the eager desire to get hold of other minds representing the false relations to truth, and not the simple and disinterested ones. Proselytising pharisaism is the first shadow of that great manifestation of the tyrannical aspect of truth, or man's idea of truth which afterwards became so terrible a distortion of Christianity. Deep concern for human souls would never have produced spiritual despotism or persecution; it was a selfish relation to truth to begin with which produced these; it was the lapse of the human heart from charity to pride in the matter. The vindictive punishment of error did not arise from the sense of value of truth, but from men holding truth, or their idea of it, as a selfish treasure; contrary opinions threatened their hold of this treasure: its forced acceptance rooted them in possession of it. The propagation of truth became the pride of dominion over souls.

One would not of course exclude from the sphere of religion the motive of *esprit de corps:* it is undoubtedly a great stimulus, and in its measure is consistent with all simplicity and singleness of heart; but in an intense form, when the individual is absorbed in a blind obedience to a body, it corrupts the quality of religion; it ensnares the man in a kind of self-interest; and he sees in the success of the body the reflection of himself. It becomes an egotistic motive. There has been certainly an immense produce from it; but the type of religion it has produced is a deflection from simplicity; it may possess striking and powerful qualities, but it is not like the free religion of the heart; and there is that difference between the two, which there is between what comes from a second-hand source and from the fountain head. It has not that naturalness (in the highest sense) which alone gives beauty to religion.

Again, those who feel that they have a mission may convert it into a snare to themselves. Doubtless, if, according to St. Paul, "he who desireth the office of a bishop desireth a good work," so one who has a mission to do some particular work has a good office given him. Still, where life is too prominently regarded in this light, the view of life as a mission tends to supersede the view of it as trial and probation. The mission becomes the final cause of life. The generality may be born to do their duty in that station of life in which it has pleased God to call them; but in their own case the mission overtops and puts into the shade the general purpose of life as probation; the generality are sent into the world for their own moral benefit, but they are rather sent into the world for the benefit of that world itself. The outward object with its display and machinery is apt to reduce to a kind of insignificance the inward individual end of life. It appears small and commonplace. The success of their own individual probation is assumed in embarking upon the larger work, as the less is included in the greater; it figures as a preliminary in their eyes, which may be taken for granted; it appears an easy thing to them to save their own souls, a thing so to speak for anybody to do.

What has been dwelt upon hitherto as a source of false magnifying and exaltation of human character, has been the invisibility of men's motives. But let us take another source of mistake in human judgment.

Nothing is easier, when we take gifts of the intellect and imagination in the abstract, than to see that these do not constitute moral goodness. This is indeed a mere truism; and yet, in the concrete, it is impossible not to see how nearly they border upon counting as such; to what advantage they set off any moral good there may be in a man; sometimes even supplying the absence of real good with what looks extremely like it. On paper these mental gifts are a mere string of terms; we see exactly what these terms denote, and we cannot mistake it for something else. It is plain that eloquence, imagination, poetical talent, are no more moral goodness than riches are, or than health and strength are, or than noble birth is. We know that bad men have possessed them just as much as good men. Nevertheless, take them in actual life, in the actual effect and impression they make, as they express a man's best moods and highest perceptions and feelings, and what a wonderful likeness and image of what is moral do they produce. Think of the effect of refined power of expression, of a keen and vivid imagination as applied to the illustration and enrichment of moral subjects,—to bringing out, *e.g.*, with the whole force of intellectual sympathy, the delicate and high regions of character,—does not one who can do this seem to have all the goodness which he expresses? And it is quite possible he may have; but this does not prove it.

There is nothing more in this than the faculty of imagination and intellectual appreciation of moral things. There enters thus unavoidably often into a great religious reputation a good deal which is not religion but power.

Let us take the character which St. Paul draws. It is difficult to believe that one who had the tongue of men and of angels would not be able to persuade the world that he himself was extraordinarily good. Rather it is part of the fascination of the gift, that the grace of it is reflected in the possessor. But St. Paul gives him, besides thrilling speech which masters men's spirits and carries them away, those profound depths of imagination which still and solemnise them; which lead them to the edge of the unseen world, and excite the sense of the awful and supernatural; he has the understanding of all mysteries. And again, knowledge unfolds all its stores to him, with which to illustrate and enrich spiritual truths. Let one then, so wonderful in mental gifts, combine them with the utmost fervour, with boundless faith, before which everything gives way; boundless zeal, ready to make even splendid sacrifices; has there been any age in which such a man would have been set down as sounding and empty? St. Paul could see that such a man might yet be without the true substance—goodness; and that all his gifts could not guarantee it to him; but to the mass his own eloquence would interpret him, the gifts would carry the day, and the brilliant partial virtues would disguise the absence of the general grace of love.

Gifts of intellect and imagination, poetical power,

and the like, are indeed in themselves a department of worldly prosperity. It is a very narrow view of prosperity that it consists only in having property; a certain kind of gifts are just as much worldly prosperity as riches; nor are they less so if they belong to a religious man, any more than riches are less prosperity because a religious man is rich. We call these gifts worldly prosperity, because they are in themselves a great advantage, and create success, influence, credit, and all which man so much values; and at the same time they are not moral goodness, because the most corrupt men may have them.

But even the gifts of outward fortune themselves have much of the effect of gifts of mind in having the semblance of something moral. They set off what goodness a man has to such immense advantage, and heighten the effect of it. Take some well-disposed person, and suppose him suddenly to be left an enormous fortune, he would feel himself immediately so much better a man. He would seem to himself to become suddenly endowed with a new large heartedness and benevolence. He would picture himself the generous patron, the large dispenser of charity, the promoter of all good in the world. The power to become such would look like a new disposition. And in the eyes of others too, his goodness would appear to have taken a fresh start. Even serious piety is recognised more as such; it is brought out and placed in high relief, when connected with outward advantages; and so the gifts of fortune become a kind of moral addition to a man.

Action then, on a large scale, and the overpowering effect of great gifts, are what produce, in a great degree, what we call the canonization of men—the popular judgment which sets them up morally and spiritually upon the pinnacle of the temple, and which professes to be a forestalment, through the mouth of the Church or of religious society, of the final judgment. How decisive is the world's, and, not less confident, the visible Church's note of praise. It is just that trumpet note which does not bear a doubt. How it is trusted! With what certainty it speaks! How large a part of the world's and Church's voice is praise! It is an immense and ceaseless volume of utterance. And by all means let man praise man, and not do it grudgingly either; let there be an echo of that vast action which goes on in the world, provided we only speak of what we know. But if we begin to speak of what we do not know, and which only a higher judgment can decide, we are going beyond our province. On this question we are like men who are deciding irreversibly on some matter in which everything depends upon one element in the case, which element they cannot get at. We appear to know a great deal of one another, and yet if we reflect, what a vast system of secrecy the moral world is. How low down in a man sometimes (not always) lies the fundamental motive which sways his life? But this is what everything depends on. Is it an unspiritual motive? Is there some keen passion connected with this world at the bottom? Then it corrupts the whole body of action. There is a good deal of prominent religion then, which keeps up its character, even when this motive betrays itself; great gifts fortify it, and people do not see because they will not. But at any rate there is a vast quantity of religious position which has this one great point undecided beneath it; and we know of tremendous dangers to which it is exposed. Action upon a theatre may doubtless be as simple-minded action as any other; it has often been; it has been often even childlike action; the apostles acted on a theatre; they were a spectacle to men and to angels. Still what dangers in a spiritual point of view does it ordinarily include—dangers to simplicity, inward probity, sincerity! How does action on this scale and of this kind seem, notwithstanding its religious object, to pass over people not touching one of their faults, leaving—more than their infirmities—the dark veins of evil in their character as fixed as ever. How will persons sacrifice themselves to their objects? They would benefit the world, it would appear, at their own moral expense; but this is a kind of generosity which is perilous policy for the soul, and is indeed the very mint in which the great mass of false spiritual coinage is made.

On the other hand, while the open theatre of spiritual power and energy is so accessible to corrupt motives, which, though undermining its truthfulness, leave standing all the brilliance of the outer manifestation; let it be considered what a strength and power of goodness may be accumulating in unseen quarters. The way in which man bears temptation is what decides his character; yet how secret is the system of temptation? Who knows what is going on? What the real ordeal has been? What its issue was? So with respect to the trial of griefs and sorrows, the world is again a system of secrecy. There is something particularly penetrating, and which strikes home in those disappointments which are specially not extraordinary, and make no show. What comes naturally and as a part of our situation has a probing force, grander strokes have not; there is a solemnity and stateliness in these, but the blow which is nearest to common life gets the stronger hold. Is there any particular event which seems to have, if we may say so, a kind of malice in it which provokes the manichean feeling in our nature, it is something which we should have a difficulty in making appear to any one else, any special trial. Compared with this inner grasp of some stroke of Providence, voluntary sacrifice stands outside of us. After all the self-made trial is a poor disciplinarian weapon; there is a subtle masterly irritant and provoking point in the genuine natural trial, and in the natural crossness of events, which the artificial thing cannot manage; we can no more make our trials than we can make our feelings. In this way moderate deprivations are in some cases more difficult to bear than extreme ones. "I can bear total obscurity," says Pascal, "well enough; what disgusts me is semi-obscurity; I can make an idol of the whole, but no great merit of the half." And so it is often the case that what we *must* do as simply right, and, which would not strike even ourselves, and still less anybody else, is just the hardest thing to do. A work of supererogation would be much easier. All this points in the direction of great work going on under common outsides where it is not noticed; it hints at a secret sphere of growth and progress; and as such it is an augury and presage of a harvest which may come some day suddenly to light, which human judgments had not counted on.

It is upon such a train of thought as this which has been passing through our minds, that we raise ourselves to the reception of that solemn sentence which Scripture has inscribed on the curtain which hangs down before the Judgment-Seat—"The first shall be last, and the last shall be first." The secrets of the tribunal are guarded, and yet a finger points which seems to say—"Beyond, in this direction, behind this veil, things are different from what you will have looked for."

Suppose, *e.g.*, any supernatural judge should appear in the world now, and it is evident that the scene he would create would be one to startle us; we should not soon be used to it; it would look strange; it would shock and appal; and that from no other cause than simply its reductions; that it presented characters stripped bare, denuded of what was irrelevant to goodness, and only with their moral substance left. The judge would take no cognisance of a rich imagination, power of language, poetical gifts and the like, in themselves, as parts of goodness, any more than he would of riches and prosperity; and the moral residuum left would appear perhaps a bare result. The first look of divine justice would strike us as injustice; it would be too pure a justice for us; we should be long in reconciling ourselves to it. Justice would appear, like the painter's gaunt skeleton of emblematic meaning, to be stalking through the world, smiting with attenuation luxuriating forms of virtue. Forms, changed from what we knew, would meet us, strange unaccustomed forms, and we should have to ask them who they were—" you were flourishing but a short while ago, what has happened to you now?" And the answer, if it spoke the truth, would be—" nothing, except that now, much which lately counted as goodness, counts as such no longer; we are tried by a new moral measure, out of which we issue different men; gifts which have figured as goodness remain as gifts, but cease to be goodness." Thus would the large sweep made of human canonisations act like blight or volcanic fire upon some rich landscape, converting the luxury of nature into a dried-up scene of bare stems and scorched vegetation.

So may the scrutiny of the last day, by discovering the irrelevant material in men's goodness, reduce to a shadow much exalted earthly character. Men are made up of professions, gifts, and talents, and also of themselves, but all so mixed together that we cannot separate one element from another; but another day must show what the moral substance is, and what is only the brightness and setting off of gifts. On the other hand, the same day may show where, though the setting off of gifts is less, the substance is more. If there will be reversal of human judgment for evil, there will be reversal of it for good too. The solid work which has gone on in secret, under common exteriors, will then spring into light, and come out in a glorious aspect. Do we not meet with surprises of this kind here, which look like auguries of a greater surprise in the next world, a surprise on a vast scale. Those who have lived under an exterior of rule, when they come to a trying moment sometimes disappoint us; they are not equal to the act required from them; because their forms of duty, whatever they are, have not touched in reality their deeper fault of character, meanness, or jealousy, or the like, but have left them where they were; they have gone on thinking themselves good because they did particular things, and used certain language, and adopted certain ways of thought, and have been utterly unconscious all the time of a corroding sin within them. On the other hand some one who did not promise much, comes out at a moment of trial strikingly and favourably. This is a surprise then which sometimes happens, nay, and sometimes a greater surprise still, when out of the eater comes forth meat, and out of a state of sin there springs the soul of virtue. The act of the thief on the cross is a surprise. Up to the time when he was judged he was a thief, and from a thief he became a saint. For even in the dark labyrinth of evil there are unexpected outlets; sin is established by habit in the man, but the good principle which is in him also, but kept down and suppressed, may be secretly growing too; it may be undermining it, and extracting the life and force from it. In this man then, sin becomes more and more, though holding its place by custom, an outside and coating, just as virtue does in the deteriorating man, till at last, by a sudden effort and the inspiration of an opportunity, the strong good casts off the weak crust of evil and comes out free. We witness a conversion.

But this is a large and mysterious subject—the foundation for high virtue to become apparent in a future world, which hardly rises up above the ground here. We cannot think of the enormous trial which is undergone in this world by vast masses without the thought also of some sublime fruit to come of it some day. True, it may not emerge from the struggle of bare endurance here, but has not the seed been sown? Think of the burden of toil and sorrow borne by the crowds of poor: we know that pain does not of itself make people good; but what we observe is, that even in those in whom the trial seems to do something, it yet seems such a failure. What inconstancy, violence, untruths! The pathos in it all moves you. What a tempest of character it is! And yet when such trial has been passed we involuntarily say—has not a foundation been laid? And so in the life of a soldier, what agonies must nature pass through in it. While the present result of such trial is so disappointing, so little seems to come of it! Yet we cannot think of what has been gone through by countless multitudes in war, of the dreadful altar of sacrifice, and the lingering victims, without the involuntary idea arising that in some, even of the irregular and undisciplined, the foundation of some great purification has been laid. We hear sometimes of single remarkable acts of virtue, which spring from minds in which there is not the habit of virtue. Such acts point to a foundation, a root of virtue in man, deeper than habit; they are sudden leaps which show an unseen spring in a man, which are able to compress in a moment the growth of years.

To conclude. The Gospel language throws doubt upon the final stability of much that passes current here with respect to character, upon established judgments, and the elevations of the outward sanctuary. It lays down a wholesome scepticism. We do not do justice to the spirit of the Gospel by making it enthusiastic simply, or even benevolent simply. It is sagacious, too. It is a book of judgment. Man is judged in it. Our Lord is judge. We cannot separate our Lord's divinity from His humanity; and yet we must be blind if we do not see a great judicial side of our Lord's human character;—that severe type of understanding, in relation to the worldly man, which has had its imperfect representation in great human minds. He was unspeakably benevolent, kind, compassionate; true, but He was a Judge. It was indeed of His very completeness as man that He should know man; and to know is to judge. He must be blind who, in the significant acts and sayings of our Lord, as they unroll themselves in the pregnant page of the Gospel, does not thus read His character; he sees it in that insight into pretensions, exposure of motives, laying bare of disguises; in the sayings—"Believe it not;" "Take heed that no man deceive you;" "Behold, I have told you;" in all that profoundness of reflection in regard to man, which great observing minds among mankind have shown, though accompanied by much of frailty, anger, impatience, or melancholy. His human character is not benevolence only; there is in it wise distrust—that moral sagacity which belongs to the perfection of man.

Now then, as has been said, this scepticism with regard to human character has, as a line of thought, had certain well-known representatives in great minds, who have discovered a root of selfishness in men's actions, have probed motives, extracted aims, and placed man before himself denuded and exposed; they judged him, and in the frigid sententiousness or the wild force of their utterances, we hear that of which we cannot but say—how true! But knowledge is a goad to those who have it; a disturbing power; a keenness which distorts; and in the light it gives it partly blinds also. The fault of these minds was that in exposing evil they did not really believe in goodness; goodness was to them but an airy ideal,—the dispirited echo of perplexed hearts,—returned to them from the rocks of the desert, without bearing hope with it. They had no genuine belief in any world which was different from theirs; they availed themselves of an ideal indeed to judge this world, and they could not have judged it without; for anything, whatever it is, is good, if we have no idea of anything better; and therefore the conception of a good world was necessary to judge the bad one. But the ideal held loose to their minds—not as anything to be substantiated, not as a type in which a real world was to be cast, not as anything of structural power, able to gather into it, form round it, and build up upon itself; not, in short, as anything of power at all, able to make anything, or do anything, but only like some fragrant scent in the air, which comes and goes, loses itself, returns again in faint breaths, and rises and falls in imperceptive waves. Such was goodness to these minds; it was a dream. But the Gospel distrust is not disbelief in goodness. It raises a great suspense indeed, it shows a curtain not yet drawn up, it checks weak enthusiasm, it appends a warning note to the pomp and flattery of human judgments, to the erection of idols; and points to a day of great reversal; a day of the Lord of Hosts; the day of pulling down and plucking up, of planting and building. But, together with the law of sin, the root of evil in the world, and the false goodness in it, it announces a fount of true natures; it tells us of a breath of Heaven of which we know not whence it cometh and whither it goeth; which inspires single individual hearts, that spring up here and there, and everywhere, like broken gleams of the Supreme Goodness. And it recognises in the renewed heart of man an instinct which can discern true goodness and distinguish it from false; a secret discrimination in the good by which they know the good. It does not therefore stand in the way of that natural and quiet reliance which we are designed by God to have in one another, and that trust in those whose hearts we know. "Wisdom is justified of her children;" "My sheep hear My voice, but a stranger will they not follow, for they know not the voice of strangers."

WAR.

MATTHEW XXIV. 7.

"*Nation shall rise against nation, and kingdom against kingdom.*"

THE relations of Christianity to war are certainly at first sight an extraordinary enigma. For what do we see? those who are spiritually one with another, and brethren in Christ, killing each other deliberately, on an immense scale, by weapons and engines which have been long and systematically improved with a view to the highest success in destruction; the contrivance of which indeed has strained to the very utmost the invention and ingenuity of Christians. Nor is this mutual slaughter, by the law of the Church, the slightest break in Christian union and fellowship; the Communion of the Church absolutely unites one side spiritually with the other. When then, having first looked upon Christians fighting one another with the eye of custom, taking it as a matter of course, wanting no explanation, we have suddenly become alive to the strangeness and startlingness of the fact; we then turn right round and forthwith suppose that there must be some very *extraordinary* explanation. But there is no other than an ordinary explanation to give.

The Christian recognition of the right of war was contained in Christianity's original recognition of *nations*, as constituting at the same time the division and the structure of the human world. Gathering up the whole world into one communion spiritually, the new universal society yet announced its coalescence with mankind's divisions politically; it was one body of one kind, in many bodies of another kind. It did not interfere with the established fabric of human society; its ancient inclosures, those formations of nature or events which collected mankind into separate masses, those great civil corporations into which mankind was distributed; in a word with *nations*; it gathered up into itself not only the unions but the chasms of the human race, all that separated as well as all that united; all that divided, and by dividing created variety and individuality in our human world. The nation was one of those wholes to which the individual man belonged, and of which he was a part and member; it existed prior to Christianity, and was admitted into it with other natural elements in us; Christians were from the outset members of States; and the Church could no more ignore the State than it could the family. And as one of those wholes to which the individual belonged, a sentiment and affection attached to it; Christianity admitted this sentiment; it gave room for national feeling, for patriotism, for that common bond which a common history creates, for loyalty, for pride in the grandeur of the nation's traditions, for joy in its success.

There is indeed a jealousy in some schools of

thought of this national sentiment, as belonging to members of the Church Catholic, as if it were a sentiment of nature which grace had obliterated; as if a universal spiritual society had left far behind such lower rudiments of humanity, and it were a mark of a relapse into heathenism to express any particular interest in your own country. The universal society claims the whole individual affection of the man; the Catholic has ceased to be patriotic, and become a citizen of the Church only. This is the idea; but just as there are no two more different landscapes than the same under altered skies; no two ideas are wider apart than the same under different circumstances for realising them. In Heaven, all is one spiritual society only; but here, if besides the Church there is the nation, the effacement of the national sentiment is an artificial and violent erasion of a fact of nature. We see all the difference in such a case between the vision of an angel and a fanatical or pedantic theory. It appears to belong to such theories to impoverish the minds which they absorb. Nature punishes with dryness the spirits that reject her; even their spiritual citizenship issues forth stamped with utter insipidity, a piece of the most technical, barren, and jejune mechanism.

The question, indeed, whether Christianity admits of the national sentiment is part of the general question whether Christianity adopts nature. To one class of zealous religious minds everything connected with nature has looked suspicious; poetry, art, philosophy, have not only had the taint of original evil which they bear, but they have only and simply appeared sinful. And to this view of them it has been replied that Christianity does not abolish, but purify and consecrate nature. Nature enriches, nay, makes the material which religion is to penetrate. Christianity is not a flame which burns in a pure vacuum and a void. The soul has natural feelings and affections for it to feed upon; as the rich unguents of the wood feed the flame. So with respect to the national sentiment. It is part of the great inheritance of nature. The nation is one of those natural wholes to which man belongs, as the family is another. He is annexed to it; and a sentiment arises out of that annexion. He belongs to it by the same great law of association, though in a further stage of it, upon which the tie of the family depends.

It may be said that the tie of country is not inculcated in the New Testament, which, on the other hand, everywhere speaks of us as members of the Church which it contemplates extending over the whole world. But if it does not expressly form an article of teaching in the New Testament, we still cannot argue from the omission as if it were rejection, and gather from the absence of direct injunction to it that it is obsolete under the Gospel. It must be observed that the argument of Hooker, by which he met the Puritan formula —that in the matter of Church order and ceremonial whatever was not enjoined in Scripture was wrong,— applies to the *ethics* of Scripture as well. Hooker said that Scripture, by leaving out, did not *condemn*, but only sent us back to the ground of reason and natural law. And to those who would argue that Scripture prohibited some affection, or sentiment, or bond, because it omitted the injunction of it, the answer is the same. The New Testament, *e. g.*, says very little about duties to equals, and enlarges upon duties to inferiors, upon charity, condescension, and compassion to the poor, the sick, and the afflicted. But we may not suppose from this that duties to equals are not very important duties, not even that they are not the more trying class of duties, and the most pregnant with discipline, and that the society of equals is not a more searching ordeal to the character than intercourse with the poor, who do not try our pride or challenge our jealousy. Nor may we suppose that if Scripture omits special injunctions to patriotism, it therefore cancels or prohibits it. It only sends us back to the law of nature and reason on this head.

The Christian Church then recognised and adopted nations, with their inherent rights; took them into her inclosure. But war is one of these rights, because under the division of mankind into distinct nations it becomes a necessity. Each of these is a centre to itself, without any amenableness to a common centre. Questions of right and justice must arise between these independent centres; these cannot be decided except by mutual agreement or force, and when one fails the other only remains — not that it necessarily settles questions rightly indeed, because it is force and not right which decides; but the right side makes the trial. In the act, then, of recognising and including within herself, nations, collecting within one spiritual area so many different independent political sources, the Christian Church necessarily admitted also war within her pale. Together with the nations there comes also within the Church the process of *national* settlement of questions — that which in nations corresponds to judicial proceedings between individuals—*i.e.*, war. For, if Christians only use, in resorting to it, a natural right, the use of this right does not exclude them from the Church; which is to say, that Christians fight each other in full spiritual communion. Such an issue the primitive Christian perhaps hardly foresaw; and could the veil of time have been lifted, and a European field of battle been shown him, he could hardly have believed the picture; but it is still the result of a natural right which Christianity had begun with admitting.

Christianity does not admit, indeed, but utterly denounces and condemns the motives which lead to war,—selfish ambition, rapacity, tyranny, and vanity; but the condemnation of one side is the justification of the other; these very motives give the right of resistance to one side. And, inasmuch as the Church has no authority to decide which is the right side,—is no judge of national questions or of national motives, not having been made by her Divine Founder a "judge or a divider" in this sphere, the Church cannot, in her ignorance, exclude the other side either. The Church therefore stands neutral, and takes in both sides; that is to say, both sides fight within the bond of Christian unity. She only contemplates war forensically, as a mode of settling national questions, which is justified by the want of any other mode.

This independence of nations is not of course the

ultimate account of war, which is human passion and misapprehension, but only an account of it as differing from the peaceable settlement of disputes between individuals.

'It must be observed that individuals are enabled to settle their disputes peaceably by the fact of being under a government. It is not that individuals are less pugnacious than nations, but they are differently circumstanced. Being under a government, they are obliged, if they do not voluntarily come to terms, to accept the arbitration of a court. Nobody supposes that the suitors for justice in our courts agree with the judge when he decides against them. They think him in error, but they submit because they are obliged. Every judgment of a court is backed by the whole force of the nation, as against the force of the individual who dissents. Individuals then are able to settle their disputes peaceably, because they are governed by the nation; but nations themselves are not governed by a power above them. This then is the original disadvantage under which nations are placed as regards the settlement of disputes; and in consequence of which, force takes the place of justice in that settlement. We are struck at the very first with the enormous, the almost incredible contrast between the mode in which individual disputes are decided, and that in which national disputes are; they appear hardly to belong to the same age, or to the same world; it is to appearance all the difference between civilisation and barbarism. And yet the whole difference springs from one distinction in the situation of the two,—that there is a government of individuals provided in the world, but not a government of nations. The aim of the nation in going to war is exactly the same as that of the individual in entering a court; it wants its rights, or what it alleges to be its rights; but it is not in the situation in which the individual is of being compelled by force to accept the decision of a judge upon them. For indeed a court of justice possesses, only in reserve, exactly the same identical force as that which exerts and demonstrates itself in war. It is one and the same force in principle; only in the court it is confessedly superior to all opposition, and therefore has not to make any demonstration of itself, *i.e.*, it acts peaceably. In war it has to make a demonstration, to come out, *i.e.* its action is warlike. It acts as a contending force; because it is only as a superior force that it is effective; and its superiority can only be proved by contention. It exists in its compressed form in the court, like the genius shut up in the chest in the eastern legend; in war it rises to a colossal height, like the same genius when let out. In civil government the force of final resort is a stationary force at the nation's centre; in war it is a moving and nomad force, going about the world, and showing itself by the proof of the event in battle, in whatever place the occasion may arise; but it is the same force in different circumstances.

It may be observed that such an account of war, as arising from the want of a government over the contending parties, applies in reality to civil wars as well as to national; only in the former case the headship over the contending parties has given way for a time; in the latter it never existed.

So far we have been dealing with wars of self-defence; but self-defence by no means exhausts the whole rationale of war. Self-defence stands in moral treatises as the formal hypothesis to which all justification of war is reduced; but this is applying a considerable strain to it. When we go further, we find that there is a spring in the very setting and framework of the world, whence movements are ever pushing up to the surface—movements for recasting more or less the national distribution of the world; for establishing fresh centres and forming States into new groups and combinations. Much of this is doubtless owing to the mere spirit of selfish conquest; for conquest as such is change and reconstruction; but conquest does not account for the whole of it. There is doubtless an instinctive reaching in nations and masses of people after alteration and readjustment, which has justice in it, and which rises from real needs. The arrangement does not suit as it stands; there is want of adaptation; there is confinement and pressure;—people kept away from each other that are made to be together; and parts separated that were made to join. Thus there is uneasiness in States, and an impulse rises up toward some new coalition; it is long an undergrowth of feeling, but at last it comes to the top, and takes steps for putting itself in force. Strong States then, it is true, are ready enough to assume the office of reconstructors, and yet we must admit there is sometimes a natural justice in these movements, and that they are instances of a real self-correcting process which is part of the constitution of the world, and which is coeval in root with the political structure which it remedies. They are an opening out of political nature, seeking relief and proper scope in new divisions; sometimes reactions in favour of older union, disturbed by later artificial division. In either case it is the framework of society forced by an inward impulse upon its own improvement and rectification. But such just needs when they arise must produce war; because a *status quo* is blind to new necessities, and does not think such an alteration to be for the better, but much for the worse. Then there are wars of progress; they do not belong to the strict head of wars of self-defence; but so far as they are really necessary for the due advantage of mankind and growth of society, they have a justification in that reason. And as Christianity at its commencement took up the national divisions of mankind, with war as a consequence contained in them, so it assumes this root of change and reconstruction with the same consequence—this fundamental tendency to re-settlement, this inherent corrective process in political nature.

It is this judicial character of war, and its lawful place in the world, as a mode of obtaining justice; it is the sacred and serious object, which *so far* attaches to war, which gives war its morality; and enables it to produce its solemnising type of character. For we should keep clear and distinguished in our minds the moral effects of war, and the physical. These are apt to be confounded under such expressions as the horrors of war. But the horrors of war are partly bodily torment and suffering, which are dreadful indeed, but dreadful as misery, not as sin. War is hateful as a physical scourge, like a pestilence or a famine; and again, it is hateful on account of the passions of those who originate it, and on account of the excesses in those who serve in it. But if we take the bad effects on those who serve in it by themselves—it is not impossible to exaggerate them, at least by comparison: for while war has its criminal side, peace is not innocent; and who can say that more sin is not committed every day in every capital of Europe than on the largest field of battle. We may observe in the New Testament an absence of all disparagement of the military life. It is treated as one of those callings which are necessary in the world, which supplies its own set of temptations, and its own form of discipline.

There is one side indeed of the moral character of war in special harmony with the Christian type—I refer to the spirit of sacrifice which is inherent in the very idea of the individual encountering death for the sake of the body to which he belongs. There is a mediatorial function which pervades the whole dispensation of God's natural providence, by which men have to suffer for each other, and one member of the human body has to bear the burden and participate in the grief of another. And it is this serious and sacred function which consecrates war. Without it, indeed, what would war be but carnage; with it, war displays in spite of its terrible features, a solemn morality. The devotion of the individual to the community stands before us in a form which, while it overwhelms and appals, strikes us with admiration. That the nation may rise the individual sinks into the abyss; he vanishes as a drop that waters the earth, yet he does not murmur; it is his function, it is his appointment, it is an end to which he is ordained; the member is bound to the body, the unit exists for the good of the whole. In a battle itself, a mass moves, advances, wins, and occupies without one look to its gaps; a remorseless identity carries it through it all; the whole is the same, while the parts disappear at every step; and the great unit moves on without a pause to its goal. So it is with the nation itself; before it is the glorified whole, and behind it are the strewn and scattered fragments everywhere upon the ground. The nation pursues its road to greatness, and to the individuals it only belongs to say, Ave Cæsar, morituri te salutant. Thus is history formed, thus do great States rise, and thus is national sentiment cemented. The whole wins at the cost of the members : and the life which is gone, and whose place knoweth it no more; that which is effaced and expunged from the tablet,—the vanishing, the perishing and lost, is the solid rock on which a nation is founded. Certainly one asks—what and who is this mighty enchantress, that can so chain the spirits of mankind, so fascinate, so transport them; that can claim such service, and impose such martyrdom? Is it anything tangible, visible? Can you see the nation, can you feel it? You cannot. It is all around you, but impalpable as the air; you cannot take hold of it; the individuals are there, but the whole eludes your grasp. The nation is nowhere,—an abstraction. It exists only in idea; but ideas are the strongest things in man; they bind him with irresistible force, and penetrate his affections with supreme subtlety.

War is thus elevated by sacrifice; by the mixed effect of glory and grief. There is in it that action just before death which so interests the human mind. All that a man does upon this extreme boundary of vision appeals to us; what he said, or did, how he looked, his expressions and signs upon the verge of that moment awaken our curiosity; it seems as if he were *in* another world, when he was so *near* one. So in war there is just that conflux of splendid action upon the very edge of life, which rouses curiosity and emotion; the figures move upon the extreme line of a shifting horizon, in another instant they are below it; yet the flame of energy mounts the highest upon the moment of the eclipse. There is a miraculous outbreak of power and will, which gathers all into a point; then all is over, and the man is gone. The old Saxon poet, though he deals with war of the rudest kind, though it is the storming of a mound, or battle of boats up some creek, is carried beyond himself in contemplating the superhuman energies with which life goes out; the action in which man vanishes from earth; and unable to express his emotion in words, fills up his blank intervals with inarticulate sounds, to serve as the signs of what is unutterable. It is true there is inspiration in numbers, in men acting at once and together; it is a marvellous prop to human nature. "The fear of death," says Montaigne, " is got rid of by dying in company; they are no longer astonished at it; they lament no longer." There is a strain in solitary action when a man is thrown upon himself, which is too much for him, fellowship in danger relieves it. And there is excitement doubtless in a crowd, an indefinite mass of human beings; it fills the mind; the spectacle is stirring and absorbing; and a crowd has this singular effect too, that so far from lessening the individual in his own eyes, which one would imagine before that it must do, on the contrary it magnifies him; he appends it to himself; he does not belong so much to it as it to him. Still though it is assisted nature which acts on these occasions, it is nature assisted by natural means. Thus have the scenes of war figured as a kind of supernatural borderland of action, in human sentiment; they have left an impress upon the memorials of the city and the field, and as associations and memories their place would be missed in the roll of the past; while the self sacrifice of war has also produced a class of virtues, which cannot well be spared in the portrait of man.

And as the individual fights *for* a whole, so he fights against a whole too: the hostile aim passes through the individual, as a mere necessary incident, to rest for its real object upon the impalpable generalisation of the nation, which disperses itself in the air, and defies our grasp. As respects the individuals it is simply a problem of force, which is working itself out, by means indeed of those individuals on each side as exponents, but wholly irrelevant of any regard to them as persons. It works itself out, just as an argument does, nor is there more hatred in force than there is in reasoning. It is a means to an end—that end being the establishment of a right, as the end of an argument is the establishment of a truth. Thus, take two hostile armies, and the total amount of anger is in almost spectral and unearthly contrast with the hideous mass of injury. It is like a tempest without a wind. The enmity is in the two wholes—the abstractions: the individuals are at peace.

But there is a sad counterpart of the self-sacrificing encounter of death on the part of the individual for the body,—the mere animal defiance of death. We know that man can, by custom and constant hardening, be at last rendered callous to the fear of death; but the result sometimes is, so far from a good one in man, a terrible and wild outburst of evil nature in him. So long as he was under the fear of death there was something to restrain him; there was something hanging over him; there was something before him which he dreaded; he was under a yoke and felt it; but when this last check is flung off, then he triumphs wildly in his freedom, and tramples upon law. This is the effect of the exultation of conquering the dread of death in the base and carnal heart; it lets the whole man loose; and in the rule of corruptio optimi pessima, just as the victory over the terror of death, in self-devotion produces the highest state of mind, so the mere animal conquest of it produces the lowest.

Is war to be regarded then as an accident of society,

which may some day be got rid of, or as something rooted in it? Imagination earnestly stretches forward to an epoch when war will cease; and first, it has been said that the progress of society will put an end to war. But, in the first place, human nature consists of such varied contents that it is very difficult to say that any one principle, such as what we call progress, can control it. Old feeling starts up again, when it was thought obsolete, and there is much that is wild and irregular in man, however we may think we have subjugated and tamed him. There is an outburst when we least expect it. "Canst thou draw out leviathan with a hook? will he make a covenant with thee? wilt thou take him for a servant for ever?" "I have never seen," says the great philosopher I have quoted, speaking of himself as the human creature, and with that roughness which is peculiar to him, "I have never seen," he says, "a more evident monster or miracle in the world than myself: a man grows familiar with all strange things by time and custom; but the more I visit and the better I know myself, the more does my deformity astonish me, and the less I understand of myself." Therefore the pretension of any one principle like that of material progress to control entirely this being, to make a covenant with him, and take him as a servant for ever, is on the very face of it an absurdity. But what are we to say when progress produces war, instead of stopping it? It is true that progress has stopped wars arising from that petty class of causes—court and family intrigues. So much popular power has done. But if progress stops war on one side, it makes it on another, and war is its instrument. Certainly it would be as easy to justify the crusades on the principle of self-defence, as it would be to justify two of the three great European wars of the last dozen years on that principle. They were wars of progress; wars of a natural reconstructing scope. So in the East war has been war of progress; forcing two empires that have shut themselves up, and excluded themselves from the society of mankind, out of their artificial imprisonment and insulation, and obliging them to come out into the world, and take at any rate some part and place in it.

But again, and principally—the progress of society doubtless increases by comparison the barbarous aspect of war as an instrument; but does it provide any other instrument by which nations can gain their rights? Any other process of obtaining justice, however rough this one may be, and however chance its verdicts?

The natural remedy for war then would appear to be a government of nations; but this would be nothing short of a universal empire, and can this be accomplished by any progress? It is indeed a physical improbability. The Church, indeed, in the Middle Ages put forth pretensions to this power; the Roman Empire was in its day an approach to it; and so are all large conquests in their degree, keeping the nations under them distinct, but only partially self-governing, and depending on a centre. Nor is the dream of a universal government or empire confined entirely to such shapes, or to such sources. Great popular causes, powerful tides of opinion, as they spread and advance over the world, tend to level the barriers of nations, to reduce patriotic sentiment, and to throw open the whole of human society into one vast area, in which the interests of collective humanity alone reign. The first French revolution was such a movement; it bound together the disciples of revolutionary philosophy all over the world, and tended to erect one immense brotherhood, whose common ground was stronger and more connecting than their differencing one; the union of ideas more forcible than the separation of country. At the present time that vast common fellowship, coextensive with the world—the great uniting bond of labour, man's universal yoke, has produced a move in a like direction; and even in Spain, which so long idolised its own blood, the International Operative Society proclaimed, upon the late question of the election to the throne, a total freedom from prejudice, and entire indifference to the distinction of nations, and whether their king was to be Spanish or a foreigner. But whatever approach may occasionally take place toward a relaxation of the national tie, the alternative is still an inexorable one between independent nations and a universal empire; and as a universal empire is impossible, the division of nations only remains. The waves of universalism can only dash themselves in vain against that rock; they cannot possibly shake the seat of distributed power and government; and by a fortunate necessity nations must ever form the barriers and breakwaters in that boundless ocean of humanity, which would otherwise drive with irresistible and wild force in the direction of particular great movements and ideas; they are the groins which divide the beach, whose whole immeasurable expanse of sands would otherwise crowd up into overwhelming piles and masses.

We thus fall back again upon independent States, which must decide their own rights, otherwise they are not full and integral States; they have not that autonomy, that freedom from all subordinateness to an authority above them, that self-sufficiency, which the peremptory logic of our well known statutes claims for them in the statement that "by divers old authentic histories and chronicles, it is manifestly declared and expressed that this kingdom of England is an empire, and so hath been accepted by the world, with plenary, whole, and entire power, authority, prerogative and jurisdiction, and final determination in all causes." But such states meet equal rights in other states, for the conflict of which no solution is provided but war.

The idea has risen up indeed at various times of a modification of the autonomy of States by the erection of a court of arbitration, which would be a universal government upon this particular point; but though no well guided State would disturb the world for secondary points, or refuse a neutral's judgment upon them, it is difficult to see how, upon a question vitally touching its own basis and safety, it could go upon any other sense of justice than its own. Take an individual, what a natural keen sense he has of the justice of his own case. How he is penetrated through and through with its grounds and reasons, into the full acquaintance with which he has grown gradually and naturally, having had time to see the facts in all their relations: An individual then certainly does accept the judgment of a neutral on his cause in the person of a judge, and surrender his own sense of the justice of his case; but he is compelled to do so. A nation is not compelled to do this; if it doubts then whether an indifferent spectator who would have to apply a hard, forced attention to its cause would do adequate justice to its rights, it is asking a great deal that it should give up its own judgment of its own rights to the judgment of that other. A nation knows it does justice to its own case; it cannot be sure that another will do so. It is not partiality to self alone upon which the idea is founded that you see your own cause best. There is an element of reason in this idea; your judgment even appeals to you, that you must grasp most completely *yourself* what is so near to you, what so intimately relates to you; what, by your situation, you have had such a power of searching into. The case is indeed something analogous to an individual surrendering his own moral judgment to another. He may do so if he is not certain; but if he feels certain it is almost a contradiction to do so.

It may be said, why may not a nation give up its rights on a principle of humility and generosity as the individual does? But to impose such humility as this on a nation would be to impose on it something quite different in ethical constitution from the same humility in an individual. An individual's abandonment of his rights is what the very words grammatically mean—the individual sacrificing himself; but a nation's abandonment of its rights means the individual sacrificing the nation; for the nation only acts through individuals. The individual is humble not for himself but for another, which is a very different thing.

It is thus that every prospect which the progress of society appears to open of eradicating war from the system of the world, closes as soon as we examine it. It may indeed be admitted that even under all the existing defects of the world's system, a great diminution of war might arise from an improvement in one particular in the public mind of nations; their judgment in estimating the strength of rival national causes and movements. In an age, *e.g.*, when the clouds of war gather round the cause of national concentration, the interested neighbour-state that is conscious its own relative greatness is challenged by it, should be able to calculate the strength of that cause and its susceptibility of resistance. We in this country, *e.g.*, have long had this measuring faculty with respect to the strength of our own internal public movements and causes; an acute sense of their growth, and when they reach a point at which they cannot be resisted; and thus civil war has been forestalled by opportune concession. Did such a subtle perception exist in nations with respect to the strength of these national causes outside of them, nations too could reasonably judge when these reached an irresistible strength; and so war would be forestalled between nations.

It is the lack of such a perception as this to which we may trace the cause of the recent terrible war close to our shores. In that case, on the one side there were the fragments of a mighty nation determined to reunite; and on the other side there was a splendid nation, accustomed to supremacy, resolved to prevent a combination which would challenge that proud position. But to stop that reunion was an impossibility; that reunion was rooted in the action of a century, in a whole age of gradual drawing close; it was too deeply fixed in the will of the people, had too strong a hold over their hearts; it had turned the point of resistance. Yet this was what the other nation did not see; one man alone saw it, and he was its Ruler. It came out afterwards, indeed, that even he had not the knowledge of particulars, but he had that intuitive judgment and fine balancing faculty which sometimes acts in its place. He stood upon the shore, and to his importuning subjects, who bid him order back the wave, replied that he could not. But his will was not equal to his penetration, he did what, a thousand times before him, the acute, the discriminating, and the philosophic have done, gave way to the impetuous and blind; and he had soon to retire from the uproar and conflict of empire, to meditate in solitude and isolation on the use of being wise.

But though nations may advance in judgment, what sign is there that the progress of society ever can alter the existing *plan of* the world, or rather want of plan, from which war comes—viz., a want of all head to the nations and states of the world,—that progress can give natural society a vertex which nature has not given?

Are we then, progress failing us, to look for a cessation of war from the side of Christianity? The question has often indeed been asked tauntingly, and it is a favourite fact which is called in evidence against revelation—why has not Christianity done away with war? But if an alteration in the system of the world would be necessary in order to stop war; if there is an irregularity in the structure of natural society, a void and hiatus in the fabric as it is—that is no deficiency which Christianity is required to correct. It is no part of the mission of Christianity to reconstruct the order of the world; that is not its task, or its function. It assumes the world's system and its want of system; its system as regards individuals, its unsystematic condition as regards nations; it does not profess to provide another world for us to live in. Yet this is the work which those in reality impose upon it who ask triumphantly, why has not Christianity stopped war? Progress has not done it, within whose sphere it rather is. Without indeed any correction of the structure of the world, a universal change in the temper of mankind would stop war. But Christianity is not remedial to the whole of human nature, but only to those hearts that receive it.

It might, indeed, as well be asked—why has not Christianity done away with civil government as carried on by force, and by the infliction of punishment, chains, and death? Yet we do not blame it for not having substituted love for compulsion here; and why should we blame it for not having done so in the case of nations. War and civil force are branches of one common stock, however wide apart in their mode of demonstration. Civil government with its sword is a kind of war with man; war, with its settlement of questions, is a kind of government of man. Can we indeed historically separate civil government and war, with reference to the ultimate basis of the force which each respectively applies? Civil government has practically arisen out of conquest, which collected the scattered fragments of human society together, bound together independent tribes, and congregated mankind in a sufficient mass to admit of it. And yet, though apparently war yields neither to the secular principle nor the religious, but keeps its place in the future obstinately, some go on thinking of this world as advancing to some indefinite state of perfection.

Prophecy indeed has foretold the time when nations should beat their swords into ploughshares, and their spears into pruning-hooks, when nation shall not lift up sword against nation, neither shall they learn war any more. But this total change pictured by the prophet does not in truth apply to war only; it applies just as much to the civil government of the world. He foresees a reign of universal love, when men will no longer act by terror and compulsion; but this is just as much against the chains and death of civil government as it is against war. Prophecy has two sides. On one side it says, a great renovation is coming, the slough of inveterate corruption will be cast off, peace and love will reign, and there will be no more war. On the other hand, prophecy says, it will always be the same—things will go on as they do —the world will not change; man will not cease to sin; iniquity will abound up to the very end; and there shall be wars; nation shall rise against nation, and kingdom against kingdom. Such are the two voices. Separately, the one is all vision, the other all matter of fact. But we cannot take these two prophecies separately; we must take them together; they are two sides of a whole. Prophecy speaks as a whole, of which the oppositions are interpretations. A kingdom of peace there will be; but when the prophet seems to associate this paradisal era with earth, then apparent prophecy is corrected by a later supplement. As we approach the Gospel time, the sublime and supernatural scene remains, but its locality alters. To the Jewish prophet earth was heaven; they mixed together in one landscape; but the two worlds under the Gospel light divided, and the visible was exchanged for the invisible, as the *place* of the prophetic realm of peace. With respect to this world, later or Gospel prophecy is, if one may so say, singularly unenthusiastic; it draws no sanguine picture, is in no ecstasy about humanity, speaks of no regeneration of society here; it uses the language of melancholy fact.

It was open to Christianity at starting to adopt and impose a higher law than the necessities of society allowed. Community of goods is better than the appropriation of them, and the renunciation of the sword better than the use of it, provided only these agree with the necessities of society. It was open, therefore, to Christianity to have prohibited property and war. But such a course would have been in the first place wrong, if we may so speak; because the higher law which is right if it agrees with the necessities of society, is wrong if it contradicts them; and in the next place, though a sect can afford to be arbitrary and exclusive, and to disown natural rights, Christianity, if it had done so, would have been abandoning its mission to embrace the world. There was therefore an inauguration of an era, a symbolical fragment, and expression by action of the law of love, in the shape of a passing scene of community of goods; but Christianity fundamentally assumed the right of property, and assumed the right of war. The right of property was open to the greatest abuses; the right of war was a great evil to prevent a greater; but they were *necessary*—absolutely necessary, therefore Christianity did not shrink from them.

But Christianity at the same time only sanctions war through the medium of natural society, and upon the hypothesis of a world at discord with herself. In her own world war would be impossible. And this mixture of Christianity with an alien hypothesis it is, which makes Christian war so portentous a fact—almost like a picture of Manichean dualism, in which the empire of light and darkness, order and confusion, spirit and matter, divine peace and self-conflicting uproar, coalesce in one creation. In Christian war, upon each one is the Holy Spirit's seal of peace, and on the mass wild nature's stamp of discord. It is indeed a humiliation, and we shrink back from it; but Christianity is obliged to act upon the assumption of that world which as a matter of fact exists, not upon the assumption of her own ideal world.

When Faustus, the Manichean, argued with Augustine for his own idea of Christianity against the Catholic one, he said in effect—I want to release Christianity from degrading alliances: *your* Gospel is too accommodating; it descends to the lowest connections, and rises upon the very rudest basis of the Jewish law and its low and sanguinary morality; rid Christianity of this coarse foundation, and shift it to a basis of sublime Magianism instead, and I will join you. What Faustus objected to was the actual junction in which the Divine Spirit of revelation in the Jewish law placed itself with the rudimental and coarse ideas of a rude age. But though Divine revelation might have come out as a pure ethereal flame, floating in air to feed some few fastidious spirits, and neglecting the mass, that was not its temper; and Augustine declined to change the Jewish for a sublime Magian foundation for Christianity.

Now the rights of natural society are not to be put upon a par with the rude ideas of early ages; still Christianity does undoubtedly drag an enormous weight with her in the adoption of these natural rights with their consequences. We speak of Christianity joining the world in the age of Constantine; but indeed, antecedently to any particular relations to courts or states, Christianity is weighted with human nature; is burdened by having to act upon an alien hypothesis; and has to admit within its pale a state of relationships full of dreadful disorder. Yet it stoops to conquer; it grapples with the coarse elements of human nature, descends to the dust with man, to raise him out of it; and accommodates its celestial birth to a worldly sojourn.

Lastly, Christianity comes as the consoler of the sufferings of war. The general only regards his men as masses, so much aggregate of force; he cannot afford to look at them in any other aspect; he has only two things to look at, the end and the means, he cannot pause between them to think of the life individual; it would carry him into interminable thought; it would be meditating as a sage, not acting; the idea is overwhelming, and it would paralyse him; he may admit it just for a moment, like Xerxes, but he must dismiss it instantly. No! force is all he has to do with; if he thinks of the persons he totters; if he pities, he is gone. But the Church takes up the mass exactly where he left off; at the units in it,—the persons. Every one of these had his hopes, his interests, his schemes, his prospects; but to some a wound, a loss of limb, in a moment altered all. Christianity comes to him as comforter, and shows how even that loss may be a gain. Every one of them has his home, where he is thought of, where he is somebody. If he has fallen, Christian hope alleviates the sorrow of that home. Thus the aspect of man as a mass was true for a purpose only, and false in itself. To some, to think of humanity as personal seems a dream and romance; that it is an aggregate, a whole, is the matter of fact; but to the Church this last is the dream, the first is the fact. Mankind is all mass to the human eye, and all individual to the Divine.

NATURE.

Psalm CIV. 1, 2.

"*Thou art become exceeding glorious; thou art clothed with majesty and honour. Thou deckest thyself with light as it were with a garment: and spreadest out the heavens like a curtain.*"

NATURE has two great revelations,—that of use and that of beauty; and the first thing we observe about these two characteristics of her is, that they are bound together, and tied to each other. It would not be true, indeed, to say that use was universally accompanied by beauty; still, upon that immense scale upon which nature is beautiful, it is beautiful by the self-same material and laws by which she is useful. The beauty of nature is not, as it were, a fortunate accident, which can be separated from her use; there is no difference in the tenure upon which these two characteristics stand; the beauty is just as much a part of nature as the use; they are only different aspects of the self-same facts. Take a gorgeous sunset; what is the substance of it? only a combination of atmospheric laws and laws of light and heat; the same laws by which we are enabled to live, see, and breathe. But the solid means of life constitute also a rich sight; the usefulness on one side is on the other beauty. It is not that the mechanism is painted over, in order to disguise the deformity of machinery, but the machinery is itself the painting; the useful laws compose the spectacle. All the colours of the landscape, the tints of spring and autumn, the hues of twilight and the dawn—all that might seem the superfluities of Nature, are only her most necessary operations under another view; her ornament is but another aspect of her work; and in the very act of labouring as a machine, she also sleeps as a picture. So in the sphere of space — the same lines which serve as the measure of distance, to regulate all our motions, also make the beauty of perspective.

But if the first thing we observe respecting use and beauty is, that they are united in their source, the next thing we observe is, that in themselves they are totally separate. These two effects of nature are as totally different and distinct facts as can be conceived. Who could possibly have told beforehand that those physical laws which fed us, clothed us, gave us breath and motion, the use of our organs, and all the means of life, would also create a picture? These two results are divided *toto cœlo* from each other. These laws go on employing themselves upon plain hard work, till we become suddenly alive to their throwing off, in this working, a magnificent spectacle, as if by some happy luck. We can, as spectators, abstract the picture from the mechanism. The picture does not feed us, clothe us, fill our lungs, nourish our nerves and centres of motion. Although the picture is a pure derivation from, although it is essentially united to, the working apparatus, it is a completely distinct conception from it. We see a surprising co-existence of two characters in nature, but we see no reason why they go together, why they should be bound to each other; and it seems to be a kind of duplication of the identity of nature, and a work of magic, as the same facts are metamorphosed from use into beauty, and *vice versa*. We have not the slightest conception of the common root in which these enormous diversities unite, the unity to which they mount up, the ultimate heading out of which both branch, the secret of their identity.

To go to the fact which has called out these remarks. It is worth observing, in the history of the mind of this country, the formation of a kind of passion for scenery and natural beauty. And though great poets have led the way here, it has been caught by the mass, and the sight of nature has undoubtedly gained an extraordinary power over people's minds; witness the quantity of travelling there is, purely to get the sight of grand objects. This is rather a new feature of the world—the popular pursuit of natural beauty, the inoculation of the crowd with it; the subject entering so much into people's thoughts, and being made so much a business of. And though it might sometimes appear that there is nothing particularly serious in the current fashion, still the general sentiment shows a serious passion existing in the poetry and thought of the age, which it follows and copies.

This new passion, then, for the beauty of the external world, has strongly developed the two points in it just noticed. First, it has realised that the beauty of nature is a distinct revelation made to the human mind, from that of its use. A vast fabric of poetical language has sprung up, which has abstracted the picture in nature from the mechanism; which has separated the scenic exhibition and appeal to the eye, from the whole useful structure and apparatus, and detaching the whole beautiful surface from its framework, has hung it up as an ethereal representation in space, for mankind simply to gaze at and contemplate as a vision. The older poetical view brought in more the utility and active force of nature, its nourishing powers, wealth, comfort, and prosperity. In the newer description, without at all dismissing utility, which is a sacred thought to keep in reserve, and essential even to the full poetical view of nature, the main contemplation of the poet is still a vision, in which the marvellous surface of nature is represented. He has fixed his eye upon the passive spectacle—upon nature as an appearance, a sight, a picture. To another he leaves the search and analysis; he is content to look, and to look only; this, and this alone, satisfies him; he stands like a watcher or sentinel, gazing on earth, sea and sky, upon the vast assembled imagery, upon the rich majestic representation on the canvas.

But though this view separates the beauty from the use, the picture from the mechanism, by an act of the *imagination*, it still retains intrinsically the union of the two; and from this union a result follows. The picture becomes, by virtue of it, as immediate a derivation from the Divine Mind as the utility of nature; as much a vision of the Divine raising as the solid structure is a machinery of the Divine contrivance.

What is the religious bearing then, of this modern passion for nature in its pictorial aspect, which is a feature of the day; which is a profounder feeling than the taste and sentiment of a former age; and which has developed itself in the way which has been just described, viz., by throwing itself wholly upon the picture and spectacle in nature? The rise of this remarkable feeling in society is a fact that deserves attention in this aspect, as it cannot well be without some consequences bearing on religion.

First, then, with respect to the place which the beauty of nature has in the argument of Design from nature. When the materialist has exhausted himself in efforts to explain utility in nature, it would appear to be the peculiar office of beauty to rise up suddenly as a confounding and baffling *extra*, which was not even formally provided for in his scheme. Nature goes off at a tangent which carries her farther than ever from the head under which he places her, and shows the utter inadequacy of that head to include all that has to be included in it. The secret of nature is farther off than ever from what he thinks it. Physical science goes back and back into nature, but it is the aspect and front of nature which gives the challenge; and it is a challenge which no backward train of physical causes can meet. This applies even to the useful contrivance of nature, viz., that what we have to account for is the face of nature, that which meets the eye in the shape of obvious arrangement and collocation. The physical causes are only all the separate items traced back step after step; which is no explanation of their collocation. Thus, the more men retreat into the interior the farther they fly from the true problem, and leave altogether behind them the question—what makes the arrangement and the disposition? But the remark applies even more conspicuously to the beauty of nature. I will explain.

There is this remarkable difference between useful contrivance and beauty as evidence of an intelligent cause; that contrivance has a complete end and account of itself without any reference to the understanding of man. True, it is an object, and a very stimulating object, of the understanding, but it does not require that use of it in order to account for it; even if no single one of all those sentient beings who profit by the contrivance of nature *understand* it, still they profit by it all the same; this is a sufficient account of it; it is enough if it works, and it is not necessary for its use that it should be seen. But it is essential to the very sense and meaning of beauty that it should be seen; and in as much as it is visible to reason alone, we have thus in the very structure of nature a recognition of reason, and a distinct address to reason; wholly unaccountable unless there is a higher reason or mind to which to make it. For what but reason can address reason? I say beauty is visible to reason alone. It is remarkable that if any one asks himself—what I suppose every one has done at some time, when he has had some great spectacle of nature before him—why does this scene impress me?

—what makes the beauty of it? why should we be affected by visible objects in the way we are? by so many perpendicular feet of height or depth? by masses, projections, angles, vapour, colour, space, and extent?—that we can get no answer whatever to this question from the facts themselves. It is an entire puzzle in that direction, and like trying to look through a wall. The only accurate information which we can procure about these facts is what a surveyor or mineralogist can give us; the facts themselves are wholly inadequate to account for the poetical impression they produce; and so long as we search in that quarter only, so long it must appear senseless, that a man should be really mentally affected by this size, length, height, depth, and the other items of a scene of nature. But the glory of nature in reality resides in the mind of man; there is an inward intervening light through which the material objects pass, a transforming medium which converts the physical assemblage into a picture. It must be remarked that the whole of what any scene of earth or sky is materially, is stamped upon the retina of the brute, just as it is upon the man's; and that the brute sees all the same objects which are beautiful to man, only without their beauty; which aspect is inherent in man, and part of his reason. He possesses the key to the sight; and that which makes the appearance what it is, resides in him; and is an inner light or splendour reflected from his reason upon the surface of the universal frame of things. The type of beauty then on which the universe is framed, being essentially a relative thing, the very existence of which requires reason to see it; the existence of beauty, unless we account for the correspondence of the two by chance, is an express acknowledgment of rational mind, which cannot proceed except *from* mind.

But leaving natural beauty as a part of evidence, we will go to the mode in which it bears upon the principle of worship, and upon the religious sentiment or emotions. It is obvious, in the first place, that the beauty of nature is necessary for the perfection of *praise;* and that the praise of the Creator must be essentially weakened without it; it must be roused and excited by sight. It may seem extraordinary, but it is the case that, though we certainly look at contrivance or machinery in nature with a high admiration, still, with all its countless and multitudinous uses, which we acknowledge with gratitude, there is nothing in it which raises the mind's interest in nearly the same degree that beauty does. It is an awakening sight; and one way in which it acts is by exciting a certain curiosity about the Deity. It must be observed that the old Design language was deficient in this respect, and got too much in the direction as if we knew everything about God: He was benevolent and intelligent, wise and contriving, and studied man's bodily and social interest. But beauty stands upon the threshold of the mystical world, and excites a curiosity about God. In what does He possess character, feelings, relations to us?—all unanswerable questions; but the very entertainment of which is an excitement of the reason, and throws us upon the thought of what there is behind the veil. This curiosity is a strong part of worship and of praise. To think that we know everything about God is to benumb and deaden worship; but mystical thought quickens worship; and the beauty of nature raises mystical thought. So long as a man is probing nature, and in the thick of its causes and operations, he is too busy about his own inquiries to receive this impress from her; but place the picture before him, and he becomes conscious of a veil and curtain which has the secrets of a moral existence behind it; interest is inspired, curiosity is awakened, and worship is raised. "Surely Thou art a God that hidest Thyself." But if God simply hid Himself and nothing more, if we knew nothing, we should not wish to know more. But the veil suggests that it *is* a veil, and that there is something behind it which it conceals. It thus raises a curiosity about God, whose character is so faintly, just hinted, and then wrapped again in darkness. But it is this which composes what we call mystical feeling. The mystical idea of the Deity is only in fact the moral idea of Him, with curiosity superadded— curiosity grasping the existence of the unknown, but knowing it cannot be gratified as to what it is.

This is one great effect then of that whole bolder view of nature as a picture, which more recent poetical thought has struck out. It is the tendency of a highly civilised age to object to mystery in religion, but it is significant and worth observing that the same bar is not put to it in nature. Poetry is allowed to border upon the horizon of mysticism, the privilege is given to it, and it is admitted that it may do so with truth, with taste, and with good sense. Mystical feeling has indeed always, alike in its highest and in its lowest forms, flourished upon exteriors; a sight has suggested the unseen; and the ancient hierophant initiated men into his sanctuary of wisdom by a succession of sights. If then any great movement of thought in an age summons forth a great spectacle, or opens men's eyes to one which before they had not so fully seen, still more, if it converts the universe into a great sight; such a movement will infallibly engender mystical thought. The sight will act as a spell and fascination on men's minds, and though it will roll the unquiet or the listless round and round in a dream of mere idle wonder and speculation, it will in others kindle the spark of worship and praise.

But again, nature is partly a curtain and partly a disclosure, partly a veil and partly a revelation; and here we come to her faculty of symbolism, which is so strong an aid to, and has so immensely affected, the principles of worship. There can be no doubt that it is natural for us to regard the beauty and grandeur of nature as not stopping with itself, but bearing a relation to something moral, of which it is the similitude and type. We do so by an inherent force of association, which we cannot break from. Certainly no person has a right to fasten his own fancies upon the visible creation, and say that its various features mean this and that, resemble this or that in the moral world; but if the association is universal, if we cannot even describe nature without the help of moral terms—solemn, tender, awful, and the like—it is evidence of a natural and real similitude of physical things to moral.

If we are asked for an explanation indeed of this—how it is that what is physical can resemble what is spiritual, and how there can be such a translation of one thing into another—we cannot say; we cannot explain, as we just now said, why material objects impress the imagination; and so we cannot explain why material objects are emblematic. We can only say that the interpretation is part of our reason. The child in its nurse's arms catches at a ribbon, or its eye is caught by something that shines. It is the beginning of a process in the mind of man which makes material sights and objects first beautiful and then emblematic, first fine images and then moral images—a process which starts with a physical impulse and ends in spiritualising nature, and giving a soul to the world of mere measures and sizes—lengths and breadths, heights and depths, lights and shadows.

We cannot, for instance, but note that remarkable desire which seems to be innate in all,—grave and gay, serious and thoughtless alike—the desire to be solemnised. People like being awed, they enjoy it; it is almost like a physical pleasure to them; they relish being silenced for a moment by some grand object, some striking sight in nature; one of those great forms and magnitudes in nature, one of those altitudes, one of those abysses. The crowd find awe a pleasant sensation; they will travel a great distance for it, and to gain some overpowering impress. Why is this? What can it be that makes even the trifling and volatile like of all things to be awed. The multitude does not show any great sympathy with solemn ideas in ordinary life; they do not seek them, their happiness does not depend on them. Yet to be solemnised by an outward spectacle, to have it done for them, is delightful.

Now this craving for the transient awe inspired by some grand object is undoubtedly connected with the chronic disquiet of man's mind, his want of control over his thoughts. This constitutes a normal restlessness; he is carried off in mind here, there, and everywhere, as different images fly past him, coming he knows not whence; he is surrounded by floating hosts of shadows, which call him off at any moment from his tack, and beckon him to follow them. Even in his engaged states, when he is tied to some object, side currents are perpetually interfering with him, and slipping into the empty interstices of his thoughts. He would fain break away from the yoke of his own levity, but the fatigue of resistance brings him under it again, and he finds he cannot cope with the tyrant. His passions take advantage of his feebleness, and add a stimulus to the caprice of nature; they crowd in upon the vacant mind, and open tracts of desultory fancy; they suggest, they insinuate, they provoke; they raise obnoxious images, the pursuit of which leads to fresh irrelevant flights. Thus the inner life of man is a struggle with volatility and disorder, which issues in a law of restlessness, under which he still nourishes a perpetual longing for some satisfying repose. This is what he craves; and could some new grandeur be discovered in nature, which could by its own irresistible impress quell the whole discord of his mind, could he count upon some sight which would petrify him and strike him dumb with amazement, he would go half over the world to see it.

Awe then is a pleasurable sensation, for this simple reason, that there exists at the bottom of every one's mind the idea of a great Being to whom awe is due. It is evident that there must be a pleasure springing from all the feelings which fulfil and express real relations,—the proper relations of one being to another; awe is the feeling which expresses the relation to the Great Being above us; and therefore there must be a real pleasure attaching to awe. A mock awe, or even an awe merely professed and put on, when it is not really felt, out of good behaviour, is a burden; but the real sensation must, in the very reason of the case, be one of the pleasures of nature. And therefore it does not require seriousness to feel the pleasure of awe; even the light-minded and thoughtless can feel it when circumstances and objects produce it for them; because they cannot prevent themselves having their own nature, and this is an accompaniment of that nature. Nothing indeed can speak more clearly to the religious sense in man than this pleasure of being awed. What does it mean without it? It is nonsense. Unless reason divines a superior Being to whom awe is really due, it is unaccountable that it should be pleasant.

To give then physical greatness the power of imparting this awe, there must be a radical association in our minds *of* physical greatness *with* this existence above us; the mere physical thing could not do it of itself; taken by itself it is nothing, only matter. It can only, in the reason of the case, act by means of an interpretation which it gathers in passing through our minds. And this interpretation cannot be of our own making, otherwise it could not command our choice; as we made it, so we could throw it off. If it was our own artifice we should find it out; or not let it cheat us. It is in our nature then. It is not arbitrary, but independent of our will. And so when men are solemnised by mere quiet and ordinary means —solitude, the shadows of evening, moonlight, and the like, it is impossible that these mere physical conditions of matter can affect the feelings in any way, except it is that they collect a signification in passing through our mind, receive the stamp of an implanted association, and are linked on to the spiritual realm by an obscure medium which is too far below for us to get hold of.

And from these observations we may see in what sense the glory of nature, or that great picture which proceeds, together with the mechanism of nature, from God, is a manifestation of God. Nature is sometimes spoken of in a pantheistic corporeal manner; as if it were a kind of bodily manifestation of the Divine Being, analogous to that garment of the flesh which encircles the human soul, and is the instrument of expression to it. But the manifestation of the Deity which takes place in the beauty of nature rests upon the ground and the principle of language. It is the revelation of the character of God in the way a material type or similitude can be. But a type is a kind of distinct language—the language of oblique and indirect expression, as contrasted with direct. We may remark that indirect language is an important and real section of language, and it grows up and comes to great perfection in cultivated society,—the meaning of the speaker being conveyed by an angle to its destination. It is indeed unfortunate that that which is so beautiful and delicate a branch of speech in itself, should have been enlisted with such special success in the service of malice, and that when we go for the most perfect forms of it, we turn unconsciously to the polished conflicts of hostile minds; that it is there we should see at its greatest advantage that mechanism of diction which acts so obliquely, that while the effect is completely reached, the agency seems quite unconscious of the cause: the mere situation of a word speaks, and unexpected light glances from the dullest corners. But indeed language is everywhere half sign; its hieroglyphics, the dumb modes of expression, surpass the speech. All action indeed is, besides being action, language; if you do a thing for another, that is language; if you do not do it, that is language; and if you half do it, that is language too. A look gives the warning and the hope; a look gives the threat and the promise. Fragments are the very pick of expression—that reality which just comes to the surface for a moment, the light which just breaks upon the countenance, and is swallowed up in night again, and in the mask of custom, —what we call nature—is like something fluctuating in darkness, which is just called up to the surface by an eddy, and is engulphed in the depth again. It only exists in broken gleams and vanishing hints, and the proverb is true which says, the half is more than the whole; fragments mean most.

Imagine, then, this distant language, this transparent veil of enigma or hint carried into the exalted region of communication between the Supreme Being and the creature, and we have what is in fact the language of nature as a picture. If symbolism indeed has no natural basis, if the association of material images with moral is entirely arbitrary and artificial, then there is no language in nature; but if, on the other hand, there is a consensus and uniformity in the interpretation of physical things, *i.e.*, the mode in which our feelings are affected by them; if no people have ever existed to whom the sky has not suggested one set of ideas; if God has always spoken with one voice—not literally indeed in the thunder—but in the impress of awe and solemnity which He has attached to the thunder; if love, joy, peace, hope, have attached to the same features of nature everywhere; if there is general agreement in these impresses, and they proceed inevitably from God's own work in the construction of our minds, then there is language; and language in something more than a metaphorical sense, a true communication and indication according to the medium employed. The cypher is not unintelligible; it lets out something. The Great Spirit, speaking by dumb representation to other spirits, intimates and signifies to them something about Himself, for if nature is symbolical, what it is symbolical about must be its author. The Deity over and above our inward conscience wants His external world to tell us He is moral; He therefore creates in nature a universal language about Himself; its features convey signals from a distant country, and man is placed in communication with a great correspondent whose tablet he interprets. And thus is formed that which is akin to worship in the poetical view of nature. While we do not worship the material created sign, for that would be idolatry, we still repose on it as the true language of the Deity.

In this peculiar view of nature,—the mind fastening upon it as a spectacle or picture,—it is to be observed that there are two points in striking concurrence with the vision-language of Scripture. First, Scripture has specially consecrated the faculty of sight, and has partly put forth, and has promised in a still more complete form, a manifestation of the Deity to mankind, through the medium of a great sight. This view only breaks out in fragments in the Old Testament, and may be distinguished from its ordinary language. The ordinary language is the praise of God's works as the evidences of His contrivance and goodness; " in wisdom has He made them all;" His works are His instruments, His servants, and His ministers; they do His bidding; they tremble at the look of Him; they praise and adore Him; fire, and hail; snow, and vapour; wind and storm fulfilling His word: mountains, and all hills; fruitful trees, and all cedars: beasts, and all cattle; worms, and feathered fowl. But so far, though giving ample *proofs* of His power and benevolence, nature does not symbolise and figuratively manifest the Deity.

But this latter view breaks through the clouds, and emerges into light when nature is spoken of as the garment and robe of the Deity, when the glory of the Lord covers the tabernacle; when Moses is permitted to behold from the cleft in the rock the skirts of the Divine glory. Especially does the idea of a visible manifestation come out in the prophetic visions, where the splendid gleams and colours of nature, sapphire and amber, rainbow and flame, are collected together, and combined in an emblematic figure and shape, in order to make "the appearance of the likeness of the glory of the Lord."[1] "And when I saw, says the Prophet, I fell on my face, and I heard the voice of one that spake." But the scattered rays of pictorial representation which only occasionally pierce through the clouds of the Old Testament, are gathered into one focus in the New, they converge and are absorbed into an ineffable, eternal appearance, in which God will ever be seen as He is, and they issue in the doctrine of the *Visio Dei*. It must be remarked by everybody, that the glory of the future state of the Christian revelation is always put before us not as an inner consciousness or mental communion simply,—not as an absorption into ourselves within, but as a great spectacle without us; the spectacle of a great visible manifestation of God. It is a sight, a picture, a representation, that constitutes the heavenly state, not mere thought and contemplation. The glorified saint of Scripture is especially a beholder; he gazes, he looks; he fixes his eyes upon something before him; he does

[1] Ezekiel i. 28.

not merely ruminate within, but his whole mind is carried out towards and upon a great representation. And thus Heaven specially appears in Scripture as the sphere of perfected sight; where the faculty is raised and exalted to its highest act, and the happiness of existence culminates in vision. Whatever then may be the real and full meaning of these great emblematic representations in Scripture, it is not putting any strain upon the poetical attitude toward nature on which we are commenting, or giving it a theological interpretation, to observe that so far as it converts nature into a great spectacle, and an emblematic spectacle which is significant of, and manifests and expresses, the Divine Mind, so far it concurs with Scripture language, and gives its witness to the principle of the Scriptural representation. It couples in an extraordinary way high fruition with sight, and it raises up a manifestation of the Deity by an emblematic spectacle or picture. But such a vision in Nature is in intimate sympathy and correspondence with the visions of prophetic illumination. Prophetic illumination collects the splendours of nature into a particular figure and outline, which is the special conception of the Prophet's mind; while Nature herself is a picture which fills all space,—the union of height, depth, magnitude, colour, light, and shadow. The masses group, the clouds and vapours roll; and earth, sea, and sky, combine in one great scene of representation. But the natural picture has in its measure the same office which the conceived one has, and performs in its measure the same part of similitude and symbol.

Secondly, it must be remarked, as another principle in the Scriptural representation, that the act of seeing a perfectly glorious sight or object is what constitutes the spectator's and beholder's own glory. The future life is called a state of glory in Scripture, and it is called such not only in reference to the world in which it will be enjoyed, which is a glorious world, but also with regard to those who enjoy it; who attain to glory as a personal state. This personal state is enjoyed by them then on this principle, that they are glorified as spectators of glory, that beholding Majesty is their own exaltation, and adoration their own ascent. But this latter is certainly the principle of nature, and it is inculcated by all who vindicate the place and office of nature as a spectacle. No one was ever struck with wonder and admiration in beholding the works of God, no one was ever impressed strongly by the beauty and majesty of the visible creation, without at the same time feeling an accession of rank and elevation to himself from the act. There is an ambition which is gratified by admiration; and true admiration is a kind of glory to the admirer; because the person rises in it to the level marked out to him as a spectator, he is equal to his post, and his perceptions do justice to the object. It raises him in his own sight. All strong fruition is indeed a kind of glory to men; they are magnified to themselves by it; and there is a false and debased copy of this when the extravagance of even sensual joy is an obvious exaltation of the man in his own eyes, and he feels a sort of glory reflected on him from the effervescences of his own spirit; when the swell of passion seems to give him a kind of superior being, and to endow him with greatness and strength; when the mere sense of license raises him to the clouds; when mere excitement flatters, and the very breath of novelty lifts up. For what lifts men up in their own idea is often not anything they have done themselves, but something outside of them; some spectacle, some public commotion, some public triumph; the imagery of kingdoms and empires, which is raised up by some event; the sight of multitudes. These produce a false swell of inward exaltation. The true sense is produced by high joys, which are gratifications of perceptions of high objects, such as those of creation. It attaches unconsciously to the act of praise—praise of goodness that we know or read of, and especially to the highest act of praise, when a whole congregation sings the praise of God. Every single member of the congregation that joins with heart and soul in such praise feels himself raised by the act; he has the sense of being himself lifted up in it, and endowed with rank; and the ascent of the heart upwards is reflected upon himself.

It is thus that the admiration of the beauty of nature strikes a sort of balance with the scientific analysis of nature in the general effect upon the religious mind of an age. The tendency of the analysis of nature is to reduce the idea of the Deity in men's minds to a negation, and to convert the First Great Cause into a mere physical force. But the admiration of nature as a creation of beauty, on the other hand, tends to support the moral idea of the Deity, to excite a curiosity and interest about His character, and so far to sustain the mystery of the Gospel disclosure of His character. One and the same age has developed, in a signal manner, both of these principles; two influences have gone forth from it, and the physical idea of nature from analysis, and the mystical and imaginative idea from the picture, have contended within its bosom, and sometimes within the same minds. The impression from the visible world, as a chain of material causation, has been more or less counteracted and counterbalanced by the visible world as a spiritual sight. A spiritual fact ever before us is a spiritual memento, and beauty is a spiritual fact, because it altogether hinges upon a spiritual principle within us, and only exists as an address to it. And so we generally find that no one set of ideas is allowed to domineer and monopolise ground in any age, but, when one rises to power, another is provided to meet and check it.

But though the outward face of nature is a religious communication to those who come to it with the religious element already in them, no man can get a religion out of the beauty of nature. There must be for the base of a religion, the internal view, the inner sense, the look into ourselves, and recognition of an inward state,—sin, helplessness, misery; if there is not this, outward nature cannot of itself enlighten man's conscience and give him a knowledge of God. It will be a picture to him, and nothing more. It is an introspection on which all religion is built; the Psalms and St. Paul alike witness to it—man going into himself and seeing the struggle within him; and thence getting self-knowledge, and thence the knowledge of God.

I will take the most refined and intellectual sense of beauty, as inspiring a kind of religion; when a man who feels the need of some kind of religion, submits himself to the influence of the sublime picture of nature, goes about with it everywhere before him, rests his eyes on it, and yields himself like wax to its impress, passively imbibing all the feeling which it has to impart to him. Here then is a state of mental affection, which is so far like religion that it contrasts widely with the life of the man of the world,—its selfish strife and ambition, and vulgar trifles. And as such a contrast it doubtless gives satisfaction to the contemplative spirit who yearns for some sacrifice, and can challenge for his special devotion that attribute of religion which consists in being unworldly. Yet how far is such an interest and fascination from being religion! and how weak is outward nature compared with the inner sense which has been just mentioned, as a power to awaken the mind, to give it spiritual vigour, to bring out its true instincts and presages, and give force to its vision! A life of passive admiration is but a dream, and external Nature is thus rather an enchantress who magnetises the human spirit than an inspirer into it of energy and strength. There is nothing prophetic in the spectacle of nature, as thus seen. It is curious how men who, simply from this standing point, admire nature, have before them perpetually what they themselves call a vision of celestial beauty, and yet this celestial vision never points to any real heaven. The scene of Nature soothes and entrances, and then melts away. The future is a blank, or a dark enigma to them. So little does the glory of mere outward nature prophecy. It is that inner sense alone, which, struggling in darkness, under the yoke of weakness and sin, has, out of the conflict of a hidden war, pierced to the realms of eternal day.

Or take the more striking and conspicuous case of the great Atheistic poets, and what is the issue of a religion of natural beauty here? First discord, and then despair. On the one side is their astonishing insight into the glory of the external world; they dive into the very heart of it, and are as absorbed in the vision of beauty before their eyes as if they were prophets, whose minds had been attuned by the Divine Creator Himself into sympathetic union with His creation; such is the power of the Sight upon them; on the other hand is the very spirit of blasphemy; so that one moment they adore like the cherubim, in the next they cry out like the vexed demoniacs, and say, —"'What have we to do with Thee,' Thou God of heaven and earth?" How are we to account for this madness, for this dreadful schism in the minds of these men, which splits them, as it were, in two beings? The cause of this discord in their own spirits was, that they themselves cut nature into two, and took its beauty separated from its law. They took the picture, the external vision, without the inner yoke, and divided the Spirit of Nature from the Divine Lawgiver. They then worshipped the Spirit of

M

Nature. The poet stained his soul with every sensual excess, but the sense of beauty was his counterpart of grace; it renewed and purified him; he thought he could wash in its fount and be clean, that he could wipe off his guilt as by a baptism; he plunged into it polluted, and rose up purified: so long as he could intensely admire, it was enough; the act of communion with nature was his restoration and forgiveness. He sinned, he worshipped; he sinned again, he worshipped again; every time he was absorbed in the sight of Nature, he had been taken out of himself and exalted to heaven. It was the seal of recognition, and for a few short moments he felt at peace with himself and his Creator.

The passionate sense of beauty was thus the religion of these men; but because they made it their religion, on that very account it utterly dissatisfied them. For how was beauty itself to interpret the other part of nature, or the *law*? They came straight from the scene without, which fascinated and enraptured them, to look upon a dark struggle within, which scandalised them; and they had not a single reason in their minds—I will not say to account for this yoke of weakness and misery, for nobody can do that,—but for submitting to it. They were like men who were obliged to turn away from some smiling and luxuriant landscape to look within the bars of a frightful dungeon. The inner man was simply a dreadful enigma to them; the strife within, which the apostle describes, was regarded in the light of an insupportable grievance, and of a crime in the constitution of things. Had the mystery of sin preceded in their minds the glory of nature, they would have reconciled the two; but coming *from* glory first, they then recoiled and started back from the dark mystery; they loathed their own image; they could hardly believe it was their own likeness; then when they saw it was, they rebelled. And "who made self-contempt," one asked, taunting the Creator. He placed himself in a dilemma, for the answer is obvious,—If you think this estimate of yourself untrue, why do you hold it? If you think it true, why do you complain of it? How can you convert sin, which you acknowledge to be in yourself, into accusation against another? But the outward world idolised, spoiled these men for the inward, and in anger they fell back upon a Manichean God, who was lovely in nature and unjust in man.

When men have started from outward nature, when they have used it as a foundation, and made it their first stay, its glory has thus issued in gloom and despondency; but to those who have first made the knowledge of themselves and their own souls their care, it has ever turned to light and hope. They have read in Nature an augury and a presage; they have found in it a language and a revelation; and they have caught in it signs and intimations of Him who has clothed Himself with it as with a garment, who has robed Himself with its honour and majesty, has decked Himself with its light, and who created it as an expression and manifestation of Himself.

THE WORK OF THE SPIRIT.

JOHN III. 8.

"*The wind bloweth where it listeth, and thou hearest the sound thereof, but canst not tell whence it cometh, and whither it goeth: so is every one that is born of the Spirit.*"

TWO main characteristics of spiritual religion, or the religious temper which belong to the dispensation of the Spirit as distinguished from that of the law, are given in Scripture. One is, that it resides in the affections and not only in the conscience. "Being made free from sin," says St. Paul, "ye became the servants of righteousness." We are the slaves of sin when our inclinations are so strong on the side of sin that we cannot resist them. We are the slaves of righteousness then when our inclinations are equally strong on the side of good. The same truth is conveyed in many other forms, as where he says, "Reckon ye also yourselves to be dead unto Sin but alive unto God." Death unto sin implies utter indifference and insensibility to the attractions of sin, an absence of all inclination to do what is wrong, as distinguished from mere abstinence on the ground of conscience. The torpor and coldness of death are employed to represent the utter absence of sympathy with evil in the perfected soul which wants life and animation in this direction; a holy defect which contrasts so strongly with the keen vicious sensibilities of the natural man, who is in his turn a mere corpse in relation to good, wholly impenetrable to its motives and incapable of feeling its pleasures. It is constantly assumed in the Epistles that Christians are in this state of death unto sin and life unto righteousness. They are addressed as if they were; not of course that they all were in point of fact, but that this was the religious disposition belonging to the dispensation of the Spirit, and that those who were under the dispensation were to be supposed to have the disposition. Christians were no longer under the yoke of the law, because their duty had ceased to be a yoke imposed on them from without, and had become a labour of love in which they delighted. The Epistles abound in expressions which describe the spiritual temper as being of this kind—viz., as having very much the characteristics of what we call a *natural* disposition. A natural disposition acts without effort or formality, not doing its work in a set way, because it is enjoined, and because it is right; but spontaneously, and from choice. The spiritual temper acts in the same way, with the freedom and unconstrained manner of a second nature. A new birth, indeed, is the very name which is given to it.

This is a test of the superior or spiritual disposition, which approves itself to our common sense. We apply indeed the same criterion elsewhere. The test of true *admiration* is *pleasure*—pleasure in looking at the object or scene which we admire. We are all of us acquainted with the state of mind in which we see something to be admired in a work of art or grand spectacle of nature, and yet cannot make ourselves *feel* it. We try every means to rouse and quicken our perceptions, and give warmth to them, but there still remains, in spite of all our efforts, only a cold sense of something grand or beautiful which stands obstinately on the outside of our minds and will not enter into them. But it is evident that this is an inferior state of the intellect; because, if we really and properly *saw* the beauty we should *feel* it, and therefore pleasure is the criterion of true admiration. The same test, perhaps, applies in a degree to other perceptions besides those of taste; for all truths, even the most abstract and subtle truth in mathematics or metaphysics, is, by the very constitution of the human mind, perceived— when it really is perceived — with a quick and pungent feeling, which is of the nature of the highest pleasure. In the same way the criterion of the highest and perfect moral state of mind is pleasure,—when good acts are not only done, but when we take pleasure in doing them. We are certainly bound to do them whether we like it or not; and obedience, for conscience sake, which is carried on against inclination, is deserving of all praise, and is constantly urged upon us in Scripture; but it is still an inferior moral state compared with that in which the inclinations themselves are on the side of good. For, looking into the real nature of the case, we cannot but call it a state of servitude when a man's affections do not go along with his work, but he submits to duty as a yoke which a superior power or law imposes on him, even though that law be revealed to him through his own conscience.

It is indeed impossible that this superior or spiritual state of mind, in which inclination goes entirely along with duty, can be fully attained by any one in this life. It never can be simply pleasant to resist a bodily appetite, and yet we have those appetites so long as we remain in the flesh, and they have always a tendency to excess, which must be checked and struggled against. And the same may be said of various passions of the mind, which are actually part of our nature, and therefore cannot be got rid of; which have also attached to them, and always must have in our present state, the same tendency to excess. But to some extent this spiritual condition of mind may be realised in this life, because, if on the one side we have appetites and passions which are neutral in themselves, and tend to inordinateness in the indulgence of them, we have also on the other, moral and spiritual affections which are in themselves good; so that, if these affections are properly developed in us, they constitute our duty and our pleasure at the same time: our pleasure, because they are our affections; our duty, because they are good ones. Take, for example the principle of compassion in our nature. Here is an affection, the admirable and beautiful operation of which is, that it gives the person who feels it pleasure even in the very act of ministering to and succouring pain. There can be no doubt that a compassionate person derives a true gratification from the exercise of his affection, and that a sensation that comes within the truest definition of pleasure is elicited in his mind at the very point of contact with suffering in which the act of that affection places him. Such being the operation then of the affection of pity, one person will perform actions of charity and minister to the relief of others under the positive influence of, and from the impulse of that affection; another will perform the same acts, but he will not do them from feeling so much as from a sense of duty, and because he recognises the law which commands us to relieve our distressed neighbour. It is evident that the former is the superior or spiritual state of mind, because it is the characteristic of the dispensation of the Spirit that under it men act from elevated affections and from an impulse given them within, and not only from obedience to a law. The latter, on the contrary, though performing what is acceptable to God, is still under the law, as acting from obedience to an outward command which is not as yet identified with his inclinations and feelings, and, as it were, incorporated in his nature.

Though when we say that the spiritual disposition is like a natural disposition in its mode of working, it is not meant that it is no more than a natural disposition in substance. To take the instance of compassion again—it is evident that this affection, as possessed by a Christian under the new dispensation, is much superior to the natural affection as it would exhibit itself in a heathen. There would be a great difference in the tone of the affection; its depth and refinement corresponding to the immense difference in the object of it—his wonderful nature and prospects, as disclosed by revelation; which represents him as an immortal being passing through trial to another world, and possessing a soul, as well as a body: a soul which claims our sympathy with it in its own peculiar sufferings amid those awful risks which agitate it, and obscure it with fears, and forebodings and apprehensions for the future.

The second characteristic of the spiritual disposition, as described in Scripture, is quite in harmony with the first, and indeed follows from it, "Thou canst not tell whence it cometh." Besides what we have just spoken of, and what we may call its naturalness, it has an *unknown source*, we cannot create it ourselves and by our own will, and that for the very reason that it *is* this natural kind of disposition. For if it resides specially in the affections and inclinations, it is plain these are what we cannot produce in ourselves by an effort of the will. Upon one theory, indeed, even acts of the will spring from an unknown source, and even our own wills are not determined by ourselves; but all agree that we cannot make our own *feelings*. We can make ourselves perform certain acts by an effort of the will, but this is a very different thing from making our inclinations go along with them. It is evident then we do not possess this power over ourselves. How often indeed do we wish we did, when we know we ought to feel something which we do not feel, when we are conscious of doing something coldly and indifferently which we ought to do with real heart. Human nature covets the possession of feelings, and men strain after them, and would fain persuade themselves that they have them when they have not. They borrow from the world of illusion, and enjoy emotions which fictitious scenes have the power of raising within them; but when the stimulus of illusion is withdrawn, and that curious mechanism within us stops which enables us to appropriate and assimilate for the time an external pathos, when they are thrown back upon themselves, they find how dead their nature is; and how cold, awkward, and artificial, at the very next call of real life upon it, is the mind which was just now feeling intensely upon a borrowed basis.

Are we then to stop here; to say that our affections are simply out of our power, and that if we have them it is well, if not we cannot help it? To leave the subject standing thus would be far from satisfactory, and would hardly be in accordance with the exhortations in Scripture to strive after the spiritual disposition and good affections, as if they were in some way connected with our wills, and our use of them. It is evident that we want then some distinction here, to enable us to reconcile an apparent discrepancy and fill up the obvious void which is left in this matter of obtaining affection.

The first explanation to which we have recourse is the simple doctrine of habits—that although we cannot by an effort of the will produce an affection or inclination at the *time*, a succession of such acts will at last produce it; that it is of the nature of habit to make acts easier and easier, till what was at first distasteful at last becomes pleasant. But although this is a good explanation of certain results in morals there appears to be a point in which it fails in the present case, and that just the turning-point. For is it true that habit, solely and of itself, does even produce positive inclination or affection? undoubtedly habit is a great facilitating principle, making the will perform certain acts more easily and as a matter of course, which at first it did with difficulty; but what is the actual nature and composition of the habit when it is formed? The act which is facilitated by repetition is not, by the very supposition, an act of feeling or affection properly speaking, otherwise it would not have needed an acquired facility at all. It is an act of self-control by which the mind forces itself to do a particular thing in spite of a disinclination to do it. But this act, let it be ever so often repeated and facilitated by repetition, can never become a feeling, but must always remain in substance what it was to begin with—an act of self-control—only made easier instead of more difficult; it cannot pass into another thing from what it was at first. But though acquired habit is not strictly speaking *in itself* of the nature of a feeling or affection, it has a connection and an important one with the due growth of the feelings, in this way—that it removes obstructions which stand in the way of their coming out and obtaining their proper place in the character. There is undoubtedly a root of love at the bottom of the human heart, which it has received from God, and which only requires the removal of the pressure of other matter upon it to bring it out as the true part of the man. But there is too apt to be an immense pressure upon it, as we can plainly see. There is the pressure upon it of selfish aims and desires of all kinds, low cares, jealousies, enmities, and the general agitation of worldly life. It is impossible that this implanted feeling, or love, can come out as a real force and power in our nature so long as it is overwhelmed and crushed by a mixed mass of secular and indifferent motives which occupy the whole mind;—while the mind is a prey to every malicious thought that takes hold of it, to envious thoughts, to irritation, to mean propensities, covetousness, bodily appetites, selfish ease and indolence. There must be acts of the will to resist this adverse occupation of the mind, to remove these bad feelings and passions; then, in proportion as the ground clears, and room is given to the good ones, these good feelings and affections have a natural tendency of their own to come up and take possession of the vacant space. It is because the good part of our nature has been kept down by a weight upon it that it has not acted; it begins to act as soon as the weight upon it is removed, and it is allowed to rise. Thus, though it is true that we cannot make ourselves feel at the time by an act of the will, acts of the will do eventually—not create feeling, indeed, for feeling is a divine gift—but elicit it and bring it into play, by removing the obstructions to it. And thus the formation of habits will in the end practically be the growth of feeling too. And this is the relation in which the doctrine of habits, in ethics, will stand to the doctrine of good and holy affections as the basis of the character laid down in the new

Dispensation. The formation of habits by acts of the will against inclination is indeed the working of the law by which the mind is prepared for a higher state, in which feeling, and inclination itself moves it to good; that feeling being moreover, now that God has called it forth by His preparatory grace, quickened and raised by the direct impulses of the Holy Spirit.

The way in which feeling or inclination is obtained thus bears perhaps some analogy to the way in which knowledge is obtained. It is a common remark that, in difficult matters especially, we do not obtain knowledge at the actual time of study and investigation; I mean that the point of view which solves a difficulty, that first act of insight which makes us conscious that we have exchanged ignorance for knowledge, does not perhaps ordinarily come at the exact time when we are laboriously examining a subject. Every student knows the immense powers of passive resistance in a subject, how barren and fruitless even long periods of application often are, how insoluble the knot remains, and how obstinately stationary thought continues amid constant restless efforts to advance. But these barren periods are not mere wastes, and are not without their fruit, though it does not come at the time. Somehow or other, the mind subsequently finds itself cleared, and able to see its way better; and the insight it wants is apt to come almost without trouble, and by a kind of impulse when it does come. It would seem that there was some great obstruction to the intellect which had to be removed by a sort of blind struggle before an opening to the light could be obtained. One writer, to explain such cases, has supposed a law by which, after the intellect has been once put in vehement motion by great efforts, an unconscious working of the instrument takes place, so that an actual growth or process of mind is going on within us, of which we are not aware, of which light or knowledge is the result. So subtle an hypothesis at any rate witnesses to a curious phenomenon to be accounted for, which is indeed by no means rare, but a very common one. It is a part of even the schoolboy's experience, who is surprised at finding difficulties clear up themselves as it were, after much hard work which was at the time barren. This appears indeed to be the ordinary way in which knowledge does come to us. If there is no exact analogy this will serve at least as an illustration of the way in which a good inclination rises up in a man, and love takes the place of a mere sense of duty. The Law is a schoolmaster to bring us to Christ. And this is a point of view which singularly ennobles and elevates a great deal of hard and dry discipline which appeared to the person to do nothing at the time, and to raise no feeling or warmth in him. This barren work had all along a latent fruitfulness, and was only separated by an interval from its prize. When we look, for example, at the condition of the poor, who are so peculiarly connected in Scripture with the new dispensation, and see the quantity of dry discipline their hard life imposes on them, attended by nothing whatever inspiring; and requiring simply endurance, we are enabled to see a promise in all this labour — a promise of brightness.

Such a rule, however, as that love or feeling follows in a certain proportion to acts of the will, would not profess to contain the whole truth on this mysterious subject. For, not to go into the question what acts of the will themselves spring from, with which we are not concerned in the present inquiry, Scripture appears in many parts to represent the growth of the spiritual principle or love in the human heart as the pure work of the Holy Spirit, in a sense rather contrasted with acts of the will being the cause which brings it out. Nor ought we to attempt to explain away the natural meaning of this part of Scripture language which agrees, indeed, as we can hardly help observing, with some remarkable facts in the world of human character around us. I do not see why we should object to admit—what even the religious thought of heathens had no reluctance to allow—that some persons are, even in point of character, if we may use the expression, favourites of heaven. Some persons certainly appear to have a nature richer in good than others, and to have that well of spiritual water deeper; that is to say, there is a difference which we cannot wholly account for by acts of the will. In some even this strength of the spiritual affections appears to clear the way for them altogether from the first. I mean, that some persons certainly exhibit from the first dawn of their existence as moral agents, a spiritual type that is not only a law written in their hearts, but an implanted goodness and beauty of character which carries them instinctively to that good which others reach only by many struggles and perhaps many falls. Such have many of us seen—sometimes in humble life, faithful and devoted, loyal to man and full of melody in their hearts to God, their life one act of praise; sometimes in a higher sphere, living amid the pride of life, but wholly untouched by its spells; free and unensnared souls, that have never been lighted up by the false lights and aspirations of human life, or been fascinated by the evil of the world, though sympathising with all that is good in it, and enjoying it becomingly; who give us, so far as human character now can do, an insight into the realms of light, the light that comes from neither sun nor moon, but from Him who is the light everlasting. Some such, perhaps, have some of us seen, and watched their course even up to that time when the tabernacle which veiled the spirit dissolved, and left us wondering;—and tracking the line of light left on our memory. How or why have these victors gained their crowns without the disfigurement and alloy of that struggle which leaves its stamp on so many? We know not. It is a mystery to us. But we must recognise the fact that it does please the Almighty to endow some of his creatures from the first with extraordinary graces. It may be partly perhaps to show us what goodness is in its most admirable form,—in the form that is, in which it will exist in another world; that of the real nature of the man. Those who acquire goodness by much struggle and effort have their high merit, but it must be admitted that they do not always show goodness off to the best advantage; it is apt to be defective in the 'amabile quiddam;' to betray too much in them the machinery of its growth, and to be in some degree formal or artificial in tone; but another kind of formation more immediately from above corrects the impression, and reveals in some degree what virtue is in its natural and eternal form. And let us, on this day, which is dedicated to the praise of the Holy Spirit, and celebrates the commencement of His great dispensation, thank Him for these admirable creations of His, the saints who exhibit His own immediate handywork, by the sight of whom He designs to teach and to inspirit us.

Again, from striking cases of implanted goodness, we may pass to a Divine gift which is more generally bestowed. We find ourselves surrounded by the greatest variety of character in the world, and even the varieties of good character are almost infinite, no one good person being perhaps exactly like another. Such variety, however much difference of education and circumstances may contribute to it, must be due in some degree to an original and implanted difference in minds and constitutions. This propriety then, or characteristic in the individual, which he receives from a Divine source, is a sacred deposit with him to be done justice to, and guarded and developed naturally, and not to be submitted to any Procrustean process, even of disciplinarian moulding, which others may dictate to him. Different duties, tasks, positions in life, suit different minds, according to their original type or cast. It is no liberty, but proper prudence and proper self-respect for persons to feel their way independently toward such a line of life and duty as agrees with this original propriety of constitution. We are not bound, indeed, to be accurately acquainted with, and conscious of, our own type, and the habit of contemplating ourselves is hardly to be encouraged; still persons, if they are only true to themselves, instinctively know to some extent what suits their character and what does not, and have an insight into their proper and genuine capabilities; and by following up this insight and allowing it to direct them to a suitable mode of life and course of action, they preserve the truth and characteristic stamp of their own nature.

It is indeed this original propriety or root within us, which, whilst it is a Divine gift, is at the same time most *ourselves*—this pre-eminently constitutes the man, and unites in itself opposites, that which comes most from without and most from within at the same time. The preservation of it is the only security for the continuance of what is most precious and sterling in character. For though we should not deprive any form of conscientious life of its praise, it is difficult to believe that there is not something morally as well as intellectually defective in the act of one man giving himself up to be moulded by another;—that such an act is not feeble, below the level of our nature, and unjust to the design of our creation. And though those who adopt this step, and attach themselves to an absorbing system which makes life a course of formal taskwork, without room for choice or play of will, may honestly appear to themselves to be choosing the highest form of humility and self-denial, such a plan of life does not appear to produce the strong moral fibre that other more natural forms of probation well sustained do ; not to say that it is singularly apt to become a prey to many littlenesses, and especially to a certain childish form of pharisaism ; a poor issue indeed of a well-intended scheme of life.

This observation of what is original and characteristic in men, suggests too a reflection with respect to the use of imitation. We are doubtless to imitate others so far as they possess moral qualities which are of general and common service. Example is in this sense of the highest use ; and such imitation does not in the least interfere with the natural character of the copier, who can engraft in perfect agreement these common qualities upon the individual stock ; but to imitate persons as such, their particular type or character, is to fail in justice to ourselves. There is nothing to be gained by such imitation, for after all we cannot make ourselves other persons. That peculiar character which we admire in another would become quite a different one in ourselves could we achieve the most successful imitation. The copy could never have the spirit of the original, because it would want the natural root upon which the original grew. We ought to grow out of our own roots ; our own inherent propriety of constitution is the best nucleus for our own formation. This fitness, whatever it be, whether a higher or a humbler one, is the gift of the Holy Spirit, which we must stir up and bring to maturity. In the cultivation of the intellect certainly, persons make great mistakes from not finding out what their natural talent really is; sometimes even supposing it to be the opposite of what it is, because the desire to imitate some gifted man, who has been made a prominent object in their eyes, has made them inattentive to the composition of their own minds; and something analogous to it appears to be the case in morals.

In conclusion, there is a qualification which has already been referred to, and which certainly ought not to be lost sight of whenever that characteristic of the dispensation of the Spirit is placed before us, which has been the subject of this discourse; viz., its making an inclination within, and not a law from without, the basis of the religious life. It is not to be supposed that such a high state of mind as this can be realised to the full in this life. We must not be so unjust, indeed, to the present operation of the Holy Spirit as not to acknowledge that many Christians do show in a considerable measure the stamp of the dispensation of the Spirit, that they serve God and do works of righteousness from heart and inclination, and because their affections are enlisted on the side of what is holy and good. But the truth must be admitted, that many who belong visibly to the dispensation of the Spirit, are still inwardly under the Law in this sense, that their inclinations are not yet on the side of God's service, and that, if they perform their duty in any degree, it is only in obedience to a law, of the penalties of which they stand in just and proper fear, but not on the spiritual principles of love. Indeed, are not *all* Christians, whatever advance they may have made, to a great extent still under the law in this sense, that their affections are not yet wholly set upon things above, that there is much in their own minds against which they have to fight, and that duty is still a struggle and an effort to them. The new heart and the new spirit is the promise indeed of the Gospel, but that promise is only fulfilled, as some other Divine promises are, with an accommodation to those drawbacks and obstacles which the heart of man itself presents to the complete fulfilment. There is some characteristic frailty at the bottom of every human heart whose hold may have been loosened, but which does not yet move before the influence of grace. It remains even in eminent servants of God, and impedes the freedom of their service, making it often a severe and an irksome task.

And this consideration affects the question of the language which Christians may lawfully use about themselves and their own possession of spiritual graces. We may observe a tendency sometimes in persons of zeal and forwardness in religion to suppose that they can speak highly of their own spiritual gifts and graces, provided they do it with thankful acknowledgment that this goodness is the work of grace in them, and received from the Holy Spirit. But this is surely a very hazardous and inconsistent use to which they turn the dispensation of the Spirit, to use it as enabling persons to speak highly of their own state. Self abasement, as illustrated by the parable of the sanctified Publican, and the Guest at the feast, is specially and peculiarly the law of the Gospel. But it is not a sufficient fulfilment of this law that a person should speak to the fact of his own eminent graces, only appending the recognition of Divine power as the cause of them. The great test of humility is our estimate of the fact of our condition. If this estimate is high, then to whatever origin we may attribute it, we do not practically fulfil the law of self-abasement laid down in the Gospel. Rather it is founding a species of self righteousness on this very law.

There is perhaps a natural tendency in men of enthusiastic minds to assume (and this for their party and school as well as for themselves) too high a spiritual growth, because they can call it a spiritual growth and not a legal one, inducing a great luxuriance, and a want of due sincerity and truth in estimates; all because there is this salvo as to the source of gifts. The proper safeguard against these pretensions which advance unconsciously in the mind is a strict attention to facts—those serious facts which so much limit the new heart and the new spirit as actually possessed in this life—the deep faults of character which appear to survive all present influence of the Holy Spirit, the confession of which can alone in any sense neutralise them. These are serious things to think of, and the recollection of them should subdue this spirit of self-congratulation. Let men remember what they really are, and see themselves *as* they are. See how much, even when they have attained to a sense of spiritual things, old faults go on, only under new shapes; how little way they have made in truly spiritual, unselfish affections and inclinations; and how little, in any important sense, they have advanced beyond the Law, even while they live under the Gospel.

THE ATONEMENT.

Hebrews x. 5.

"Sacrifice and offering thou wouldest not, but a body hast thou prepared me."

IT must strike any person, as something that wants accounting for, how it is that a doctrine which has called forth the moral affections of man so strongly, and presented so sublime and transcendent an object for them, as that of the Atonement has, should of all criticisms in the world be specially subjected to the charge of being an immoral doctrine. It is based, it is said, upon injustice. Had the Christian body then, simply accepted this doctrine in a neutral spirit, or with a respectful indifference, this charge might not have seemed so strange, but if it has won human hearts, and appealed to the highest moral feelings, such an estimate is perplexing. And it must be noted that injustice is of all immoralities not the one most easily condoned. It creates boundless hatred, and those who commit it themselves have the greatest objection to it in others. There can hardly be said to be a more unpopular vice. What can be the reason of this extraordinary discord in the estimate of this doctrine? Is it not that the Christian body has taken the doctrine as a whole, with all the light which the different elements of it throw upon each other, while the objection has only fixed on one element in the doctrine, abstracted from the others. The point upon which the objector has fixed is the substitution of one man for another to suffer for sin; but he has not taken this point as it is represented and interpreted in the doctrine itself, but barely and nakedly, simply as the principle of vicarious punishment. Thus stated then —that one man can be guilty of the crime, and another punished in his stead, that a criminal can suffer penalty by deputy, and have sentence executed upon him by substitute, this notion of justice is a barbarous and untenable one. We cannot say that God could, agreeably with his moral attributes, be satisfied with the punishment of an innocent man in simple exchange for the punishment of a guilty one—that his justice could possibly regard punishment apart from the person to whom it is due; be appeased by pain as such, without reference to the bearer of it; and be contented, so long as it was suffered, that another than the criminal should be the sufferer. We could not admit such an idea as this into our own moral nature, and therefore cannot assign such a principle of action to God. It is to be observed that, according to this idea of sacrifice for sin, it is not in the least necessary the sacrifice should be voluntary, because the whole principle of sacrifice is swallowed up in the idea of vicarious punishment; and punishment, vicarious or other, does not require a voluntary sufferer, but only a sufferer. The victim may be willing or unwilling;

it matters not, so long as he is a victim; he endures agony or death in fact, and that is all that, upon the principle of mere substitution, is wanted. It was this low and degraded idea of sacrifice which had possession of the ancient world for so many ages, and which produced, as its natural fruit, *human* sacrifices, with all the horrible and revolting cruelties attending them. For, indeed, it was impossible that an idea of sacrifice, which simply demanded a substituted person's suffering; which assumed that the more suffering there was the more expiation there was, and which did not care the least whether that suffering was voluntary or involuntary; it was impossible that this idea of sacrifice could rest contented with brutes as the victims. The blood of bulls or of goats sufficed for the Mosaic law, because the atonements of that law were only typical and figurative; but assume that the sacrifices of mere substitution really take away sin, and then they will go farther. They did go farther: they proceeded to claim *men*. Brutes were comparatively free from the power of suffering; their ignorance and want of reason protected them; they could not foresee their fate, and were led up unconscious to the altar, only to receive at one stroke their sentence and their release. But human beings could suffer; they could suffer because they could foresee, and therefore their sacrifice was the more availing and the more powerful in proportion as it was the more dreadful. Thus human sacrifices became a general institution over the ancient world, and the page of history is stained by the dark acts of that remorseless superstition—though not indeed without a protest from the high thought even of pagans. Ancient poetry mourned the Virgin of Aulis, and echoed, age after age, with ever fresh compassion, the sad strain, knowing how it would appeal to all human hearts;—the image of the tender daughter of the royal house, dragged by men's hands trembling to the altar, speechless, except with the piteous glance of her eyes, with which she smote her sacrificers.

But we must remark that for the great development of the idea of atonement, understood nakedly as vicarious punishment, we have to go to the new world. When the Spaniards conquered Mexico they found a gigantic and elaborate system of human sacrifices which exceeded all that had appeared in history. The annual ceremonies of sacrifice consumed several days, and the immolations of victims counted not by thousands but by tens of thousands. It was the function of the Mexican government, and devolved upon what may be called the Home Office, to expiate the sins of the whole population of Mexico; and so radically was the sacrificial system made a state object, that it affected even the foreign policy of the empire; and Montezuma, when he was asked by the Spanish general why he had omitted to conquer a certain independent republic, which was close at hand, replied, that if this State were part of his empire he could not go to war with it; but that he must have captives of war for victims to his gods. The blood of human victims thus flowed in such torrents that not a single sin could escape expiation in the whole empire of Mexico, and the monarch, as representative of the interests of his subjects, could point to most conspicuous success. But it was not only the quantity of the victims, but the refinement of the suffering, which showed the fructification of the original idea of atonement by simple substitution. The Aztec ritual prescribed upon solemn festivals, with horrible exactness, the most exquisite preliminary tortures. But the pains of imagination were also brought into requisition,—the agonies of a long anticipation and of a fixed prospective period, during which the victim lived with the certainty of a dreadful death before him. In one special case of annual sacrifice, the victim was solemnly devoted a year beforehand, the day was known, the exact ceremony and process of the death was known, up to the very moment when life must vanish. But in the meantime the victim lived surrounded with delights,—in the most delicate and refined luxury, amidst the pomp of retinue, the sweetness of music, the fragrance of flowers, and the incense of admiring crowds. He lived in the dreadful mockery of a kind of paradise, which he knew was to give place at an appointed moment to the most barbarous death, and in the meantime was to heighten, by the contrast of its present charms, the horror of the close. Tantum religio potuit suadere malorum. Such subtlety of cruelty was the issue of the idea that a mere substitution could be a sacrifice for sin; pain, due in justice to one, be escaped by simple transference to another.

As if, indeed, the Almighty could ever possibly be appeased by a struggling victim, dragged up in horror and agony, to be a sacrifice for sin against his will, recoiling at every step from the purpose to which he was devoted! As if an unwilling sacrifice for sin could ever possibly *be* a sacrifice for sin! But this idea was totally and for ever extinguished by the Gospel idea, when it was revealed that love was of the very essence of sacrifice, and that there could not *be* sacrifice without will. A victim then appeared who was the real sacrifice for sin. But how surprised would all those offerers of human victims have been had this real human victim, the only man who really was such, been pointed out to them. Here was no earthly altar, no expiatory form, no visible priest; nobody could have told, either from his life or from his death, that he was a victim; He died by the natural course of events as the effect of a holy and courageous life operating upon the intense jealousy of a class; he died by civil punishment: and in heaven that death pleaded as the sacrifice that taketh away the sin of the world. But that sacrifice was a willing, a self-offered sacrifice.

The circumstance then of the victim being a self-offered one, makes, in the first place all the difference upon the question of *injustice* to the *victim*. In common life and most human affairs the rule is that no wrong in justice is done to one who volunteers to undertake a painful office, which he might refuse if he pleased. In accepting his offer this would not indeed always apply; for there might be reasons which would make it improper to allow him to sacrifice himself. But it cannot be said that it is itself contrary to justice to accept a volunteer offer of suffering. Is it in itself wrong that there should be suffering which is not deserved? Not if it is undertaken voluntarily, and for an important object. Upon the existence of pain and evil being presupposed and assumed, there are other justifications of persons undergoing it besides ill-desert. The existence of pain or evil being supposed, there arises a special morality upon this fact, and in connection with it. It is the morality of sacrifice. Sacrifice then becomes, in the person who makes it, the most remarkable kind of manifestation of virtue; which ennobles the sufferer, and which it is no wrong doing in the universe to accept.

But this being the case with respect to voluntary sacrifice, the Gospel sacrifice is, as has been said, specially a voluntary and self-offered one. It must be remembered that the supernaturalness of the sphere in which the doctrine of the Atonement is placed, affects the agency concerned in the work of the Atonement. He who is sent is one in being with Him who sends. His willing submission, therefore, is not the willing submission of a mere man to one who is in a human sense another; but it is the act of one who, in submitting to another, submits to himself. By virtue of His unity with the Father, the Son originates, carries on, and completes himself the work of the Atonement. It is His own original will to do this, His own spontaneous undertaking, His own free and undictated choice. The peculiar nature of the agency concerned in the act of the Atonement is thus a guarantee to the willingness of the victim, and defines that willingness as being that of a volunteer from the first. And it must be observed that we have nothing to do with defending the mystery in the act of the Atonement in defending the justice of the act. Upon the question of the justice or injustice we must take the act as it is stated to be in the account which is given of it, whether that account belongs to the natural or supernatural order, the intelligible or mysterious.

The willingness of the sacrifice has then a very clear result with respect to the question of justice as regards the *victim*. But now with regard to the effect of the act of the Atonement upon the *sinner*. It will be seen, then, that with respect to this effect the willingness of a sacrifice changes the mode of the *operation* of the sacrifice, so that it acts on a totally different principle and law from that upon which a sacrifice of mere substitution acts. A sacrifice of mere substitution professes to act upon a principle of a literal fulfilment of justice, with one exception only, which is not thought to destroy but only to modify the literal fulfilment. It is true the sin is committed by one and the punishment is inflicted upon another; but there is sin, and there is punishment on account of sin, which is considered a sort of literal fulfilment of justice. But a voluntary sacrifice does not act upon the principle of a mock literal fulfilment of justice, but upon another and totally different principle. Its effect proceeds not from the substitution of one person for another in punishment, but from the influence of one person upon another for mercy,—a mediator upon one who is mediated with.

Let us see what it is which a man really means when he offers to substitute himself for another in undergoing punishment. He cannot possibly mean to fulfil the element of justice literally. What he wants to do is to stimulate the element of mercy in the judge. Justice is not everything in the world; there is such a thing as mercy. How is this mercy to be gained, enlisted on the side you want? By suffering yourself. You thereby soften the heart of the judge. The judge only accepts the act as a stimulant to mercy; it does not occur to him to accept it as a literal fulfilment of justice. The judge has the element of mercy in him; it is drawn out of him by the mediating suffering of another person for the guilty one.

The Gospel then puts before us the doctrine of the Atonement in this light, that the mercy of the Father is called out toward man by our Lord Jesus Christ's generous sacrifice of Himself in behalf of man. Now I have nothing to do here with the mystery of this transaction; the question is the morality of it—how the act of one person can alter God's regards toward another. This has given occasion to a charge of immorality against the doctrine of the Atonement; and it exhibits God as altering his feeling toward one being in consequence of the act of another. This is wrong, it is said. What has that one person's act to do with another person? How can it affect him, or influence our regards toward him?—it would be unjust in God to be affected by so entirely irrelevant a consideration. But it would certainly appear that we do ourselves something much akin to this in our relations toward others who have done anything wrong; and think it natural and *right* to do so. It is undoubtedly a fact of our nature, however we may place or connect it, that the generous suffering of one person for another affects our regards for that other person. It is true that the sufferer for another, and he who is suffered for, are two distinct persons; that the goodness of one of these persons is not the property of the other; and that it does not affect our relations toward another upon the special principle of justice; that, upon that strict principle, each is what he is in himself and nothing more; that the suffering interceder has the merit of his own generosity, the criminal the merit of his crime; and that no connection can be formed between the two on the special principle of justice. And yet, upon whatever principle it is, it is a fact of our nature, of which we are plainly conscious, that one man's interceding suffering produces an alteration of regards toward the other man. Take even a criminal before a judge, and suppose the fact just brought to his notice that a remarkable suppliant for this criminal has appeared—a suppliant so interested in this person, so absorbed in his pardon, as to be an absolute sacrifice to his own love, so as entirely to give himself up for him, and offer to undergo his death if the other only can escape:— suppose this, and is there any criminal in the world that would not be in a way consecrated by such love? Does not such love shed a halo, a glory, round the object of it? Is there any one upon earth so vile but that some reflection of the virtue of such transcendent affection must reach him?

But it will be said this is true as far as feeling goes, but it is a weakness, a confessed weakness; this impulse is not supported by the *whole* of the man. Can you carry it out, it may be said; can you put it into execution? We cannot, for very good reasons, that civil justice is for civil objects, and in the moral sphere final pardon is not in our province. But because this particular impulse to pardon cannot be carried out or put into execution, it is not therefore a weakness. It is something true and sincere which speaks in our nature, though it cannot be embraced in its full bearings and in its full issue. Even if it is a fragment, it is a genuine fragment. It exists in us as a true emotion of the mind, a fact of our true selves; it is a fact of nature, in the correct and high sense of the word. It is not disclaimed upon appeal; it stands its ground; nor, because it is a fragment, does it turn out upon inspection spurious. There is something which truly passes from suffering love to him for whom it suffers; something which is communicated to the criminal; a new regard to him which is an advantage to him. He looks different after it from what he did before. There is a transition of some kind in our minds. There is a pacifying influence upon the appetite for punishment. That another, and such another, is interested in him;—does that for him which he could not do for himself; it is rank to him; a new position. That there is an alteration of feeling toward him in consequence of another's act, and that the love of another to him can move toward pardon, is a fact of our nature.

This is only, indeed, an instance of one department of that general law of mediation which we observe in life and in nature. The whole law of association, e. g., is a law of mediation in the way of enlisting feelings for us, by means external to us. The laws of association do in fact plead for persons from the moment they are born; men have advocates in those they never knew, and succeed to pre-engaged affections, and have difficulties cleared away before them in their path. The air they breathe intercedes for them, the ground they have trod on, the same sights, the same neighbourhood. What is the tie of place, or what is even the tie of blood, to the essential moral being; it is a wholly extraneous circumstance; nevertheless these links and these associations, which are wholly external to the man, procure regards for him, and regards which are inspired with strong sentiment and affection. So good deeds of others, with which persons have nothing in reality to do, procure them love and attention. The son of a friend and benefactor shines in the light of others' acts, and inspires, before he is known, a warm and approving feeling. These are instances of mediation, in which what others do raises the regard toward yourself, puts you in an advantageous light, and creates a good will toward you. And though it is another, still it is only another step in this particular line of mediation, when, by its own suffering, mediating love alters regards toward one who has contracted guilt. It is indeed denied in some quarters that the parallel of mediation in nature extends to such a case as this. It is said, if you examine what mediation in nature in the behalf of the guilty really is, and what it amounts to, you will find that it applies only to the physical consequences of sinful actions as actions, and not to the moral consequences of such actions as *sins*. A man by a course of profligacy loses his health, and by a course of medical discipline recovers it; a man wastes his property, and is rescued from ruin by the intervention of his friends. These are cases in which one train of physical consequences is checked by the operation of another; but you do not find in nature, it is said, any case of mediation in which the *moral* consequences of sin are interfered with—its punishment as sin, as being of ill desert: and this must be put down therefore as a contradiction to our moral nature—that any act of one man can affect the moral result of the sin of another, or affect our regards toward that man as a guilty person. But though this limit in the mediation of nature is asserted, it appears to me to be asserted contrary to obvious facts. Mediation does appear, in particular cases, to advance beyond physical consequences to moral; as where, as has just been described, suffering love, pleading for another person, clearly has the power of appeasing our appetite for his punishment; and introduces fresh regards toward that other person.

This, that has been described, is the principle upon which the sacrifice of love acts, as distinguished from the sacrifice of mere substitution; it is a principle which is supported by the voice of nature and by the law of mediation in nature; and this is the principle, which the Gospel doctrine of the Atonement proclaims.

The effect of Christ's love for mankind, and suffering on their behalf, is described in Scripture as being the reconciliation of the Father to man, and the adoption of new regards toward him. The act of one, *i.e.*, produces this result in the mind of God toward another; the act of a suffering Mediator reconciles God to the guilty. But neither in natural mediation nor in supernatural does the act of suffering love, in producing that change of regard to which it tends, dispense with the moral change in the criminal. We cannot, of course, because a good man suffers for a criminal, alter our regards to him if he obstinately remains a criminal. And if the Gospel taught any such thing in the doctrine of the Atonement, it would certainly expose itself to the charge of immorality. But if there is no mediation in nature which brings out mercy *for* the criminal without a change *in* him, neither on the other hand, for the purpose of the parallel, do we want such. Undoubtedly there must be this change, but even with this, past crime is not yet pardoned. There is room for a mediator; room for some source of pardon which does not take its rise in a man's self, although it must act with conditions.

But viewed as acting upon this mediatorial principle, the doctrine of the Atonement rises altogether to another level; it parts company with the gross and irrational conception of mere naked material substitution of one person for another in punishment, and it takes its stand upon the power of love, and points to the actual effect of the intervention of suffering love in nature, and to a parallel case of mediation as a pardoning power in nature. When, then, objectors urge, against the doctrine of the Atonement the contradiction which it is to reason, that one man can be punished in the place of another, and assume a simple and naked substitution of one person for another, as the essence of the doctrine of the Atonement, it should be observed that this is going back to an ignorant and barbarous form of the doctrine as the true representation of it; when a completely new and purified form of it has come in in the Gospel doctrine of the Atonement. That doctrine was, in fact, as much a reform upon the *pagan* doctrine of substitution, as the Gospel was upon paganism, in religious truth in general. The doctrine of Scripture, so far from being the doctrine of mere substitution, is a protest against that doctrine; it makes accurate provision for moral claims; it enforces conditions on the subject of the sacrifice; it attributes a reasonable and rational ground of influence and mode of operation to the sacrifice. But objectors treat a doctrine which is, in fact, an harmonious balance and adjustment of truths, as if it were the same with the coarse and rude violation of common sense, which the pagan atonement represented. It is as though—if one may compare secular things with sacred—some correct statement of diplomacy or reasoning had been charged with a rude blunder wholly out of its scope. They make a mistake in the object of their attack; they mistake their doctrine, and have got hold of the wrong one. They are attacking the pagan doctrine, and think they are attacking the Christian one. The scope of their attack suits very well as against the savage and antiquated notion of mere substitution ; but their weapon is powerless, and cuts the air as against the Christian idea.

There is, however, undoubtedly contained in the Scriptural doctrine of the Atonement, a kind and a true kind, of *fulfilment* of justice. It is a fulfilment in the sense of appeasing and satisfying justice ; appeasing that appetite for punishment which is the characteristic of justice in relation to evil. There is obviously an appetite in justice which is implied in that very anger which is occasioned by crime, by a wrong being committed ; we desire the punishment of the criminal as a kind of redress, and his punishment undoubtedly satisfies a natural craving of our mind. But let any one have exposed himself thus to the appetite for punishment in our nature, and it is undoubtedly the case, however we may account for it, that the real suffering of another for him, of a good person for a guilty one, will mollify the appetite for punishment, which was possibly up to that time in full possession of our minds ; and this kind of satisfaction to justice and appeasing of it is involved in the Scriptural doctrine of the Atonement. And so, also, there is a kind of *substitution* involved in the Scripture doctrine of the Atonement, and a true kind ; but it is not a literal but a moral kind of substitution. It is one person suffering in behalf of another, for the sake of another : in that sense he takes the place and acts in the stead of another, he suffers that another may escape suffering, he condemns himself to a burden that another may be relieved. But this is the moral substitution which is inherent in acts of love and labour *for* others; it is a totally different thing from the literal substitution of one person for another in punishment. The outspoken witness in the human heart which has from the beginning embraced the doctrine of the Atonement with the warmth of religious affection, has been, indeed, a better judge on the moral question than particular formal schools of theological philosophy. The atoning act of the Son, as an act of love on behalf of sinful man, appealed to wonder and praise : the effect of the act in changing the regards of the Father towards the sinner, was only the representation, in the sublime and ineffable region of mystery, of an effect which men recognised in their own minds. The human heart accepts mediation. It does not understand it as a whole; but the fragment of which it is conscious is enough to defend the doctrine upon the score of morals.

Have we not, indeed, in our moral nature a great deal to do with fragments. What is mercy itself but a fragment which we do not intellectually understand, and which we cannot harmonise and bring into consistency with justice. Guilt is the direct consequence of a crime having been committed, it means that fact; it therefore cannot, as far as we can see, be taken from the man so long as the crime *has been* committed; and the old proverb said it was *the* thing the gods themselves could not do—to make what had been done, not have been done. It is therefore a profound and absolute impossibility that a man ever can be relieved from guilt at all by the light of speculative reason. We only know mercy as a practical state of feeling—that when an offender exhibits certain conditions we go through a certain change of mind concerning him, which is the stage of mercy. But if mercy is a fragment justice is a fragment too; you cannot carry justice out. It is not a whole, it is not a consistent thing. If mediation as a pardoning power then is a fragment of our moral nature—felt, but not knowing the way to act it out; a part of natural feeling not reduced to system; we say no more of it in substance than we do of justice and mercy. With respect to mercy, we have practical feeling about it which we cannot resist, and which we think right; and with respect to mediating love as a motive to mercy, we practically feel it to be a true motive as a part of us; that, as an ingredient in our nature, we cannot help acknowledging the power of one person's love to affect our regards to another, and unconsciously transfer a certain merit from the loving person to the loved. We cannot carry out this principle into any whole developed action; but it is a true element in our nature, and it affects us in a true way in our relations to guilt. Justice is a fragment, mercy is a fragment, mediation is a fragment; justice, mercy, mediation as a reason of mercy—all three; what indeed are they but great vistas and openings into an invisible world in which is the point of view which brings them all together.

There can of course be, and has been, a punctilious and narrow view of justice which only takes in the single idea, extracting it from the whole setting and context in which it naturally stands. This rigid and pedantic idea of justice has been a very persistent foe of Christianity and has always dogged its steps. It was the favourite argument of the Pelagians, and has been of various Deistical schools; but the error was obvious, that it was making a whole of what was only a fragment. The Pelagians were always harping upon one chord: they never got out of a groove of one single idea about justice in connection with merit; that all goodness must be a man's original own making; that inspiration was unfair, atoning love irrelevant. So a school of Deists have only seen one moral principle in things—justice, and converted mercy into justice, as man's due. All this is the teaching of men who can only see one idea in human nature; according to this idea of justice the sacrifice of a mediator is an act of high moral virtue, but the state of the criminal is not touched by it; they are separate facts, without any bearing upon each other; each is what it is; each merits what he merits. But the human heart takes in all the great vistas and reaches of human reason; one true element in us agrees with every other.

The doctrine of the Atonement is the doctrine which most of all comes into collision with, and declares most unextinguishable war with, materialistic ideas of the Deity; and for this very reason, as often as the materialistic side is by circumstances made the prominent one in our minds, and we are made to realise the visible infinity and unbroken law of the physical universe,—at such times, confronted by the iron empire of a mechanical immensity, we feel at the moment the whole account of the Atonement come as a surprise upon us. Material infinity is in fact a scene—the world appearing in a certain light and aspect to us. Well, if when the universe appears in this aspect to us —if while looking on a dreadful expanse of impersonal vacancy, the action of the Atonement suddenly demands a place in this world, is there not a clash? What room is there for this most awful, most grand, most sublime, most pathetic and glorious—if we may express heavenly things in human language—adventure amid the laws of nature? The reign of material fact, the *sort* of reality *that* is, throws an unsubstantial visionariness on the other plane of history; and the drama of the Atonement hangs like a beautiful picture in the sky, too good to be true. For it is characteristic of the Atonement that it is not only a doctrine but a history: it is a drama; it has action, it has parts, it has personages, it has place and scene. There is a Father and there is a Son; the Father sends the Son to be the Saviour of the world; the Son comes down from heaven to save it; enters this world, lives a life of sorrow in it; dies as a sacrifice for it; He rises from the dead, returns to heaven, and sits at the right hand of God, above all principality and power, and might and dominion, and every name that is named, not only in this world but also in the world to come. Visible fragments then of this sublime story are witnessed to; but in what heaven and earth did the whole take place? None that we see; none that science knows of; there is no place for it within this sphere of space in which we are. In no material sky did the Father give the commission to the Son. In no material sky does the Son now sit by the throne of the Father. This whole action took place in another heaven than that we see. Within this sphere of space, and to one who does not cast his eye in any sense out of it, it looks no part of the real world, it looks out of place; the whole story is one grand incongruity; a splendid illusion; ready to melt away and evaporate, like any creation of cloud or colour, the first occasion any one probes its solidity.

Hence then it is that some see only in the account of the Son of God's Atonement for the human race, a religious form of one of those legends which have followed the dawn of human sentiment and poetry. This has been, they say, the favourite type of the romance of all ages. There is a captive in chains, there is an oppressor, there is a deliverer from a far country; he exposes himself to hardships and death for the sake of the fallen; he conquers, he restores the enchained to freedom, and wins for himself glory and triumph. And is not this, they say, the story of the Atonement? And if so, what is it all but like soothing the ears of children with ancient rhymes, or sending them to sleep with the sound of soft music and murmuring voices? What is it but, when facts desert us, having recourse to dreams, believing in poems, and feeding on imagery?

Undoubtedly the story of the Atonement can be so

represented as to seem to follow in general type the poetical legends and romances of the infantine imagination of the world. In *details*—what we read in the four Gospels—not much resemblance can be charged, but a summary can be made so as to resemble them. And what if it can? What is it but to say that certain turning ideas, Divine and human, resemble each other; that there is an analogy? The old legends of mankind represent in their general scope not mere fancy, but a real longing of human nature, a desire of men's hearts for a real Deliverer under the evils under which life groans. The whole creation groaneth and travaileth in pain together until now. But more than this, do not they represent real facts too? These legends of deliverers would never have arisen had there not been deliverers in fact; the fabulous champions would not have appeared had there not been the real; it was truth which put it in men's heads to *imagine*. Doubtless, in all ages, there were men above the level, who interposed to put a stop to wrongs and grievances; for, indeed, the world would have been intolerable had it been completely given up to the bad. The romances of early times, then, reflect at the bottom what are facts; they reflect the action of real mediators in nature, who interposed from time to time for the succour of mankind in great emergencies. When, then, a heavenly mediation is found to resemble in general language an earthly one, what is it more than saying that earthly things are types of heavenly. We do not suppose that the two worlds, visible and invisible, are absolutely different and heterogeneous in fundamental structure ; we believe that they are upon one type, only that the type is carried out in an infinitely higher manner in the heavenly world than in the earthly. What wonder then if, when the highest of all mediators, the Mediator between God and man appears, the outline of His work comes out in the language of the Christian creed, as resembling the outline of some great earthly mediation ; in that sense in which what is heavenly can resemble what is earthly. "He for us men came down from heaven ; He was made man ; He was crucified for us. He suffered ; He was buried ; He rose again ; He ascended." So long as these words stand, and they are words of Scripture as well as of the Creed, so long must the Atonement recall to us images of high earthly mediations ; so long must the doctrine of the Atonement remind us of facts and of ideals in the history and mind of man. It is impossible to prevent these words from bringing back the burden of other histories—the home of grandeur and peace left, the dark and dreadful contest entered, the victory, the rescue, and the exaltation. But is this any reflection upon the doctrine of the Atonement? Or is it not rather the glory of that great doctrine that all these high earthly types of what is noble in action point so naturally to it, and that it fulfils all the highest conceptions and aspirations of the human mind.

So rooted is the great principle of mediation in nature, that the mediatorship of Christ cannot be revealed to us without reminding us of a whole world of analogous action, and of representation of action. How natural thus does the idea of a Mediator turn out to be? Yet this is exactly the point at which many stumble; pardon they approve of; reconciliation they approve of; but reconciliation by means of mediation is what they cannot understand. Why not dispense with a superfluity they say; and why not let these relieve us from what they consider the *incumbrance* of a mediator? But this is not the light in which a mediator is viewed by the great bulk of the human race. It has appeared to the great mass of Christians infinitely more natural to be saved with a Mediator than without one. They have no desire to be spared a Mediator, and cannot imagine the advantage of being saved a special source of love. They may be offered greater directness in forgiveness, but forgiveness by intervention is more like the truth to them.

It is this rooted place of a Mediator in the human heart which is so sublimely displayed in the sacred crowds of the Book of Revelations. The multitude which no man can number are indeed there all holy, all kings and priests, all consecrated and elect. But the individual greatness of all is consummated in One who is in the centre of the whole, Him who is the head of the whole race, who leads it, who has saved it, its King and Representative, the First-Born of the whole creation and the Redeemer of it. Toward Him all faces are turned; and it is as when a vast army fixes its look upon a great commander in whom it glories, who on some festival day is placed conspicuously in the midst. Is there humiliation in that look because he commands them? there is pride and exaltation, because he represents them. Every one is greater for such a representative. So in that heavenly crowd all countenances reflect the exaltation of their Head. Of that countless multitude none forgets that he has been ransomed, but none is lowered by the thought. The ransom has been given by their Head, and man has been rescued by man. The air of Heaven is perfumed with the fragrance of an altar, and animated with the glory of a great conquest. The victory of the Mediator never ceases, and all triumph in Him.

OUR DUTY TO EQUALS.

ROMANS XII. 16, 17.

"*Condescend to men of low estate. . . . Provide things honest in the sight of all men.*"

HOOKER'S great principle may perhaps be applied to the moral as well as the ceremonial question —that the omission of a point in Scripture does not decide against it, but only throws us upon the law of reason in the matter. Scripture ethics may perhaps be affected by this principle as well as Scripture law respecting Church forms. I mean by Scripture ethics here, not so much duties themselves, as the comparative rank of different duties—that we cannot judge from the comparative omission of this or that class of duties in Scripture, that therefore anything is decided as to its importance, or that it does not rank so high as some other class of duties which stands forward more prominently. Thus the New Testament says comparatively little about duties to equals, and enlarges upon duties to inferiors, compassion for the poor, sympathy with the afflicted, indulgence to the weak and the like —upon what we may call generally the condescending life; *i.e.* a voluntary descending from our own level to that of others. With respect to those who are as strong as themselves, as rich as themselves, as clever as themselves, and know as much as themselves, and have as many advantages in short of body and mind as they have—in a word about men's equals; it does not say much. But we may not infer from this that duties to equals do not rank as high and are not as trying a class of duties as those to inferiors or to sufferers. We may not infer even that they are not a more trying class of duties; we can infer nothing at all about it. What if the former are a more searching ordeal of the character than the latter? There is nothing at all against this estimate in Scripture, from the fact that it says less about them and more about the other; because Scripture in omitting, comparatively, express mention or inculcation of one class of duties may still assume the whole truth about them; and what that truth is, is left to our natural reason to decide. If Scripture singles out particularly one class of duties, it may be not to give it intrinsic pre-eminence, but because, as a supplement to former ethics, it needed special notice. What may be called the condescending life was comparatively a new branch of morals; it therefore demanded a prominent place in that page of Scripture in which, as a large and fully developed law of morals, it was for the first time brought forward. But Scripture in the particular expansion it gives to our duties to the poor and the inferior, institutes no comparison between the merits of the two, and decides nothing as to the superiority of the class of duties it calls special attention to over the class it comparatively omits.

This is not a subject altogether without a special interest in the present period of our Church, during which this branch of Christian work, which involves the relationship to the poor, the sympathy with them, and what we may call generally the condescending life, as distinguished from the life amongst equals, has been so largely and so profitably developed. We may say in brief that the peculiar scope of our Church ethics for the last thirty years has been the culture of works of compassion. It may be said, and we may rejoice in saying it, that great numbers have devoted themselves specially to a life of compassion and charitable exertion in the cause of the sick and poor. It has been a most remarkable instance of extraordinary development in a particular field of labour and energy in a church; and doubtless the historians of our Church in a future day will pay a marked tribute to it. Nor need we confine the special expansion of this branch of Christian work by any means to the rise of formal institutions; it has penetrated as a general spirit into our parishes and through society.

This striking manifestation cannot be observed without awakening much thought and many reflections upon the singular power which Christianity has exhibited in this field of employment. What a new life of the affections it has called into existence! The conspicuous and commanding use indeed which Christianity has made of the principle of compassion, is a characteristic of it which must strike everybody. And in addition to the obvious moral fruits which are involved in the employment of such an affection, it is impossible not to see what an enormous move was made in the furtherance of the greatest happiness principle, when this affection was taken up and converted into practice, and made a part of the individual's life. It is impossible not to see that numbers who never would have been happy in any other way, have been made happy and satisfied by the habitual exercise of compassion; by a life spent in more or less degree in that employment. Is not one struck with the astonishing stupidity of paganism in throwing away, as hardly looking at it, such an engine, such an instrument of gratification of the most deep, insinuating, and penetrating kind;—winding itself into the inner soul. Why, instead of that philosophical horror of perturbations; instead of all those quaint formulæ about compassion as an infirmity, an ægritudo, which one reads as one would the curious pedantic jargon of an obsolete world, separated from us by cycles of ages, why, instead of talking, did it not fasten at once and eagerly upon such a prize as a *motive;*—such a fortunate and such an invaluable discovery, such a gain to life—the life even of the agents themselves? It is obvious, upon the mere face of it, that compassion is a very remarkable principle; and one remarkable in this very point of view, that it converts into a pleasure to the individual that which is of incalculable advantage to society,—the alleviation of pain and misery. There could not be a more striking instance of things being double one of another, than that, there being sadness in the world, there should be an affection which derives its very gratification from sadness, and is carried toward the relief of it by an impulse which becomes pleasure in the act; *pleasure* as the very consequence of *pain*, because it is pain that calls forth that special form of love, and with the form of love the special delight that accompanies that form. And thus Montaigne says, that there is a spice of cruelty in compassion, because it requires pain to gratify its own special nature. There being, however, this peculiar affection in us, which was obviously of such immense practical power for dealing with this world as we find it, nay, which converts the very evil of the world into a material for exercising man and his affections; and not only exercising them but gratifying them;—how was it that the old world so entirely overlooked this wonderful practical instrument, rejected the compassionate life, and talked in a way about compassion in which men in a dream would talk about something,—with feeble idle remarks; dealt with it with a vapid superciliousness and a querulous emptiness which did not enter into its nature, or interpret the scope of the affection, or see the work it could do. This vast power in the world lay dormant, and had nothing given it to do. It acted of course as a natural affection in human hearts, whatever philosophers might say, and had its influence as such. It was the consoler of human sorrows, the softener of human trials. That it must be always, nature will always claim its own; but no public work was given it in the economy of the world,—it was not brought out.

And we may remark how paganism has blunted and suppressed even the natural virtue. One sees an instance of this in the religious rite of Hindooism, in leading the aged and infirm to the banks of the Ganges, and there leaving them to be carried away by the next rise of the waters. The religion had doubtless its own account to give of such a cutting short of human life : it might say it saved a great deal of bodily pain and suffering by it: what one observes is the total blindness it shows to the immense resources of compassion, the power of the virtue to convert its material into gratification. For does not age and infirmity under the point of view which compassion takes, become the subject matter of a quantity of daily cares and attentions, which interest, which soothe, and which satisfactorily engage the minds of the younger generation ? To cut off then the natural end of life was to cut off that which the virtue of compassion specially appropriated as its own, and with which it was fully able to deal and designed to deal. How much was lost to human life by this violent arrangement : and so by the Spartan expedient of cutting off at birth the maimed and the sickly forms of human life, so as not to encumber the State with unprofitable members, which required its nourishment, and did not repay it by service. The Spartan idea of human life was one of strict compensation. It demanded an equivalent. Can you pay us for it ? If so, the State will feed you. But you must fight for the State if the State is to keep you. This was the bargain. The Spartan had not the slightest conception of the State putting itself to expense and trouble for physically useless unproductive life. Did the born-maimed or feeble claim the right to live? The claim was not admitted. To be fed and to do nothing for his food was not one of the rights of man. This was the hard compact of Sparta with human existence. But what utter barrenness was there in the conception! What a loss instead of gain to the community! The principle of compassion gathers around the sick couch, interests and produces mental fruits which are ample equivalents for the want of gross power. Around the leisure of the infirm, thought, imagination, and philosophy spring up; and sick lives are centres of improving and refining influence. And a State which did not acknowledge this law consigned itself to the monotonous dulness of pugilistic strength.

Why then, when there was all this obvious power and use in compassion, could not men see it? Why did they not gladly lay hold on such a valuable instrument? The reason was they had not the heart to do it. Its nature, its scope was perfectly certain, there could be no doubt about it: it only required ordinary intellectual attention to see it; it carried its own witness with it; but there was something just on the surface which looked like weakness; it professed to act by feeling and not by strength. Therefore the pride of man did not think much of it; therefore ancient philosophy never opened the mine of happiness which lay in this principle. It was a discovery, like that of a new scientific principle, when it was made; and Christianity made it. Undoubtedly we must not forget that a life of compassion is not all happiness; it involves its own hard work; there is a great deal to do which human nature does not at first like; and there is disappointment here, as there is in other businesses of life. But there can be no doubt that this principle has added to the stock of human happiness as well as of human goodness.

It is thus that many have fled from the bitterness and disquiet of active life, from the strife and emulation of equals, to seek repose in the ministration to inferiors. They have fled to the realm of compassion for peace; knowing that there was work, but knowing that the work brought consolation and repose; knowing that there is a work which is trouble, and that there is a work which is rest. They found in man's adversity that help which they could not in his strength. So have our clergy often found in their parishes. A man enters new into the work of a parish; and, if he would confess it, he rather dreads the deathbeds; the sadness of them, the monotony of them, deprived as they are of worldly hope with its elasticity and variety;—the difficulty of health and vigour entering into the feeling of the dying. All this in prospect depresses. But the fact often turns out quite otherwise, and they are agreeably undeceived in the characteristics of a deathbed. The daily routine of parish work may be dull to a person; the calls with nothing to say, or only to say what he has said a hundred times! To deal with the stationariness of years; to do without fresh aspects, to labour on old ground wearies: but the tragic part of human life—that never fails in interest. It brings out as by some powerful chemistry the contents of men's minds, what they have in them;

it is a revealer, an awakener of hearts. It is life that deadens minds, death gives newness and freshness to them; the mask is thrown off; the day of truth has dawned, and none has seen the dawn of that day without being strengthened and freshened by it.

But while the compassionate view of man, as compared with the ordinary view of him in his health and strength as a flourishing member of this world, is characterised by a beauty of its own, it has at the same time the defect of being a protected state of mind, a state in which the mind is for the moment relieved of all its tendencies to irritation and to asperity, and thrown into a perfect quiet by an external event which does everything for it without an effort of its own.

How are we affected by a great death—the death of a great man, some leader, some man of power, who has planted himself in history? It composes and subdues us; it tranquillises us like some bell tolling, or some grave strain of music, or like evening silence. Instantly jars and discords cease, every disturbing recollection stops, and in the aspect of compassion all is forgotten that could raise the least stir or breath of air. Thus the mind is borne along in a passive train of musing, dwelling on the end and close of a splendid career, reposing on, and even in a sense enjoying, the deep peace of one great thought. Such is the soothing power of compassion that the mind under such circumstances will extract with a kind of greediness the whole strength of the sedative, and drain to the very utmost the deep power of the charm, before it lets the cup go. Such states of mind may be called eloquent; eloquent not in the form of pouring out, but drinking in—the eloquence of recipiency—drawing in deep currents of impressions. A great man gone is contemplated in all the softening light of this favouring medium of pity, which, as we are told, is akin to love. And yet we know if the man were to rise to life again, or if somebody exactly like him in character and position were to pass by, immediately every old jar would come back. Life would rob him at once of the refining hue, it would lower again, it would vulgarise again. A moment since he was all but loved, and now he is all but hated! Now it might be said, with some justice, that this is too wide a contrast in the estimate of a man for the mere accident of outward fortune to produce; that a man's character is not altered because he is alive one day and dead another; or because he is in adversity one day and in prosperity another; and that to attach ourselves to anger or to pity, according as the sun smiles upon a man or the clouds gather round him is to be slaves to the moment, and to make the judgment the creation of mere accident. But taking the compassionate view of man, as it naturally comes before us, without any stoical criticism upon it, and regarding it, as it undoubtedly is, as an extraordinary and in a sense sublime relief from all the disturbing and disquieting forces of the mind, from its pettiness, its jealousy, its egotism; it is still a state of mind which is made for us, made for us by an event; it is a sheltered state of mind; it is not our own doing; we are protected in this rest and tranquillity of the spirits, in this disinterestedness and generosity of the temper, by the circumstances of the case, which bind a chain around the passions and place us for the time under a tranquillising spell. Life is half anger, half compassion; but if the one is a fault the other is hardly our own merit.

While then the compassionate or condescending life of which I was speaking, appeals so powerfully to its own animation, and sweetnesses and intrinsic rewards, it must not be at the same time wholly forgotten, that upon this very side, and from this very source, arise its weakness and defects, as a form and sphere of discipline. The condescending life is a devoted life, but it is at the same time a protected life. It is sheltered from trials which very sharply beset the field of equals. The poor and dependent, the mourner, the desponding, the cast down—these exercise our active benevolence, but do not they unconsciously flatter us while they appeal to it; the benefit is all on one side; they are conscious of their want of power to make a return, and this want, though it is the appropriate blessing which accompanies the relation, is a blessing also, in the case of frail human benefactors, subservient to a weakness. The condescension is fully recognised, the superior is thought of, felt towards as such; as one who comes down from a higher sphere, to minister voluntarily to the inferior; this is his position, and he cannot help it; but it is a shelter also which follows him throughout his labours. He is a guarded worker, guarded upon one side of attack on which he is naturally exposed in the open world.

Everything from the grateful soothes—their looks, their words; your pride is safe; they confess dependence; and so they unconsciously confer exaltation. All gives way to you, all praises you; as received into the weak human heart even gratitude can turn into a subtle species of flattery; there is a flattery even of the dying. But in the society of equals it is specially the case that a man is exposed to the most terrible blows on the very side on which he is sheltered in the life of condescension; upon the side of his pride. He starts in the first place with a less exalted position, in a sphere of ordinary duty, as compared with a voluntary and gratuitous descent; he has his task set him; he must do it or he is punished. There is undoubtedly very deep in human nature the reluctance to acting upon compulsion; it is disagreeable to man; yet it would be very unwise to say that obligation was not very salutary to man, as distinguished from that idea which he is so fond of,—and which constitutes what may be called the natural doctrine of works of supererogation,—that very common idea between men and their own hearts that they do more than they strictly ought to do, and that life is with them a great superabundance and excess beyond the rule of right and duty.

And when we go into particulars: in the life of equals a man enters upon a vast field of relations in which his humility and his generosity pass through an ordeal of special and peculiar severity; severity far greater than that which attaches to any trial of them in the relationship to inferiors; for the simple reason that a man is in competition with his equals, and he is not in competition with his inferiors. To a superficial person it might appear that the great act of humility was condescension, and that therefore the condescending life was necessarily a more humble one than the life with equals. But this is not the true view of the case. The hardest trial of humility must be not towards a person to whom you are superior, and who acknowledges that superiority, but towards a person with whom you are on equal footing of competition. In the relationship of the superior to the inferior it is the very condescension which constitutes a satisfaction to man's self-love; by his very condescension, while he gives on the one side benevolent exertion, frail man receives and gains on the other a sense of superiority. But in the relationship of equals this cannot be the case; where there is competition you yourself lose what you give to another, you fall yourself by how much you raise another.

The relations to equals are thus the more real trial of humility than the relations to inferiors; and if persons will examine into their state of mind, they will, I think, find that their own feelings and sensations will verify this comparison. The sense of defeat, the pangs of wounded pride, the mortification of aims and aspirations,—these witness to the sharp ordeals which the life of equals produces; while certainly if these are borne well, they constitute a safer guarantee to a real humility of character than any condescension to inferiors in the nature of the case can. So that it stands to reason that humility is much more tried by equals than it is by inferiors. Do not equals in fact make the appropriate, the special, and the only effective correction to pride? The individual in truth comes into the rough open air as soon as he gets among his equals. He comes into contact with his own weaknesses, and finds out his own failings in a way in which no condescending life could have acquainted him with them. And amongst other things he finds out how much harder it is to be fair to an equal than ever so generous to an inferior. For it is the same with generosity as it is with humility. Generosity is more tried by an equal than it is by an inferior, for the same reason that it is so with humility—viz., that you are in competition with your equals, and are not in competition with your inferiors. We know that the great obstruction to generosity in our nature is jealousy—at least with regard to such advantages as touch our pride. It would be easy to be generous to the intellectual claims of other people, to their merits, to their character, were there no element of jealousy in ourselves. But compassion is relieved from this trial; compassion cannot be jealous; its work is with one who lies at its feet, who deprecates the slightest comparison. How generous then will a man be to the fallen; but let the man get on his legs again, and it will sometimes be hard to him who has been so superabundantly generous even to be barely just. It is thus that generosity to an equal is more difficult than generosity to an inferior. And while one who condescends to another beneath him is sheltered from all comparison and has his pride safe, he who is generous to an equal is generous at the risk of his own loss and fall by comparison; he does him justice at the cost of himself suffering for it. There is thus often a want of generosity in the apparent generosity of preferring inferiors to equals, the unsuccessful to the successful. They are preferred because they do not come into competition with you: so they must fail in order to please you. Thus an ungenerous temper may be easily fostered under the guise of generous condescension; and it is in fact often fostered under the pretensions of Christian humility, when a man is exceedingly desirous that everybody else should undergo the benefit of humiliation, and does not go very closely into his own heart, to examine what his motive is in that desire.

And when we go from what a man has to do to others, to what he has to suffer from others, the contrast becomes still more marked between the two spheres. The peculiar power which malice and ability together have to inflict pain is one of the familiar experiences which every man must go through, who, with any activity, and with any scope and object in life, throws himself with force and energy into the society of his equals. It is only what he must expect. He must expect to meet those who are as able and keen-witted as himself, and he must expect that there will be disagreement, and he must expect that disagreement will bring out the disagreeable parts of men's characters. Misfortune, adversity, soften the human heart; those who have fallen, those who have never risen, the depressed, the humbled, are unconscious flatterers; they raise a man on a pedestal to himself. Not so a mass of struggling equals: even when they do what is quite natural and right, they do not do this; it would indeed be very mischievous if they did. They make, even when perfectly fair and hardly even impatient, still, severe judges. And if their aims come into collision with your own, as in a general competition they will do, this tries equity and good temper. Nor need the aims necessarily relate to private or selfish interests; the contest of opinion, political or religious, is enough. Whence do those grievances come which prey upon men's spirits, whence those wounded feelings, which last often for life? Can the miserable, the feeble, the prostrate, inflict such blows? Those sharp strokes cannot come from a quarter that we condescend to; they must be then the result of relations with equals.

To leave the realm of compassion for that of equality is indeed to leave the realm of peace for that of war. Compassion is a state of peace. It undoubtedly imposes its work, but its relations are settled, its feelings flow from the situation, emulation is over, the issue has been arrived at, and there is the serenity of the end. But cross over to the world of equality, and it is a state of war; with unfixed relations, with a struggle of interests, with a comparison of strength, and with issues which have yet to be decided. All is uncertain and fluctuating, trembling on the confines of enmity; and one man the opponent of another, the rival of another. There are the concomitants of war —the precautions, the safeguards, the modifications of reserve and suspicion.

It is thus that a life of ordinary and common probation, which is what a man generally leads when he lives with his equals, is found when examined to contain a powerful supply of the most finished and subtle weapons of discipline. It is not that this kind of life possesses an inferior arsenal, which must be put up with if we have not a better, but which has only blunted instruments of correction to furnish; but that it has the finest and largest collection of such weapons, made with consummate skill, and adapted to every want. Hardly anybody need complain of a defect and scarcity, however highly he may value them. This sphere of equals, that is to say, a life of common trial, commands the sharpest contradictions to human feeling, the finest jars, the deepest discords; this rich and ample treasury is for ever renovated with fresh forces and adaptations. It is when trials form part of our natural circumstances that they enter deepest and take most hold. The trials of the sphere of equals touch the tenderest parts, and apply the most refined tests; they find out a man the most thoroughly. It is common life that has the keenest and subtlest instruments at command. It might be thought at first that it would be the reverse; that the condescending life would have the sharp and finished tools for the formation of character, and that common life would have the dull ones; but in fact common life has the finest tools. And, whereas, when some special life turns out its workmanship, it sometimes seems as if the whole figure were cut out with one tool—the face, the body, the limbs; on the other hand common life, from the very variety and subtlety of its situations and its trials—and from the very fineness of its tools, turns out the more finished form; the workmanship has more execution and expression in it. We must accord then the condescending life its own praise, for its own devotion; but we cannot give it the superiority as an engine of discipline and trial for man's pride, for his strong and passionate will, his tendency to idolise himself, his vanity, his jealousy. Equals are more than inferiors the natural correction for self-love. And while pity has certainly effects of great beauty in its own field, still the palm of a stronger and sharper correction may belong to another sphere of training.

And as a sort of vertex and climax of the life of equals, public or political life has undoubtedly great and peculiar powers of discipline. Here it may be said, with truth, there gathers to a head all that is pointed, strong, and effective in the discipline of the society of equals; here there is everything that can force a man out of a narrow sensitiveness, out of brooding thoughts, out of weaknesses, out of vanity and egotism, and even against his will strengthen and brace him. Here the necessity of action is such that a man has not the time and leisure to acquire some faults which certain defects of character require. For it is true that some kinds of faults do seem to require quiet and leisure for their growth and education; and interruption disturbs them. And this public life does seem to exercise a kind of compulsion upon men; so that it will not endure some forms of the morbid temper in men, which flourish with considerable strength upon more retired ground. Thus take the principle of forgiveness—people giving up grudges and agreeing to forget injuries. In what a slow and sluggish stream does the temper of forgiveness flow in retired and remote regions of human life. One is almost obliged to substitute, even in the place of a stream of any kind, however sluggish, the metaphor of a dull, a torpid, and a stagnant marsh. It is the discredit of social life, in some sections of it, that injuries, whether real or fancied, hardly ever are forgiven in it; but that if once offence is taken it goes on for years and never stops; that it is cherished, and becomes more fixed as it grows older; and that it gains in passive strength and obstinacy with the progress of time. But when we turn to political and public life we see that the necessities of that life are such that they do not admit of men shutting themselves up in grudges, and that men are obliged to obey the stringent call of circumstances, which requires them to give up whatever stands in the way of salutary action; that they are compelled to exert a force over themselves, and to bend their wills under the yoke. Thus in public life we see forgiveness flowing in large and copious streams, and men agreeing to act together again, as if nothing had happened. It is an astonishing and marvellous spectacle of flexibility as compared with the rigid retention of retired life. The floodgates of pardon are opened, as the exigencies of party require; and nothing is allowed to stand in the way of large, ample, and adequate effacements and abolitions, of the very highest utility, effecting the most important and patriotic objects. And though it may be said that public forgiveness is not quite the same as private; and though it may not be the case that reconciliations on this large scale are universally accompanied by the more tender sympathies, and the touching traits of forgiveness; it is still very striking to see such a subjugation of wills, such an acceptance of discipline, and such a recognition of the fact that the necessities of things are against unforgiveness, that it must give way, that there is not room for it in a world of action, and that the good of society is inconsistent with and excludes it. Such a result is a remarkable instance of the coincidence of two laws, a moral law which dictates forgiveness to the heart, and a law of business and necessity on the part of the community which demands it as the condition of public ends.

The two spheres of trial which have been compared together in the observations which I have been making, coincide partially with the two ideas of trial which attach respectively to life viewed as a mission, and life viewed as a probation. These two aspects indeed of life are so far from being in any disagreement with each other, that they mutually involve each other. It is a part of our probation to have a duty or—if we like the term better—a mission of succour and charity; a mission to comfort, to support, and instruct others according to their needs. And again it is part of our mission in life to encounter probation in it, and to submit to trials, for our own discipline. The two ideas then are part of the same process, and imply each other. And yet a certain prominence may be given to one of them or to the other, marking the two as different main ideas of life and trial two different persons may have. Persons may regard themselves as having been sent into the world to accomplish certain public objects. They may view themselves as marked out for some great charitable work; or under a special call to make other people better. If they regard themselves then as sent into the world for the benefit of the world, they will think of this life mainly as a mission. On the other hand, if they contemplate the trial of life as bearing mainly on themselves, they will then think of it as a probation. With all our admiration then of the more sanguine and enthusiastic of these two aspects of life, we may still look upon the idea of probation as the most rich in lessons of experience and of humility.

I have said that, in comparing the sphere of compassion and the field of equals together, the one class of duties is more prominent in Scripture than the other. The place which works of compassion have in the Gospel narrative and in the constitution of the early Church,—besides particular precepts,—account for this prominence. But it is quite needless to say the ordeal of the sphere of equals is still amply represented in the New Testament. Our Lord's own life is abundant evidence of this. It is particularly to be observed that our Lord, though He instituted the great exemplar of the compassionate or condescending life, had a life with equals which ran parallel to it; I speak of course of equals in the visible sense; the learned and disputative Jews, the Pharisees and Scribes, who had cultivated systematic thought, speculation, and doctrine, and led schools and parties, were in outward appearance His equals; and He stood in regard to large classes in a relationship to equals. We call then our Lord's acts of charity and pity works, and they count among His labours; but were they not also in a still truer sense refreshments of His Spirit—holy recreation to Him? Was not the act of condescending compassion to the poor and wretched a gratification, a tranquillising pause amid the strife and toil? He looked round upon a world of equals and it was war—it was the array of hostile looks, malice and craft, the watching for openings, the preparation for assault. On His own part there was the strain of a constant caution, readiness to meet attack, vigilance against surprise, and all the effort of self-defence. But when He entered the realm of compassion, then when the ear heard Him, it blessed Him, and when the eye saw Him, it gave witness to Him; the blind cried to Him from the wayside; Zaccheus watched for Him from the sycamore; the sick woman touched the hem of His garment; He was met by the affectionateness of beseeching looks and supplicating voices. Scenes of joy rose up all round Him, the leper blazed abroad his cure, the blind man glorified God for his sight, and all the people gave praise unto God. Could all this be other than a consolatory life, inserted in the midst of a life of contest and strife? When He fed the five thousand in the wilderness, could the satisfying of the hunger of such a crowd, and supplying the natural wants of man, be other than a relief to Himself? When He sighed over the ears

He was going to open, and said Ephphatha, that sigh indeed expressed a sympathetic sorrow for a world of pain and deprivation, but the act of restoring that great faculty, could not be other than grateful to the Restorer. When He gave back the son to the mother, how could that not be a pleasurable act to Him? And when He gave the news to the people of the house— the damsel is not dead, but sleepeth; how could the delivery of such joyful news not be a joy to Himself? If, by the constitution of our nature, compassion has a particular gratification attending upon it, that gratification attended upon it in our Lord's case. These then were not His labours or His toils, they were comparatively His recreation, His pleasure, and His holiday. His life among equals, proclaiming His cause against adversaries, invincible defiance, inflexible will—this was His hard work; it was by the struggle with equals that the battle of eternal truth was fought; and by this He fulfilled the great trial of a human life. The powers of nature and the powers of Hell were conquered by His other and miraculous acts; by this struggle He conquered man. First in the succour of man, first in the war with man, first in both hemispheres of action, the Firstborn of Creation lives in the Gospel, a marvellous whole, to inspire morality with a new spirit, to soften man's heart, to consecrate his wealth. The light of ages gathers round Him, He is the centre of the past, the pledge of a future; the great Character marches through time to collect souls about it, to found new empires for the truth, and to convert the whole earth to the knowledge of the Lord.

THE PEACEFUL TEMPER.

HEBREWS XII. 14.

"*Follow peace with all men, and holiness, without which no man shall see the Lord.*"

THERE are many particular duties in which Christianity and worldly wisdom meet, both recommending the same course. One of these is the duty mentioned in the text, viz., that of being at peace with others. A wise adviser of this world tells any one who consults him as to his conduct in life, to beware especially of getting into quarrels with people. He tells him more than this. He tells him not only to avoid actual quarrels, but to cultivate a peaceful temper. The Gospel tells us to do the same. It is one of the most frequent maxims in the New Testament. The advice is the same, though the reason of it is different, as a piece of worldly wisdom, and as a Christian precept. The reason which worldly prudence suggests, is the quiet and happiness of life, which are interfered with by relations of enmity to others. The reason which religion gives is the duty of brotherly-love, of which the peaceful disposition is a part. But the frequency of the advice, under either aspect, is remarkable, and shows that there is some strong prevailing tendency in human nature to which it is opposed. Let us then examine what this tendency is, and we shall be able better to see what that state of mind is which is the opposite of it, and which ought to take its place.

When we examine, then, the tempers of men, to see what there is in them which is so strongly opposed to this precept of following peace, the first thing we observe is, that people rush into quarrels from simple violence and impetuosity of temper, which prevents them from waiting a single minute to examine the merits of the case, and the facts of the case, but carries them forward possessed with a blind partiality in their own favour, and seeing nothing but what favours their own side. This is perhaps the most prominent and conspicuous antagonist to peace and the peaceful disposition. Again, there is the malignant temper, which fastens vindictively upon particular persons, who have been either the real or supposed authors of some disadvantage. Men of this character pursue a grudge unceasingly, and never forget or forgive. They often set themselves to work to do somebody, whoever it is, to whom they bear this grudge, some positive harm; and even when they do not enter upon a regular plan of revenge, they make use of any opportunity that falls in their way to spite him. This is another and a worse source of the relation of enmity, a more irreconcilable foe to peace than even blind impetuosity.

But impetuosity and malignity are not the only tempers which are opposed to the law of peace, and to the peaceful disposition. There are some very common habits of mind, which, without being so conspicuous and decided in their manifestations, lead to a great deal of enmity of a certain kind—sometimes open enmity, sometimes, when this is avoided, still to bad relations towards others. There are many persons who can never be neutral or support a middle state of mind. If they do not positively like others, they will see some reason for disliking them; they will be irritable if they are not pleased; they will be enemies if they are not friends. They cannot bear to be in an attitude of mind which does not give active employment to the feelings on one side or the other. They are not so unreasonable as to expect that they can like persons without knowing them; but, if they know them, if they meet them, if they live near them, if they see them often, if they have dealings with them, and still do not like them; that is, do not see in them that which meets their taste—are not taken by anything in their character,—then they put themselves in a hostile relation to those persons. They see a cause of provocation in the mere circumstance that there is nothing to engage and win. And some will confess this of themselves, and confess it with a kind of pride, that they must either love or hate, either be friends or foes. It seems to themselves to be the sign of a generous character always to have positive feeling either for or against. This rule, then, of their own, has the necessary result of placing them in a kind of enmity towards numbers of persons to whom there is not the slightest real reason for feeling it, towards those who have done them no harm, and whose fault simply is, that they do not please or suit them. But it is so irksome to them to maintain an indifference and neutrality that they cannot bring themselves to acquiesce in what are, after all, the real facts of the case, which no partial or fanciful rule of their own can alter. They cannot say to themselves,—I see nothing in these persons that commends itself particularly, and therefore I do not go so far as to entertain strong feelings for them; on the other hand, there is nothing to give actual offence, and therefore there is no reason whatever why I should entertain feelings against them. I will take care, therefore, that my feelings shall correspond to the facts of the case, and though I cannot make friends of them there shall at any rate be no enmity. This rule accords with the facts of the case; the other rule, which they take, is fanciful and arbitrary,—that of a summary alternative of friendship or enmity. It is often, however, affectionate and warm-hearted tempers that adopt this rule. They enjoy the sympathy of kindred souls, the answering of heart to heart; but if they do not meet with sympathy, then the blank is not only disappointing to them but irritating. Then they relapse into enmity, as if they were ill-used because they were not suited. There is something imperious, if we examine it, in this rule; it is as much as to say—What do these persons mean by not pleasing and fitting in to my taste. On this principle many of their neighbours are eyesores to them, and the very sight of them interrupts their repose, when there is no real occasion for any such feelings; inasmuch as, if they have furnished no cause for pleasure, they have not furnished any cause for pain either.

Such is the arbitrary and fanciful rule which

people sometimes lay down for themselves in their relations with others. And now, what I want to observe is, how completely this rule is opposed to the law which the Apostle lays down, of " following peace with all men." When we examine what the relation of peace is, we find that it is exactly that relation toward others which the temper I have described has such a difficulty in adopting, and which is so repugnant to its taste. A state of peace, which is neither less nor more than peace, is this middle state to which such objection is made. It is not a state of active love and affection, for these we do not call being at *peace*, but something more ; nor is it a state which admits of any ill-feeling ; but it lies between the two, comprehending all kindly intentions, forbidding the least wish for another's injury, avoiding, as much as possible, dispute and occasion of offence ; consulting order, quiet, and contentment, but not arriving at more than this. This is the state of thing which we call being at peace with others. If we have the least wish, though we hardly express it to ourselves, for another person's harm, if we have the least resentful motive toward him, *that* is enmity; then we are not at peace with him. Peace implies the entire absence of positive ill will. The Apostle then says that this is our proper relation toward all men. More than this applies to some, but as much as this applies to all. He would have us embrace all men within our love, so far as to be in concord with them, not to be separated from them. Separation is inconsistent with Christian membership. On the other hand, he knows that more than this must, by the limitation of our nature, apply to the few rather than to the mass and multitude; he fixes then upon this, nothing higher and nothing lower; he fixes upon the middle ground of peace as our proper relation towards the many. Be in fellowship, he says, with all men, so far as to have nothing wrong in your relation to them, nothing to disunite : follow peace with all men.

Is any other principle of conduct and kind of temper indeed *fit* for this world in which we live ? Whatever those who adopt the other course may say, there is no room for it in the state of things in which we are placed. It jars with the whole frame of things. There are so many obstacles to mutual understanding in this world, and so very thin a veil is enough to hide people from each other, that if the line is adopted of being in half or incipient enmity towards all who do not reveal themselves in an attractive and amiable light to us, we shall be in this unfavourable relation towards by far the greater part of society ; some probably of excellent character, whose higher qualities are unhappily hid from us. The great mass of those even whom we know and meet with in the intercourse and business of life must be *comparatively* nothing to us. More than this, they must be often persons—even those whom we are constantly meeting must be persons— who are not made after a model that we like, persons who do not sympathise with us or elicit sympathy from us. True and genuine intercourse and communication between minds, if it could be obtained, might clear up a good deal of this cloud, and remove the barrier which separates one man from another; but this is not given, and if it were, there still remain dissimilarity of tempers, gifts, and tastes. The Apostle then lays down a plain rule with respect to the whole of this large section—viz., to be at peace with them. But what is their rule who will have no medium between love and enmity? It is a rule which evidently places them in a kind of enmity with all such as these, *i.e.*, with by far the greater number of people with whom they have to do, the great majority of their neighbours, the larger part of those whom they are constantly seeing. If not in open, they are in secret half enmity with vast numbers, inwardly judging them and warring with them in their thoughts. They are not at peace with them because they discard a middle and neutral relation as lukewarm and not suited to them. But this is exactly the relation which the Apostle has in his mind when he enjoins peace; he contemplates this very neutral and middle state they so much object to.

I have shown that there is a kind of temper and disposition which, without impetuosity, and without malignity, is still in opposition to the law of peace, and does in fact produce a great deal of latent, if not open enmity, in the world. I will now mention one or two reasons which have a great deal to do in promoting this temper. In the first place, it is very irksome to keep watch over ourselves, and to repel the intrusion of hostile thoughts by the simple resistance of conscience, when we are not assisted by any strong current of natural feeling in doing so. This is a difficult duty. But those who say that they either like or dislike, avoid and evade this duty. They only keep away hostile feelings when, in fact, this is done for them; when a strong favouring bias, a strong current of partiality in their minds, of itself excludes such feelings. The duty is under these circumstances easy of being at peace; but to be at peace where there is no partiality is not so easy. It is necessary then to keep guard against the foe, who, seeing that the heart is not preoccupied with a positive preference, struggles to gain admission into it for what is hostile. When a person then resolves either to like or dislike, this, instead of being generosity is in reality escaping a trial, avoiding a duty which would be irksome to him. Is he not slipping his neck from the yoke, and throwing off the posture of watch over himself? He says he is always at peace with another when he is partial to another. Of course he is, his own bias then keeps out enmity; but it is keeping it out when he has not this bias that constitutes the trial.

Another reason which tends to keep up the disposition which I have been describing is, that the hostile class of relations are evidently accompanied by their own pleasures in many temperaments. They furnish an excitement to them; and, at the bottom, they prefer it to a state of peace on this account, because there is agitation and a flutter of spirits in this relation; whereas peace is repose, and does not offer this play to the mind and temper. There is a kind of interest which people take in their own grievances, their own grudges, their own causes of offence at various people, their own discords and animosities, which occupies their thought—it must candidly be said—in a manner not disagreeable to themselves. They enjoy these states of mind towards others in their own way. They summon the recollections of different occasions on which, in their own opinion, their rights were neglected and their merits depreciated. They live in an universal atmosphere of contest, but they derive a certain gratification from it. Life is relieved of its tameness and tediousness; it is filled with material of interest of a certain kind, which acts as a stimulus to the mind, and promotes the play of various emotions. All this is really more pleasant to many people than peace and quiet. They would rather a great deal be in a state of irritation with any person for any reason, than feel at all dull. To be dull is the greatest trial to them. They will stir up the scene at any rate, even at the cost of renewing vexatious subjects. It breaks the level of life; it varies the flatness of it. It is a stimulant; it keeps the spirits in motion. So, too, is the *justification* of dislike; the explanation how it arose and was called for. All this is much more to the taste of many than being at peace. They are not conscious of any deep malignity, but they derive a pleasure still from the disturbance of the ground, the agitation of the elements of life, which they take care shall not subside into complete repose. In the feeling of provocation, if there is not always the sense of victory, there is at any rate always the sense of the right to victory. This is better than nothing, and they will keep alive the sense of so important a right. There shall always be something stirring to bring it forward, some occasion for reminding themselves how much reparation they deserve at the hand of others.

It was with the entire knowledge of these weaknesses and frailties of human nature, and these elements of disturbance, even in minds of average goodness, that St. Paul said—" Follow peace with all men." You must not, he says, be at peace only with those to whom you are *partial;* that is easy enough; you must be at peace with those toward whom you entertain no partiality, who do not perhaps please you, or suit you. That is the rule of peace which the Gospel lays down, and it must be fulfilled by standing guard at the entrance of our hearts, and keeping off intruding thoughts. And he says again that we must not seek excitement from the petty quarrels and discords of life, from prejudice and antipathies, and the commotion which is bred out of them. This is a poor and morbid pleasure which impoverishes and lowers every mind that indulges in it. Peace, he says, is our proper relation to all men. There is no reason why, as far as we are concerned, we should not be at peace with everybody. If even they are not at peace with us we may be at peace with them. Let them look to their own hearts, we have only to do with our own. Let us "follow peace with all men and holiness, without which no man shall see the Lord." It is not without design that these two were connected together by the Apostle—following peace and holiness. A life of enmities is greatly in opposition to growth in holiness. All that commotion of petty animosity in which some people live, is very lowering, it dwarfs and stunts the spiritual growth of persons. Their spiritual station becomes less and less, in God's sight and in man's. In a state of peace the soul lives as in a watered garden, where, under the watchful eye of the Divine Source, the plant grows and strengthens. All religious habits and duties,—prayer, charity, and mercy, are formed and matured when the man is in a state of peace with others—with all men; when he is not agitated by small selfish excitements and interests which divert him from himself and his own path of duty, but can think of himself, what he ought to do, and where he is going. He can then live seriously, calmly, and wisely; but there is an end to all religious progress when a man's whole mind is taken up in the morbid excitement of small enmities, when he derives gratification from these jarring relations to others. He ceases to reflect upon himself and to work out his own salvation; his thoughts and his cares are frittered away upon trifles. He does not follow peace, and therefore he does not follow holiness. Let him change all this, throw off these humiliating chains, and set himself once and for all free for serving God, watching his own heart, doing good to his neighbour, and raising his own soul.

THE STRENGTH OF WISHES.

MATTHEW VII. 7, 8.

"*Ask, and it shall be given you; seek, and ye shall find; knock, and it shall be opened unto you: for every one that asketh receiveth; and he that seeketh findeth; and to him that knocketh it shall be opened.*"

SCRIPTURE insists much on the power of strong wishes in spiritual things. Its language is—if men really wish to be good, they will become good; if they really wish for faith, they will get faith; if they really wish to have habitual seriousness, they will gain habitual seriousness; if they really wish to realise God's presence, they will in time do so. The power of prayer, which is so much taught in Scripture, is in fact the power of strong wishes; wishes are prayers, if men believe in God, and if their wishes are formed around His Presence. And so the text certifies in truth to the power of strong wishes. Ask, and it shall be given you; seek, and ye shall find; knock, and it shall be opened unto you. Asking, seeking, knocking—all these express earnest wishes of the heart, which have put themselves in the shape of addresses to God. If we do not become believing, or serious Christians, Scripture says it is because we have no real wish to become so. We do not ask, or seek, or knock; if we did we should obtain.

Let us only think of the keenness and force of the wishes we form with respect to various temporal advantages, whether of mind or outward fortune. What acute wishes are raised in many persons' minds by the sight of any great eminence, or splendour, or grandeur, in human stations. How does any pompous spectacle set many hearts at once wishing for and dreaming of greatness of some sort or other! And though these are often mere volatile day-dreams, still the wishes are strong though the acting power is weak; and sometimes deep desires are formed, which become fixed and powerful impulses, propelling men to the acquisition of what they desire. So with respect to mental gifts. How common it is for men to indulge their thoughts in imagining themselves possessing gifts which they have not. Upon hearing of some eloquent speech, of some bright stroke of wit, some readiness, some quickness of reply, some act of penetration, how do they long for such faculties; what would they give to be able to achieve such feats of mind! It must be observed what imitative creatures men are, and how, upon seeing particular gifts and aptnesses in others, they fasten upon them at once as objects of desire for themselves. The coming across them puts the idea into their heads, — what, if they too had these gifts; and this sets them wishing. Thus the quantity of imitation which we see in the world;—people trying to be what they see certain other persons to be, and expending themselves in efforts which are fruitless, and sometimes injurious: all this is a sure indication of the strong wishes which the human heart forms for ability to do particular things which others do; which strike or please others. Men are like the children of a town in which some jugglers, or performers of curious bodily feats, have been exhibiting; the children are seen immediately, in all the streets, imitating the extraordinary performances they have seen, obviously having caught the inoculation of the recent spectacle, and being bitten by the desire to do something which will have a likeness to it. So does the sight of success in any human faculties;—in any particular kind of address, or in science, or art, or manner,—stir up at once the natural emulation of the human heart, and set men thinking and dreaming of it, and wishing it for themselves. And so with the persuasiveness and attractiveness of different objects for different minds. Who can live in the world without becoming aware that the very air which surrounds him is cut through in all directions by wishes, eager, impetuous wishes: wishes—happy or sad, according as they promise or not their own fulfilment—flying like spirits and invisible messengers in all directions. And of this innumerable host of wishes, which constitute, we may almost say, human nature, there is hardly one which does not affect us morally. What tests of our character are our wishes! Sometimes surer tests than our acts. We act formally—conventionally. Our wishes show our hearts. Are there not occasions in life in which some secret wish which we have is one of the deepest of inward sins, lowering us more than many outward offences would do,

What then if people, instead of wishing for wit, or quickness, or dexterity, or other such gifts, with that sharpness of desire they do, could from the heart wish that they were religious; that they had religious affections, that they had the serious apprehension of the *truth* of religion, that they could believe thoroughly in another world, and in God's promises with respect to it, —the teaching of Scripture is that the strong wish for this state of mind will be itself the means of obtaining it. Only wish for this spiritual temper really and steadily, and your wish will fulfil itself. Wish devoutly, not as if your own will and power could accomplish the wish, but under a deep sense of the power of God to work what He will within us, and to move us from the bottom of our hearts to good, and your wish will be fulfilled. But the truth is that people have not in their hearts any strong wish for religious faith and affections to begin with. They think of these qualities generally as being advantageous and right; but they cannot form in their mind the strong and real wish that they themselves personally should possess them. They do not embrace the advantage of them with that sensibility and force which is necessary for making them the object of a strong wish, they recognise perhaps a great deal of position and sensible gain, even in the way of present comfort and relief, in possessing faith. For faith is not only an excellent gift, a sublime gift, but it is a gift full of present happiness; so much so, that even a worldly man will see sometimes by his mere worldly sense, that if he had faith he would have a great deal to make him happy which he has not now, and sometimes he will say that he wishes he had faith, and that he envies those that have. For let us only set before us what we now gain by it; what comfort with respect to the future; what hopes, what prosperity. The Apostle speaks of those who by reason of death are all their life long subject to bondage; and the description applies to men of the world, even when most successful. They continue, it is true, to keep up an excitement and interest in the objects of life, and yet there is a blank feeling at the bottom that there is an end of it all. Faith would give them a world beyond this one to look forward to. Why then cannot faith, if it can do so much for our happiness, be made the object of a strong wish? Why cannot a man, not as a desultory and half mocking expression, but as a real longing of his heart, say—Ah, that I had faith! The truth is he cannot, in the state of mind in which he is. He cannot even seriously or heartily *wish* for faith. His desires are preoccupied with this world; they are so completely engaged upon success in life, and the objects he is pursuing, that he cannot even form the wish for a spiritual faculty or a spiritual enjoyment. He cannot bring himself to care about it. Whereas, for the wish for faith and religious affections to be successful, it must be the first wish of the heart. Religion, while it promises so much, takes high ground in its conditions; it must be felt as the first want, as an imperious need of the soul, otherwise the wish for it does nothing, and has no power. To desire it along with earthly objects and on a par with them, is not the wish to which the promise is given, and which has been described as being self-fulfilling. No, it must have the first rank as a wish, or it has none. If there is any other desire of the soul which takes precedence of it, it is supplanted. But how can a man, in a worldly state of mind, give this rank or this place in his mind to the wish to be religious? He cannot. It is a contradiction that he should. He desires as well as acts in chains. He is not free even to wish for what is best for him; for what would give him true happiness.

More than this; does not a worldly man, while he continues such, actually even shrink from wishing for such a change in himself as would strip him of his strong worldly affections, and endow him with spiritual ones instead? Does he not regard such a change beforehand as a kind of death, as if it would deprive him of all the living and strong interests of which he finds himself now possessed, and leave him only a cold and vacant life to live; a life hardly worthy the name? Without the stimulus, and the eager pursuit of worldly objects, what is life to him. It presents itself to him as a state of impassivity and emptiness, with nothing solid in it. But if spirituality of mind does extract all this eager pursuit of worldly ends from life, he is almost afraid, in his worldly state of mind, even of wishing himself spiritual; afraid, for fear his wish should be granted; and he should really be changed into something different from what he is now; be made another person of. He clings to his present old self, as his real and true self; he dreads being made new, as if the new man would be another man, and he himself would be dead in the transition. So deep is the instinctive feeling in the human mind, of the power of a real wish in spiritual things, that a worldly man rejects it and puts it from him, should it casually occur to him, as if it would be only too sure to effect the change in him, if it stayed; and he does not want to be changed.

And yet is this anything more than sterling justice on God's part, His requiring it as the condition of imparting His converting and renewing grace to man, that man should at any rate wish for it before he receives it? Take a man who does not believe,—does not really believe; is it anything else but fair, as a condition, that he should wish to have faith, before he obtains faith? God is indeed so gracious that he gives man faith and a religious spirit upon his asking for it; but is it too much to require that he should first ask for it? There is a justice, there is a fairness in this proceeding, which must recommend itself to our natural equity. It is the least that a man can do to wish with all his heart that he had some valuable thing, if he is to expect some day to have it. How simple a condition, could man only once resolve steadily to wish for the possession of that which he knows to be his chief good; could he but cast aside, once for all, all those vain, those fruitless longings for things that are out of his reach; for gifts and faculties which only glitter and attract the eye; and wish in the sincerity of his heart for what is really to be had for the wishing—for religious faith and temper. What happiness, what comfort, what serenity of spirit, what cheerful hope is in men's power, could they but bring themselves to wish heartily for that faith from which all these fruits spring. But, as Bishop Wilson says, "they whose hearts desire nothing, pray for nothing;" and not praying they do not obtain. Desire is the first condition. "We receive grace in the same degree we desire it," says the same devout Bishop again.

Dare then to *wish* to be spiritual, is what we would say to any man of the world, who, devoted to the objects of this world, absorbed in its exciting struggles, can not bring himself even to form the wish to be another man than he is; nay, who even starts back from wishing for it, as if he were wishing for his death; who, even if, in a moment of disgust and weariness with earth at some failure of a hope, he does utter the troubled wish, recals it immediately, and almost in a desperate hurry, for fear, by some possibility, God may take him at his word, and give him a new spirit in spite of himself. To such a one might we not say—Dare, Oh! weak and faltering soul—Dare at any rate to wish to have that which is your chief good. You imagine it now to be a sort of death, but it is not this, it is life from the dead. You think now that to be spiritually minded is to be emptied of all that interests, all that invites and wins desire, all that attracts sympathy; to have the full mind, and the life which overflows with stimulus, changed for a blank void. But it is not so. The new life will be full of interests; full of desire. Dare then to *wish* to be changed, and do not be terrified like a child at the mere notion of a new state.

And to those who have doubts as to the truth of religion, may we not also ask—Do you fulfil the first condition, of wishing it to be true? If you do not, can you be sure that your reason is in a fit state to judge of the evidence of religion? Let us take the Christian doctrine of eternal life. With respect to this doctrine, so much must at least be said, that if there is any final issue of the whole of human existence which appears to us the best possible, viz., an ascent of human existence into a glorious, happy, and endless state, we are at any rate bound to wish it to be true. If we ask you at once to believe it, you say, I cannot; it is not in my power: but you cannot say you cannot wish it to be true; and if you can wish it you ought. You are under the rational obligation of wishing that to be the true issue which is really the best and highest. Will you say your action comes under the head of duty, not your wishes? You cannot say this; wishes are a very real and a very large part of duty. In such a case as this,—that the mere conception is offered to the mind, constitutes an obligation to wish for its truth. The simple opportunity for the wish is a call for it. If, in ordinary junctures an event presents itself to us as the best possible that could be, there is a call upon us to wish for that event.

Upon what ground then can it be said that the idea of a happy endless state does not of itself create the duty to wish for the truth of it? There is only one reason that can possibly justify our not *wishing* for such an issue of human existence, viz., that the idea, however beautiful and splendid, did not hold together when examined, but fell to pieces as an inconsistency; that it was a mere creation of fancy, which, like the supernatural world of children, contained impossibilities; and that there can be no obligation to wish for what is impossible. But what is there contradictory and inconsistent in the idea? Where is the impossibility of a glorious and endless existence? Is it in its endlessness? First give a reason why personal existence should ever end. At each moment of our existence it is a more natural idea to us that we should exist the next moment, than that we should not; nor is any length of that existence a reason for its end; continuance, is at every moment the unavoidable expectation of the mind; therefore eternal existence cannot help being, however stupendous, a more natural conception than a limited one. Does the impossibility lie in the glory of the life? But why should not the scale of existence rise? Is there one reason why eternal happiness should not be a real future?

If there is nothing impossible then in the wish, is not a person evidently bound to wish that this doctrine of eternal life were true. But does he wish it? That is to say, has he a real, hearty, earnest wish about it? Or does he cast it aside altogether, even as the subject of a wish? If so, is there not enough in his own want of interest about a future life to account for his want of belief in it? Is it not the condition of all right exercise of the understanding that it should be accompanied by an interest, an affection of the mind? No evidence can be seen in that strength which really belongs to it if there is an indifference to the object with respect to which we inquire. We have no right, indeed, to think a thing true because we desire it. But to be without the desire, which natural reason prompts, for a life beyond the grave, and a happy immortality, is to be without that which is necessary for setting off the evidence itself for it at its proper value. It is to labour under a moral want. A moral want may cut off from the truth ; it must diminish your chance of finding it, where the evidence itself is of a moral kind; nay, where the very desire itself in the human heart, the longing, the reaching forward toward a future existence, is a very part of the argument for it. A future state has a supreme claim upon the heart of man ; and so should take its place there as an earnest and habitual wish. If you have not got this wish, if you have not the wish for a future life, how do you deserve to believe it ? If you are so absorbed in the sense of present life that the future is not even worth a wish in your eyes ; if you have no desire for it ; how can you expect to see the deep grounds in your own being for it ? They are hidden from you. Let us pray then that we may have good wishes ; that we may desire that which is really the highest good,—the best thing for us ; and that, in order to obtain that good promise, we may be made to love that which He commands.

THE UNSPOKEN JUDGMENT OF MANKIND.

PSALM XXXIX. 1, 2.

"*I said, I will take heed to my ways, that I offend not in my tongue: I will keep my mouth as it were with a bridle, while the ungodly is in my sight.*"

SCRIPTURE speaks in two different ways about judging others. On the one hand, it says,— "Judge nothing before the time, till the day of the Lord come;" on the other hand, it says, "He that is spiritual judgeth all things;" and we are told to regard the Holy Spirit, of which we partake, as a spirit of discernment. Indeed, all the directions that Scripture gives us about distinguishing between the bad and good in this world, with reference to our own choice of society, and the duty of showing our own preference of the one to the other, imply a certain power of judgment in us relating to people's characters. Nor, if this discernment exists in Christians, can we confine it to distinguishing only gross and flagrant sinners from well-conducted men. No; it extends much further than that; it goes much deeper. Christians who are endowed with the spirit of holiness, and who have with that gift the spirit also of wisdom and knowledge, can see where the heart is right in others, and where it is not; where the aims are pure, and where they are corrupted and alloyed; where a man is a single-hearted disciple of Christ, and where he is double-minded. All this belongs to the power which " he that is spiritual" has, "who judgeth all things." Indeed, this is part of that very unconscious power which lies in goodness as such; for goodness finds out goodness in others. On the other hand, in meeting those who have mean and selfish aims; however they disguise them, and ornament them, it feels itself coming into contact with something with which it cannot join, and which repels it. So that goodness, as such, has a wisdom in it; it knows that which attracts and draws it to itself, and that which does not; it knows the character with which it is in sympathy and agreement, and that with which it is not.

What then is meant by our being told that we are to "judge nothing before the time, till the day of the Lord come;" by our Lord's saying, "Judge not, that ye be not judged;" and by other texts, "Who art thou that judgest another;"[1] "Let not him that eateth judge him that eateth not"?[2] They mean, in the first place, that we are not to judge hastily, not to judge others for small and doubtful things; they unquestionably limit and put checks upon us in judging others. There are judgments upon others which we cannot help forming, which are the voice of conscience and reason in us, which rise within us without our seeking them; and there are judgments, on the other hand, which we provoke ourselves to form, and which are arbitrary and capricious.

[1] James iv. 12.   [2] Rom. xiv. 3.

But perhaps the great law with respect to judging, which is laid down in these texts is, that judgment in this world, when it is upon the critical point of men's goodness or badness, is suspended, with respect to its *delivery;* that it is not allowed full expression and manifestation. We know that *the* Judgment will be an outspoken judgment; that it will declare and manifest to the whole world what every one is. Its openness and full exposure of all evil is to be its very characteristic. We know that there will be no reserve shown, but that every one's acts and motives will be brought to light. The tremendous disclosures which will be made at it, is indeed one of the great terrors with which it inspires us. People have understandings with themselves here. They profess better motives than they really have; and they think that all this disguise does not signify because it is not seen. But Scripture holds before us the terror of a dreadful exposure, when all the secret terms on which people ever lived with themselves here will be laid bare, and the whole interior of man's heart be laid open,—where there "is nothing secret, which shall not be made manifest; neither anything hid, that shall not be known,"[1] but "whatsoever" has been "spoken in darkness shall be heard in the light;" and whatsoever has been "spoken in the ear in closets shall be proclaimed upon the house-tops."[2] Openness, then, is the very characteristic of the Last Judgment. But—and this is the great distinction between the two—the tongue of intermediate judgment is tied. There is an embargo laid upon the delivery of it. We are not at liberty to say openly what we

[1] Luke viii. 17. [2] Luke xii. 3.

think about others, even though it may be true. This would be to forestall the great final Judgment. We have to wait. The Holy Spirit may enable us to judge, in the sense of gaining discernment of others' characters; but He does not permit us to promulgate. The manifestation belongs to the last day.

This is the meaning, then, of " the bridle, while the ungodly is in my sight." This language implies a judgment of some kind, for there must be a judgment to know the godly from the ungodly; but it enjoins a silent, a mute judgment. The Psalmist saw that, while he had a true judgment with respect to numbers of men whom he saw in the world, it was not fitting that he should proclaim it, but that he should keep it to himself; he had deep thoughts about the world, but they must not be uttered,—" I held my tongue and spake nothing; I kept silence, yea even from good words; but it was pain and grief to me." He repressed himself,— and all repression is difficult and grievous when a man is full of some truth. But he saw that the condition of things here was such that it would not admit of the unqualified divulgement of such truth as this. So he refrains; he lays a prohibition on himself; and in the mean time gives a vent to his heart, which is hot within him, in the general thought of the transciency and shortness of that state of things which lays this burden,—this pressure of a great secret upon him; which obliges him to see what he cannot witness to, and to know what he cannot divulge: " Behold thou hast made my days, as it were, a span long, and every man living is altogether vanity."

In this temper of the Psalmist, then, we observe first, a greater strength than belongs to the other temper of impetuous and premature expression,—strength not only of self-control, but of actual feeling and passion. Such a posture of mind requires for sustaining it a stronger and more intense conviction than the other does, which breaks out into immediate indignation. For, is it not weakness, when men cannot restrain and keep up their own internal decision, without expressing it vehemently, or even without expressing it at all? Yet this is often the unconscious reason why men *do* thus rush into immediate and impetuous expression. They feel as if they could not keep up their own inner judgment and moral feeling without it; they want the help of the outward demonstration, as a protection to *themselves*, otherwise they think their own inward conviction might give way. The outward expression is indeed undoubtedly a great help to us, and a designed help, when there are no reasons to the contrary, in maintaining an inward judgment. The force of our language reacts upon ourselves; it props us up, and gives us a kind of support, when the echoes, as it were, of our own hearts come back to us, and nature, if it is not startled at the sound which itself hath made, is encouraged and invigorated by it. There are those who make too large a use of this means of self-support; and yet, in itself, this particular use of outward speech, as an auxiliary to our own thoughts and our own feelings,—ratifying, and, as it were, confirming them, fortifying the conclusion of our minds,—is natural. And this, when men break into the open expression of some judgment they have formed, is often the real reason why they do so; the feeling, viz., that they want the help of the outward demonstration to sustain the verdict within. They use strong language as a protection against their own weakness, and for fear the voice within them should otherwise sink and forget itself,—the judicial voice, which stands up for good against evil. It seems to need being assured and reinforced by its own utterances, and by hearing itself speak. And this is more especially the case when others talk or write plausibly and speciously on the side of evil, and make a show in its favour. To the weak in faith it then seems as if all were lost, as if even the stronghold of their own hearts had capitulated, and even they themselves were carried away by the stream, unless they retort instantly, and are as vehement in their exposure as the others were plausible in their defence of evil. They then especially seem to stand in need of the support of their own indignant voices, in order to preserve even their own footing, and prevent themselves being carried away by the world's argument; to keep their own judgment from being overwhelmed by this great array and show on the opposite side. They feel in ten times greater want, then, of this auxiliary to their own convictions. But it is evident that to need this kind of support is part of the weakness of nature, and not its strength. It is nature distrusting the strength of its own inward feeling, as if it were not enough for firmness and tenacity unless this auxiliary were present; as if even the heart were feeble without the help of speech. And therefore what was just said is true, that this mute form of judgment requires greater intensity of feeling, as well as greater self-command, to carry it on.

The circumstances then of the world are such, that this greater strength of feeling, this silent form of judgment, is positively needed to meet them. For consider what the perpetual expression of judgment, what the constant reply to the challenge of the other side would entail. This challenge is always going on. It is impossible to live in the world without constantly hearing admiration and praise lavished on that which we know in our hearts to be hollow and inferior in character. The world generally accepts success as a test; indeed popular judgment is almost obliged to be exceedingly rough; it must take men as they stand before it at the passing moment, and if they stand well then it welcomes them; it cannot go back and retrace steps and examine foundations. It is in its very nature a most indiscriminating judge, scattering about promiscuous compliments and commendations according to men's outward circumstances, and not according to any real criterion. Can we take up a newspaper without remarking the quantity of this inevitable kind of adulation in it—this mechanical praise, which flows from a law of public opinion. If, then, the good allow themselves to be provoked and challenged by the praise of evil which goes on in the world, and if passionate language is necessary as a support to themselves against this overwhelming force and array, they will find themselves under a perpetual call to make some indignant demonstration; to exclaim or protest.

But again, to attempt the exposure of the bad in this world would be to fight with all the conditions of our state in this world for another reason. For imagine the attempt made in any one instance. We know that particular or definite crimes can be brought home to men by evidence; but suppose it is a character which we have to bring home to a man, a character which is only the general result of the facts of his life,—though any discerning person could gather it from those facts;—and how impossible it would be to bring it home to him in such a public judicial way as crimes can be. He would have explanations of this act and of that act—points of view in which to place one term of his life and another. But the rule by which explanations are accepted in public is different from that of real individual belief; if they cannot be formally disproved, then they are admitted; the test which they have to fulfil is rather an external and conventional one, than that which satisfies the conscience and sense of truth at the bottom of every one's heart; it is what society as a kind of abstraction can claim, apart from the individual. It would be found then that the charge could not keep pace with the explanation; but that the explanation would, by the laws of society, overcome it, because by these very laws, what society as such requires and is contented with, is different from that which satisfies the individual. Society, or the present system of things, requires the services of these men, and must accept them upon their own terms, which of course are that they must be regarded as men of virtue and probity, and fulfilling the moral test. Manifestation of judgment—exposure—is against the law then of such a system. A thing is true—most true *until* you say it. But if you say it, if it goes out your lips, if it is once spoken—oh! how false it becomes. The floodgates of explanation open. It is crushed, and cannot stand a moment against the full resources of a conventional defence.

But if no judgment, however true in the sanctuary of the heart, can declare itself, by the very conditions of society, this is a clear revelation of the will of God that such a manifestation must not be attempted, and that to attempt it would be to forestall His divine purpose. And then we have nothing to fall back upon but the rule of the Psalmist—the rule of a mute and silent judgment. I will keep my mouth as it were with a bridle, while the ungodly is in my sight. The ungodly are not even now, in this world, wholly without a judge sitting in the heart of the righteous and of the spiritual man, to whom the Holy Spirit has given discernment. There is a judgment going on even now, in the depths of men's minds, in their inward thoughts, which to themselves are most familiar, and which are the home in which they live. But woe to them who would draw this judgment out of its hiding-place, who would extricate it from these solemn fetters, and from this sacred prison in which it has been lodged by God's ordinance, to remain there till it will emerge to light in another world. "Know ye not," says the Apostle, "that the saints shall judge the world." We shall, doubtless, one day know the meaning of these words much better than we do now ; when God, who acts by human means and by the agency of those hearts and wills which He has moulded into harmony with His own, will bring about the great final division of mankind by means, in part, of that judgment in men's hearts which He Himself has formed, and which will at the proper time attain a full disclosure and manifestation. But now we are under the Psalmist's rule—the rule of a strong yet silent judgment; which indeed is able to keep silence, to refrain from expression, and to discard its aid or reinforcement, *because* it is strong, because the feeling which is at the bottom of it is deeper.

In the meantime men of the world are satisfied if they can meet what is called the judgment of society, that is to say, that judgment which is conventional, and which goes upon another principle and other tests than those in the heart and conscience of the individual. They are satisfied, they congratulate themselves, if they can put matters into proper shape for this tribunal; if they can please this external judge, who stands, by his very office, outside the human heart, and never enters in to scrutinise one spring of action or probe one motive. This great husk of a judgment, which avoids touching one single responsibility of the soul, and applies only tests of public convenience and arbitrary morality, is the judgment with which the man of the world is concerned. Can he meet a charge with a proper supply of such defences as are accepted and have a received forensic value in this court? Can he furnish such an interpretation of his life and conduct as this court of the world, upon its own principles, is obliged to receive? This is the judgment, and this is the acquittal which he cares about. His standard is—a successful explanation; an explanation that, by the rules of outward society, must be admitted; an explanation about which men of the world, like himself, pronounce themselves to be quite satisfied, saying that they have no desire to go further; that that is all that the community can want; that they do not for their own part wish to trespass upon forbidden ground, and to invade the sanctuary of the human heart; they leave that to a higher tribunal. *This* judgment then is all important to him; he dreads with a real terror *this* judgment being against him; he hangs upon the breath of an outward superficial interpretation of himself; and, if this is favourable, he has got all he wants; he has passed the ordeal, and he is satisfied. But is there not all this time a judgment buried in the depths of human hearts, which he does not meet and which does not clear him? Is there not an unspoken sentence upon him, a silent verdict in the consciences of the righteous and holy which goes deeper than "explanations"? And is not this mute verdict an anticipation of that judgment which will not be silent but outspoken—the disclosure and manifestation of the human heart which will take place at the last day? Nay, and is there not even a judgment in his own heart which he does not pass altogether comfortably? Is there not a voice within him which would speak if he would let it, and did not suppress it; and which, if it did speak, would scatter to the winds the superficial and conventional acquittal of men, and overthrow in a moment his technical defence? This judgment, which is hidden at the bottom of human hearts; which the righteous who welcome it, and even the wicked who suppress it, alike conceal, this is the real judgment; real, though at present only mute and expectant. Fear this judgment—for if it is against you, you are indeed in sad case. This mute judgment is on all sides of you, it surrounds you; you do not hear it or see it, but there it is. Within the consciences of men is the tribunal which condemns you. You may be carried aloft on the conventional judgment of the world, absolving you upon its own rules; your explanations may have done everything, and been omnipotent; you may stand well and without a blot, and have an external verdict supporting you everywhere, but in the inner heart of man there still sits the mute judge who discerns and speaks not. In a thousand breasts, into which thou canst not penetrate, but which are all around thee, this judge sits; he sees what thou wouldst fain hide, and interprets what thou wouldst fain obscure; he understands, he knows thee, he sees thee; even if thine hypocrisy hides thee from thyself, thou art naked in his sight. Depend not on technical acquittals then; though thou art ever so safe in the world's judgment, thou hast a judge who is still formidable,—formidable as a prophet, though he holds no court as yet upon earth. Fear this hidden adversary; and, if it be not too late, deal with him quickly whiles thou art in the way with him.

THE TRUE TEST OF SPIRITUAL BIRTH.

JOHN III. 7, 8.

"*Marvel not that I said unto thee, Ye must be born again. The wind bloweth where it listeth, and thou hearest the sound thereof, but canst not tell whence it cometh, and whither it goeth: so is every one that is born of the Spirit.*"

THIS text conveys the idea that spiritual characters spring up in an unknown way, and that we cannot account for them, or give an explanation of them, as we can of other and ordinary characters. Thou canst not tell whence it cometh or whither it goeth —this spiritual temper and disposition. It cannot be said, with any truth, of ordinary characters, that there is any mystery about them, or that they have an unseen origin; on the contrary, we know everything about them, and can explain them without difficulty. Take an ordinary man of the world—what he thinks and what he does, his whole standard of duty is taken from the society in which he lives. It is a borrowed standard : he is as good as other people are ; he does, in the way of duty, what is generally considered proper and becoming among those with whom his lot is thrown. He reflects established opinion on such points. He follows its lead. His aims and objects in life again are taken from the world around him, and from its dictation. What it considers honourable, worth having, advantageous and good, he thinks so too and pursues it. His motives all come from a visible quarter. It would be absurd to say that there is any mystery in such a character as this; because it is formed from a known external influence—the influence of social opinion and the voice of the world. "Whence" such a character "cometh" we see; we venture to say that the source and origin of it is open and palpable, and we know it just as we know the physical causes of many common facts. We may say of such a person, as we do of some well-investigated natural phenomenon, that everything is ascertained about him, and that he is fully described; as we say of some region of which we have a good and correct map.

Of many persons then, who rise to respectable positions in the world, and who fulfil their public duties, and their duties to their neighbours, in a way which satisfies general opinion, it must be said that there is nothing about their character to which the text's description—that thou canst not tell whence it cometh—at all applies. Whence it cometh we know perfectly well; all is quite plain. And this world, as it is the source whence such a character cometh, so it supplies the object or goal to which it goeth; it is the sphere of exercise for such a character, that field which it is adapted to occupy, and in which it is qualified to shine. Present life and society is the sphere for which such a character, as it were, gives itself out as meant and intended; this explains its use; this furnishes its end; it gives no hint of a destination above the objects, the employments, and the abilities of this world. Whither it goeth is thus as much *known* as whence it cometh; there is nothing mysterious in the end or scope of such a character, any more than there is about its origin; both are obvious and palpable, and contained in this world which we know, and which is before our eyes.

There is another character very different from that of a worldly man, of which we may yet say that it does not respond to the description in the text,—Thou canst not tell whence it cometh;' and that is the character of mere religious zeal. If we take religious zeal by itself simply, and apart from that Christian love which is the refinement, the purification, and the consummation of it, it is by no means a disposition with a mysterious origin, it has none of that peculiar tone and type about it which induces one to say—Where did such a character come from? What unknown inspiration communicated it? On the contrary, the origin of unpurified religious zeal is very patent and obvious. We know all about it, and there is no mystery in it. It springs up in crowds, in masses, by a kind of inoculation, and concurrence and contact of men with each other; people catching it from the motion and stir around them, in a way analogous to that in which physical affections are sometimes made to spread. There is infection in mental conditions as well as bodily; and excitement—even religious excitement—rapidly spreads from the impression of numbers, from the influence of great spectacles, from outward exhibition and displays. Mere religious zeal is a gregarious thing, and like other gregarious affections which are caught by men in company and simultaneously, we know how they arise, and there is no hidden source.

We thus observe that in the New Testament religious zeal never of itself figures as a spiritual creation, as belonging to that spiritually born temper of which the text says, "We know not whence it cometh." Mere zeal is always represented in the New Testament as a mere growth of human nature; a natural production of the human heart; not the gift of grace. Thus, throughout the Gospels, we meet with one constantly recurring instance of religious zeal; which, however, so far from receiving countenance or praise from our Lord, draws down upon itself His strongest rebukes,—the zeal of the Pharisees. There was great zeal and activity of mind in the Pharisees; they compassed heaven and earth to extend their own school; they were scrupulous, exact, vehement, and eager, about everything connected with religion. But our Lord never allowed men to suppose that strong views and impressions, and activity in circulating them, that eagerness of mind and will,—because it takes religious material as its subject, —are therefore true religion. If there is any one lesson that the Bible teaches, it is that people may show a want of religion in their treatment of sacred things, and in the kind of worship which they set up. The Pharisees are instances of what unregenerate human nature can attain to in religious character; and they are held up before us to show that mere religious zeal is not a spiritual creation, but that it is a part of human nature, which comes out, like other passions and affections of the natural man, when there are circumstances to elicit it. Thus, St. Paul says, "Though I have faith so that I could remove mountains, and have not charity, I am nothing." That is to say, mere faith, apart from a higher principle, mere strong impression, assurance, keen and vehement interest, absorption of the mind, is not a spiritual gift, it is simply a development of the natural man. It belongs to human nature, without any Divine influence being exerted upon it, to have these states and conditions of mind; and they are no more part of a spiritual birth than conditions of our senses or bodily temperament. The mind in these states may take supernatural material for its subject, because we are impressed by nature with the sense of something supernatural; but it is not itself in a spiritual state in consequence. The Ephesian crowd that shouted, "Great is Diana of the Ephesians," was under the influence of a religious zeal.

Is not the whole Jewish character, as brought before us in the Gospels and Acts of the Apostles an example of this religious zeal, which is a mere fruit of nature, and is caught in crowds. What obstinate assurance, what devotion to their law, what fierceness against any who are suspected of want of allegiance to it, do we see in them! And at the same time how gregarious is their spirit; how it acts by means of numbers. "The *multitude* of the people followed Paul, crying, Away with him;"[1] and again, when St. Paul mentioned the Gentiles, they gave him audience up to this word,[2] and then the whole crowd "lifted up their voices." Nor can we avoid seeing that there is a good deal of Jewish spirit in the religious zeal of all ages.

[1] Acts xxi. 36.   [2] Acts xxii. 22.

This kind of religious enthusiasm then, which is born of multitudes, and springs up out of commotion and contact, no more responds, than the character of the man of the world, to the text's description—thou canst not tell whence it cometh? We know whence it cometh; it has not a mysterious origin; its source is not veiled; we see it plainly; it lies exposed before our eyes. It is a part of human nature; that human nature which is ascertained and known; and the process by which it is engendered is a visible process. It does not fulfil then the text's test of spirituality. We cannot but be struck often with the way in which men of this kind of zeal betray the want of depth and substance in their character, and expose the superficiality of their enthusiasm. There is a barrenness in their minds which stunts all the truths which they take up with so much outward ardour; or, if the truths spring up in seeming luxuriance, it is not a rich growth; they run up to stalk, as the husbandman's phrase is, and their height does not show the richness, but the leanness and shallowness of the soil which grows them. At first we imagine that enthusiasm must of its own nature always be a fertile and fruitful quality of mind; that abundance will be one of its uniform signs; and that it will invariably show affinity with the divine gifts of imagination or poetry. How is it that, when we come to experience, there is often such extraordinay dullness in enthusiasm? that instead of renovating, it seems to dry up the spirit; to drain it of all its natural gifts, instead of adding life and meaning to them; and to produce an aridity of mind which shows itself by the confinement of the man's ideas, issuing in the impoverishment even of the very truths to which he devotes himself? It is that in such cases enthusiasm does not spring from that unknown source to which the text refers, but from one which is only too well known; the common kind of contact and inoculation. Hence the individual, not having any fountain of truth within himself, is simply acted upon from without; he repeats some favourite watchword; he reflects the opinion which prevails around him, or in his own section; he has no large interests in truth; he never goes out of a small circle of ideas in which he lives, to come into contact with other thought, and to lay hold upon what would really enrich him. The character of his mind thus becomes with all its zeal, dull and insipid, because his zeal is of that sort of which we *can* tell "whence it cometh," not of that sort of which "whence it cometh" we *cannot* tell. It cometh from the palpable contact with crowds and masses; its source is *not* hidden, but known.

But now, let us turn to the other side of the description. The text tells us that there is a certain character and disposition of mind of which it *is* true to say, that "thou canst not tell whence it cometh, or whither it goeth." As the wind, which rises we know not whence, and goes we know not whither, so is every one that is of this Spirit. The New Testament describes, in various parts, what this spiritual character is, its expressions and manifestations; but there is one gift which sums up all the features of it,—the gift of love or charity. This is a great comprehensive term in

Scripture, to denote a certain combination of qualities of mind, and there is a description of such a person given by St. Paul in the First Epistle to the Corinthians, which has stood as the great Christian portrait in all ages. No words, however, not even those of Scripture, can avail us, or make us understand this character, unless we have that within us which leads us to discern it when we see it, unless our own perceptions are arrested by some peculiar forms and manifestations which naturally impress us as spiritual. Without being able to express accurately all we mean by love, we recognise it when we meet it. There are those who stand out from among the crowd, which reflects merely the atmosphere of feeling and standard of society around it, with an impress upon them which bespeaks a heavenly birth. Their criterion of what is valuable, and to be sought after, is different from that of others. They do not press forward for the prizes of this world; they stand apart from the struggle in which common minds are absorbed. But they do this without spiritual pride, they think little of themselves and much of others, and they have a love of their brethren, and of all whom God has made after His own image. They have these and other great common characteristics, though they have differences of natural disposition; and exhibit the action of divine grace, each in the form in which his natural character is adapted to show it.

Now, when we see one of these characters, it is a question which we ask ourselves, How has the person become possessed of it? Has he caught it from society around him? That cannot be, because it is wholly different from that of the world around him. Has he caught it from the inoculation of crowds and masses, as the mere religious zealot catches his character? That cannot be either, for the type is altogether different from that which masses of men, under enthusiastic impulses, exhibit. There is nothing gregarious in this character; it is the individual's own; it is not borrowed, it is not a reflection of any fashion or tone of the world outside; it rises up from some fount within, and it is a creation of which the text says, We know not whence it cometh. We know indeed that, from whatever source it springs, it arises in conformity with all those truths connected with what we call freewill. But Scripture still proclaims the source of it to be mysterious, and, if we ask about it, it tells us,— "The wind bloweth where it listeth." It rises up in one person and another person, here and there; but wherever it arises it reveals itself as an individual phenomenon, not belonging to a class, or made by an education. We know the history of the worldly character, we know the history of mere religious zeal; both of these are borrowed respectively from society and from crowds; they are fully discovered and mapped out; but we do not know the history of that character which is a birth of the divine Spirit. That is the manifestation of which "thou canst not tell whence it cometh." It is indeed on account of this, and because its origin is lost in the mystery of God's spiritual creation, that the contemplation of it excites at once our awe and love. We see that the

T

character is intrinsically of such a nature that it could not possibly be engendered from the impress of society, or the infection of a multitude; that it is no earthly manufacture, and no copy or reflection of an outside pattern, but that it is an inspiration from the fountainhead of all life and goodness. And it is because we see this that we know it to be spiritual.

And as thou canst not tell whence such a character cometh, so neither canst thou tell whither it goeth. Its destination is beyond our sight. The destination of the character of the man of the world, even if he is respectable, and in his own way useful, is not specially, as I have said, an invisible one; all his qualities are obviously made for this world as their field of exercise; they do not point to, or give any token or forecast of another. But the character which has the unknown origin is itself a prophecy and presage of another world, because it seems made for it. Its source and its destination then are alike beyond our sight. We do not see that Great Spirit from which the Sons of God derive their birth; we do not see that heavenly society of the spirits of just men made perfect toward which they are journeying. Whence they come, and whither they go, we see not; and that because they are born of the Spirit.

It is thus that what is truly spiritual in man is also represented in Scripture as that which is most inward, most original, and also, in a certain true sense, most natural; that which is most his own, in distinction from being a mould given to him by others—by fashion, by the outward standard of society, by the dictation of crowds, by current views, modes of speech, and dominant phrases. We see the influences by which the man is in vast numbers of cases made; that the process of his formation is as visible a one as that of a piece of manufacture—that he comes shaped out of the hands of some great outward public machinery, power, and influence. But for this very reason that we see whence he cometh, the character does not answer to the test of what is truly spiritual in Scripture. The special criterion of Scripture is, that we do not see whence it cometh; that it springs up from a fountain of its own, that it is owing to a power which we cannot trace, which is visible only in its effect, like the wind, of which we hear the sound but know not where it comes from. Undoubtedly no Christian stands by himself without the aid of others; religion is social, and among the means which Christianity employs for the conversion of the human heart and the education of mankind, there must be the influence of masses and of numbers. But still, with all this, there is no mistaking the test by which the Gospel has discriminated what is spiritual from what is earthly in the formation of character; that it takes us away from a palpable and visible sphere of production to a mysterious one, and from an external source to an inward one.

Let us then, on this great day,[1] adore the Holy Ghost, the Lord and Giver of life; let us specially commemorate at this time His Greatness and Majesty, His power over human hearts, His work of spiritually creating and in-

[1] Preached on Whitsunday.

spiring human souls; and let us commemorate the fruits of His inspiration, the characters of the just, the pure, the unworldly, the disinterested, the simple-minded,—those who have been the salt of the earth, and the mementos of heaven, who have been born of Him. Let us thank God for those who have witnessed by their lives to the truth of Christianity, and proved their own faith in another world by not thinking much of this. And "seeing we are compassed about with such a cloud of witnesses, let *us* lay aside every weight, and the sin which doth so easily beset us, and let us run with patience the race that is set before us."

THE ASCENSION.

Hebrews ix. 24.

"Christ is not entered into the holy places made with hands, which are the figures of the true; but into heaven itself, now to appear in the presence of God for us."

"GOD hath in these last days spoken unto us by His Son, whom He hath appointed heir of all things, by whom also He made the worlds; Who being the brightness of the Father's glory, and the express image of His person, and upholding all things by the word of His power, when He had by himself purged our sins, sat down on the right hand of the Majesty on High; being made so much better than the angels, as he hath by inheritance obtained a more excellent name than they."[1] This exaltation of Christ to a throne in heaven is the event which we celebrate this day.[2] He led out His disciples as far as Bethany, and said unto them, "All power is given unto me in heaven and in earth."[3] "Go ye into all the world, and preach the Gospel to every creature."[4] "And it came to pass, while He blessed them, he was parted from them, and carried up into heaven. And they worshipped Him,

[1] Heb. i. 2-4. [2] Preached on Ascension Day. [3] Matt. xxviii. 18.
[4] Mark xvi. 15.

and returned to Jerusalem with great joy."[1] We celebrate therefore on this day the foundation, or rather the first manifestation to the world of a great Kingdom, of which our Lord is the Supreme Head. We know that He, who in the days of His flesh showed such love for man, instructing him, healing him in body and mind, and lastly suffering for him upon the Cross,—that He who founded the Kingdom of the Gospel upon earth, who was perfect man, the Exemplar of all goodness;—that He at his departure was only removed from us in respect of sensible presence, and did not cease to be connected with us; that He was transplanted to an invisible throne in heaven, where He reigns over us now, the King both of the living and the dead. Upon this throne He has two worlds under His rule; He has all those who have departed this life in His faith and fear—"the general assembly and Church of the first-born who are written in heaven, and the spirits of just men made perfect;" He has an innumerable company of angels, He has the city of the living God, the heavenly Jerusalem. He reigns over the Church triumphant. This is one of the worlds, and the fullest and the most glorious, over which He holds His sceptre. Upon the same throne in heaven, He reigns over this world below, in which man still struggles with temptation and sin. The world of immortal life and happiness is His: again, this "creation which groaneth and travaileth in pain together until now," and in which those even who have the first fruits of the Spirit, "groan within

[1] Luke xxiv. 51.

themselves, waiting for the adoption, to wit the redemption of the body"—this lower imperfect creation is His kingdom also. Thus it was, that upon our Lord's ascension to heaven it was ordained that to Him every knee should bow, of things in heaven, and things in earth, and things under the earth; and that every tongue should confess that Jesus Christ is Lord, to the glory of God the Father.

What ought to be our feelings therefore, who know that our Lord and God, who reigns in heaven, is *man* too—that he is man now; and will be for ever in the fulness of glorified human nature? Different feelings possess us as we contemplate this glorified human nature in Christ our Judge, or our Intercessor. And first, this Divine Person, who will come to be our Judge, and who now discerneth the thoughts and intents of all hearts, sees into all men's motives, penetrates into their secret wishes and aims, sees the struggle between good and evil going on within them, and the good conquering in some, the evil in others—this Divine Person who sees all this, is in a mysterious but absolutely true sense man. The whole hidden world of human interests, passions, frauds, enmities, jealousies, schemes of pride and of selfishness, however disguised, is open to the eye of One who is man. Our Judge is one who appeared as man upon earth, and who is man now, "with all things appertaining to the perfection of man's nature" in heaven. Now, how would great numbers of men who follow their wills in this world, pursue through life an avaricious and selfish scheme, give all the strength of their faculties to gain worldly ends, but who do it all under a specious outside, and have explanations and justifications of their own conduct to themselves—how would these men feel, I say, if they knew that they had to undergo an examination and an estimate from a very wise, strong-minded, sagacious, and discerning *man*, here, in this world? Would they not immediately be in a state of most painful fear and apprehension? Would they not feel it but too certain that when that *man* came to examine their whole conduct he would at once see through all the disguises under which they had cloaked their sins, that he would penetrate the wall of their self-deceit, draw their real aims from their hiding-places, expose their real motives, lay low their hearts to themselves and others, and would show beyond dispute what manner of men they really were? But if these men would be so afraid of a merely human judge, who brought with him a vigorous and acute understanding to estimate them, He who will judge them openly at the end of the world,—He who does judge them now secretly, who estimates them, who measures them—He is more than man, indeed; but He is still man. The *man* Christ Jesus now scrutinises these *men*. Our Lord in the days of His flesh, it is especially said, "knew what was in man;" He knew what was in the minds of those who came to talk to Him, to ask Him questions, laying snares for Him. Before they spoke, he saw into their hearts. He knew the secret motives upon which the Scribes and Pharisees acted, although these were covered by the most pious exterior. Their hidden thoughts were discovered to them. Well then

He who knew what was in man in the days of His flesh; He who judged man then, knows and weighs man *now* in heaven;—even the man Christ Jesus. Are we afraid, when we know we have done wrong and do not acknowledge it to ourselves, and try to hide from our conscience—are we afraid then of the judgment of a wise and good man? We are, and we must be. Man is afraid of man. We know it is so; God has made it to be so. There is nothing that people who feel they are guilty, are more afraid of than the countenance of a man who is able to find out their guilt. They would face anything rather than this; they dare not look such an one in the face. Well then, our Lord is man—He is man now in heaven, though that human nature is glorified. He who reigns in heaven and in earth, to whom all power is given, to whom every knee shall bow, is God and man too. However, then, we may fear the countenance of man, we cannot escape being judged by one who is man. He judges us now, though not openly; He looks into our hearts; He knows what is true and what is false there, what is sound and what is corrupt. Our hearts are open to one who is man; we are searched and tested by His infallible insight. "Perfect God and Perfect Man, of a reasonable soul and human flesh subsisting" He now sits upon an invisible throne of judgment, having all hearts before Him. Shall we not be afraid before Him then—the Man Christ Jesus. If we fear the face of mere man, shall we not dread the face of Him who is God and Man?

What a motive ought this to be to us to examine

ourselves, to be true to ourselves, not to tamper with our own consciences, not to cloak our sin, not to dissemble and walk in crooked ways. There is looking upon us all the time One who is man. How disturbed, how horrified we should be, if while we were plotting some bad end, carrying on some piece of double-dealing, another man near us could see into our hearts; but He who is Man does see into them. This is the result of the Incarnation; and it is a fearful result, because, as I have said, God has so constituted man that he fears man, and that the countenance of man is formidable to him. How ought we then, bearing this in mind, to change our own hearts, to purify our motives and desires, in order to meet the eye of our Lord Jesus Christ. We cannot deceive Him. He knew what was in man when he was on earth; He knows what is in man now. To the hypocrite, to the dissembler, He is a terrible Judge: "I am He that liveth and was dead; and behold I am alive for evermore, and have the keys of hell and of death." So does He speak still to all the earth. He still scrutinises the work of Christians, as when He pronounced His judgment on the Churches, recorded in the Book of Revelations. He speaks still with the same sternness to the inconsistent Christian: "These things saith the First and the Last, which was dead and is alive . . . these things saith He which hath the sharp sword with the two edges . . . I know thy works . . . *but* I have a few things against thee . . . repent, or else I will come unto thee quickly, and will fight against thee with the sword of my mouth." He still says to the

The Ascension.

man who has the show of religion but not the substance—" I know thy works, that thou hast a name that thou livest, and art dead." He still says to the half-Christian " I know thy works, that thou art neither cold nor hot: I would thou wert cold or hot. So then, because thou art lukewarm, and neither cold nor hot, I will spue thee out of my mouth." He still says to all that He is near them, and that He examines and makes proof of them, whether they really will accept him or not: " Behold, I stand at the door, and knock: if any man will hear My voice, and open the door, I will come in to him, and will sup with him, and he with Me." He still tests and scrutinises hearts, to see whether they are true or false; whether they accept Him or not; he weighs them and estimates them. Let us think of that awful scrutiny when we are tempted to dealing falsely with ourselves. It must be observed that St. John, in the Revelation, specially brings out and calls our attention to the human nature of the Great Judge : Who says, indeed—" I am the first and the last; I am Alpha and Omega: but He also says—I am He that liveth, and was dead : I am Jesus ; I am the offspring of David."

We celebrate then this day the Ascension of our Great Judge into heaven, where He sits upon His throne and has all the world before him ; every human soul, with its desires and aims, its thoughts, words, and works, whether they be good or bad. Every man who is running now his mortal race, is from first to last before the eye of Him, who as on this day ascended with His human nature into Heaven. But we also celebrate the entrance of Christ into heaven to sit there in another character,—viz., as our Mediator, Intercessor, and Advocate. He sits there as High Priest to present to the Father His own Atonement and Sacrifice for the sins of the whole world. Under the Jewish law there were many High Priests, one succeeding another. "But this man," says St. Paul in the Epistle to the Hebrews—"this man, because he continueth ever, hath an unchangeable priesthood. Wherefore He is able also to save them to the uttermost that come unto God by Him, seeing He ever liveth to make intercession for them. For such an High Priest became us, who is holy, harmless, undefiled, separate from sinners, and made higher than the heavens." And He thus sits as High Priest and Mediator between God and Man; because He *is man*. For that very purpose, indeed, "He took not on Him," we are told in the same Epistle, "the nature of Angels; but He took on him the seed of Abraham." He who is man, could plead *for* man; He who had experienced our nature, knew its trials and infirmities; He who had Himself suffered, being tempted, was able also to succour them that are tempted. He who was made like unto His brethren, was suited to be a merciful and faithful High Priest, to make reconciliation for the sins of the people.

It is our Lord's supreme place in the universe *now*, and His reign now in the worlds, visible and invisible, which we commemorate in His Ascension. We are specially told in Scripture never to think of our Lord as having gone away and left His Church, but alway to think of Him as now reigning, now occupying His throne in heaven, and from thence ruling over all. He rules in His invisible dominions, among the spirits of just men made perfect; He rules in the Church here below still in the flesh. There He receives a perfect obedience, here an imperfect one; but He still rules over all; and though we may, many of us, resist His will here, He overrules even that resistance to the good of the Church, and conducts all things and events by His spiritual providence to their great final issue. " The Lord is king, be the people never so impatient; He sitteth between the cherubims, be the earth never so unquiet." This day especially puts before us our Lord in His human nature, because it was in that nature that He ascended up to heaven. " Thou madest Him lower than the angels, to crown Him with glory and worship: Thou madest Him to have dominion over the works of Thine hands, and hast put all things in subjection under His feet." So was it accomplished on this day, when our Lord, even as the apostles beheld Him, " was taken up and received into heaven, and sat on the right hand of God."[1] "Lift up your heads, O ye gates; and be ye lift up, ye everlasting doors; and the King of Glory shall come in." Let us worship Him in that seat in heaven; let us worship Him as Judge and as Intercessor. As Judge, who sees into all hearts; and as Intercessor, who pleads our cause. Let us worship Him with fear and love, remembering both His insight into us, and His compassion for us. He pleads, as perfect and sinless man,

[1] Mark xvi. 19.

as the second Adam, for the whole of the fallen race of Adam. He is our merciful and faithful High Priest; knowing our infirmities, inasmuch as He Himself has had experience of them; and knowing the strength of our temptations, inasmuch as He Himself also was tempted. Let us worship our Lord Jesus Christ then, both with fear and love; but also remembering that in those in whose hearts He dwells, perfect love casteth out fear. We were once enemies, but now we are reconciled to the Father by Him;[1] and being reconciled unto God by the death of His Son, much more shall we be saved by His life. On this day He hath led captivity captive, and received gifts for men. By one man, Jesus Christ, the grace of God, and the gift by grace, hath abounded unto many. By the righteousness of one the free gift hath come upon all men to justification of life. As sin hath reigned unto death, so does grace reign through righteousness unto eternal life. And as by one man's offence death reigned by one; so by one, Jesus Christ, shall they who receive abundance of grace, and of the gift of righteousness, reign in life eternal.[2] Even so has He led captivity captive, and received gifts for men. He has conquered the devil, He has freed us from the chains of sin, or that power of sin in our nature which, by one man's offence, we inherit. He hath put all enemies under His feet, even death itself, which, through Him, is swallowed up in victory. These are His captives. Again, He has endowed us with grace, and with the gift of righteousness, and hath opened to us the doors of

[1] Rom. v. 10.   [2] Rom. v. 17.

heaven,—these are His gifts. Let us show our thankfulness for them by raising our hearts to Him in prayer, by endeavouring to live as citizens of heaven, and as risen with Christ; and by seeking " those things which are above, where Christ sitteth on the right hand of God."[1]

[1] Col. iii. 1.

GRATITUDE.

Luke XVII. 17.

" And Jesus answering said, Were there not ten cleansed ? but where are the nine ?

" There are not found to give glory to God, save this stranger."

THERE is perhaps no fault that men think more monstrous in other people than ingratitude. Other faults are indulgences of nature; this seems against nature. Yet the multitude of complaints that one hears from persons on all sides of the ingratitude of men towards them, shows that people may easily commit it. On the other hand, particular instances of it are carefully treasured up, as if they were rarities, and deserved special notice. The question being so often raised tells on the side of there being some difficulties in the way of this virtue, which people do not see when they think it so easy and so matter-of-course a thing. It seems to show that there is a trial of principle in the case; and that, just as in other trials of principle, unless people are careful about themselves they will fail.

Take these nine men who went their way after they had been cured of their leprosy without saying a word; not returning even to give thanks for their cure. How eager they doubtless were to obtain a cure while they were still lepers; how they longed for the removal of their disease; what promises of service were they ready to make, to the man who would and could restore them to health! What would they not give any one for such a benefit! This was a sort of gratitude beforehand, an imaginary gratitude; they thought themselves equal to any amount of grateful action, before they got what they wanted. But when they got it, what a change immediately in their whole minds! Their former feeling was the eagerness of want; when the want was gone the grateful feeling went with it. All at once their situation was quite changed, a new future, with all its contingencies, opened out before them. They could now afford to think and reflect on the possible danger they might incur by any further connection with our Lord. Jesus Christ was narrowly watched, and all those who had anything to do with Him were watched also, by the Pharisees and others who had power in their hands, and could make that power felt by those whom they suspected of any friendly relations with Him. Was it wise to commit themselves to a beginning of communication with Him? We know from St. John's Gospel that the blind man was in danger of persecution, and fell under strong suspicion, because he spoke well of Him who had cured him, and expressed himself grateful. Nay, even to receive a cure from our Lord was in itself an offence in the eyes of many. Perhaps this immediately occurred to the nine lepers; who, in consequence, thought that the best thing for themselves they could do in such a case was to take themselves instantaneously away. Or perhaps they were afraid that our Lord might have a claim upon them to be His disciples, and that He would begin to press it. Or, perhaps, as soon as ever they felt themselves like other men, they were seized with the wish to go back to their affairs, and mix with the world again. They were in a hurry to be once more men in the world, doing what other people do, and impatient of any delay which kept them a moment back from their business and their interests. Whatever their thoughts, whichever consideration occupied them, whether one or all of these new ideas crowded into their minds on the instant, the cause of it was that their supreme want had been relieved. There was room for such new interests. The longing and yearning for something withheld from them was over; they were no longer under this pressure; they were at ease; they could think, they could consider, they could look about them. And nine out of the ten made use of this moment of consideration to determine to be seen no longer in company with our Lord, and not to delay an instant a return to their place in the world. With their need of a cure their gratitude for it expired, and they did not return to give thanks.

There is another source of an ungrateful mind, which perhaps also may have had a place in the tempers of these men. As soon as ever a man gets what he wants he thinks the higher of himself. His first reflection often is—This is my due, this is no more than I have a right to; why should I be grateful for it? So the nine lepers may have reasoned: they may have said to themselves, After all, He has only made us like other men; we have a claim to be this; it is a hardship if we are not. The loathsome disease was an injustice and a grievance; health is our right; we have now got this right; but there is no reason why we need be under a burdensome sense of gratitude for it. We are only made whole.

Here, then, are a certain number of obstructions to the proper sense of gratitude, which are of considerable strength, and tell upon people's conduct. These impediments come in according to the situation in which men are placed, and sometimes one of them may act, and sometimes another. The moment when a man gets what he wants is a testing one, it carries a trial and probation with it: or if, for the instant, his feeling is excited, the after time is a trial. There is a sudden reversion, a reaction in the posture of his mind, when from needing something greatly, he gets it. Immediately his mind can receive thoughts which it could not entertain before; which the pressure of urgent want kept out altogether. In the first place, his benefactor is no longer necessary to him; that makes a great difference. In a certain way people's hearts are warmed by a state of vehement desire and longing, and anybody who can relieve it appears like an angel to them. But when the necessity is past, then they can judge their benefactor,—if not altogether as an indifferent person, if they would feel ashamed of this,—still in a way very different from what they did before. The delivery from great need of him is also the removal of a strong bias for him. Again, they can think of themselves immediately, and their rights, and what they ought to have, till even a sense of ill-usage arises that the good conferred has been withheld so long. All this class of thoughts springs up in a man's heart as soon as he is relieved from some great want. While he was suffering the want, any supplier of it was as a messenger from heaven. Now he is only one through whom he has what rightfully belongs to him; his benefactor has been a convenience to him, but no more. The complaining spirit, or sense of grievance, which is so common in the world, is a potent obstacle to the growth of the spirit of gratitude in the heart. So long as a man thinks that every loss and misfortune he has suffered was an ill-usage, so long he will never be properly impressed by the kindness which relieves him from it. He will regard this as only a late amends made to him, and by no means a perfect one then. And this querulous temper, which chafes at all the calamities and deprivations of life, as if living under an unjust dispensation in being under the rule of Providence, is much too prevalent·a one. Where it is not openly expressed, it is often secretly fostered, and affects the habit of a man's mind. Men of this temper, then, are not grateful; they think of their own deserts, not of others' kindness. They are jealous of any claim on their gratitude, because, to own themselves grateful would be, they think, to acknowledge that this or that is not their right. Nor is a sullen temper the only unthankful recipient of benefits. There is a complacency resulting from too high a self-estimate, which equally prevents a man from entertaining the idea of gratitude. Those who are possessed with the notion of their own importance take everything as if it was their due. Gratitude is essentially the characteristic of the humble-minded, of those who are not prepossessed with the notion that they deserve more than any one can give them; who are capable of regarding a service done them as a free gift, not a payment or tribute which their own claims have extorted.

I will mention another failing much connected with the last-named ones, which prevents the growth of a grateful spirit. The habit of taking offence at trifles is an extreme enemy to gratitude. There is no amount of benefits received, no length of time that a person has been a benefactor, which is not forgotten in a moment by one under the influence of this habit. The slightest apparent offence, though it may succeed ever so long a course of good and kind acts from another, obliterates in a moment the kindnesses of years. The mind broods over some passing inadvertence or fancied neglect till it assumes gigantic dimensions, obscuring the past. Nothing is seen but the act which has displeased. Everything else is put aside. Again, how does the mere activity of life and business, in many people, oust almost immediately the impression of any kind service done them. They have no room in their minds for such recollections. As soon as one great want is satisfied, another arises, and then another. Are they beholden then to any one for the past? they have put the past behind them; they are occupied with the future. Each wish, as it is fulfilled, becomes insignificant in their eyes in comparison with some other which rises up in its place: and he who fulfilled it for them vanishes from their minds too. It is all hurrying and pressing after something before them; they look not behind.

Such are the shackles upon the mind which arise out of its own wilfulness, when the law of gratitude has to be fulfilled. It seems an easy law enough in the distance; nay, a pleasant law, a law that everybody would like to acknowledge and submit to,—inclination and duty would seem to agree here; but when it comes to the point, there are so many influences to clog and impede the grateful action of the mind!—its pride, its jealousy, its busy pursuit of its own ends. These one and all weigh heavily upon it; obtruding plausible reasons why it should claim a dispensation from this law. We alter our view of the rights of the case upon second thoughts, the simplicity of the duty goes; the plain appeal to the heart is lost; petty passions and trifling thoughts and fancies reign. Everything is listened to before this one clear law of nature and religion; the higher mind in us is stifled, and gives way to the lower.

How is man to be raised above this low level, these unworthy influences, and made to hear the voice of God speaking within him?—made to acknowledge the feelings which God has implanted in him? In what way must we rescue ourselves from this dominion of petty motives which prevent us fulfilling the very plainest and most downright duty which exists? Go to Scripture and see how this duty is put before us there. How does the divine impulse of gratitude

Gratitude. 295

come forth and demonstrate itself in that single one of the ten, who "when he saw that he was healed turned back, and with a loud voice glorified God; and fell down on his face at His feet, giving Him thanks." Who can doubt that this man was far happier in his condition of mind, that he felt a more full and ample and inspiriting enjoyment of his cure, that he experienced more exquisite sensations than any of the nine who departed without uttering a word of thankfulness? His supreme joyfulness and exultation are proclaimed in the tones with which he utters them, —in the loud voice with which he glorified God. What strength of feeling is here; out of the abundance of the heart the mouth speaketh; he is not silent, he cannot restrain his voice, he cannot bear that his thankfulness should only be felt within his own breast; he must utter it; he must utter it aloud; all shall know how he rejoices for the mercy bestowed—all shall hear him thank God for what He has done for him. How superior, how much stronger his delight in God's gift, to that of the other nine who slunk away. We see that he was transported, that he was filled to overflowing with joy of heart, and that he triumphed in the sense of the Divine goodness. It was the exultation of faith; he felt there was a God in the world, and that God was good. What greater joy can be imparted to the heart of man than that which this truth, thoroughly embraced, imparts?

Gratitude is thus specially a self-rewarding virtue; it makes those who have it so far happier than those who have it not. It inspires the mind with lively impressions, and when it is habitual, with an habitual cheerfulness and content, of which those who are without it have no experience or idea. Can the sullen and torpid and jealous mind have feelings at all equal to these? Can those who excuse themselves the sense of gratitude upon ever so plausible considerations, and find ever such good reasons why they never encounter an occasion which calls for the exercise of it, hope to rise to anything like this genuine height of inward happiness and exultation of spirit? They cannot; their lower nature depresses them and keeps them down; they lie under a weight which makes their hearts stagnate and spirit sink. They cannot feel true joy. They are under the dominion of vexatious and petty thoughts, which do not let them rise to any large and inspiriting view of God, or their neighbour, or themselves. They can feel, indeed, the eagerness and urgency of the wish, the longing for a deliverer when they are in grief, of a healer when they are sick; but how great the pity! how deep the perversity! that these men, as it were, can only be good when they are miserable, and can only feel when they are crushed; that their hearts are warmed by the sensation of a dreadful *want* alone, and by the strong craving which that want engenders. Then they long for the restorer, and think they would be infinitely grateful to him; but let him restore them, and straightway they forget him. Thus it is that their wretchedness makes their virtue, and that health and security are death. They soften at the sight or prospect of a benefactor beforehand; with the reception of the benefit they harden. Yet it was never intended by the Creator that pain and extremity should be the only or the main guides to deep feeling. When we no longer need our benefactor, when we have already got from him all we want and can hope for, then we can trust the quality of the sentiment that occupies us. The craving and yearning of mere want, whatever aspect it assumed towards those who could supply it, whatever its professions or the fervour it excited in us, was no true and religious feeling. We must aim at a habit of gratitude, which has no relation to present necessities, no eye to the future. Emotional feeling towards a possible benefactor may easily be mistaken for the grateful temper; but the gratitude which fills our heart and guides our conduct when we are well and safe, forgets self, and the interests and prospects of self, in the joy of thankful remembrance. And as this grateful spirit is the source of joy, so, in a sense, it is the source of religion in the soul. The grateful spirit alone believes, because it alone acknowledges the source of its life and being, the Author and Fountainhead. The grateful spirit alone finds out God; to it alone He reveals Himself. It alone discovers its glorious Maker in its own faculties, its own perceptions, its own capacities of happiness: and with the grateful one out of the ten, it falls down before Him giving Him thanks.

THE PRINCIPLE OF EMULATION.[1]

MATTHEW V. 15, 16.

"*Neither do men light a candle, and put it under a bushel, but on a candlestick; and it giveth light unto all that are in the house.*
"*Let your light so shine before men, that they may see your good works, and glorify your Father which is in heaven.*"

IT is a difficulty with many how to reconcile the scriptural law of humility with those motives which are found practically necessary not only for what is called success in life, but even for the fair development of our natural gifts and powers. On the one side Scripture appears to discourage all love of honour or distinction; it bids us take the lowest room; do our good works in secret; not love the praise of men, nor desire to be called Rabbi;—*i.e.* not wish for deference or distinction from other people;—not let our left hand know what our right hand does. "He that exalteth himself shall be abased, and he that humbleth himself shall be exalted." This, I say, appears to be flat against all love of honour or distinction, and to be a condemnation of it. But turn to actual life and the world around us, and see if we can do without the aid of some such motive as appears to be here condemned. Can we, to

[1] This and the following Sermons were preached at anniversaries of the opening of Lancing College.

take an instance to the point on the present occasion, do without the principle of emulation in our schools? How are we to bring out boy's minds without it? How are we to unlock the treasury of intellect? What key are we to use? Can we do without what some have called "laudable ambition," in active life, private or public? Look at the most conscientious and religious of our statesmen, and say if motives of this sort have not operated upon them, and played a very important part in bringing them out as we now see them, and lain in more or less strength behind their whole course of action and service.

What are we to say then in this state of the case? Are we to say that Scripture says one thing and the practical life another? Are we to solve the difficulty on a kind of Manichæan principle that the world which God has made, and has ordained to be carried on through our instrumentality, does somehow or other require, and cannot go on *without*, the aid of a set of motives, which, according to another revelation of His will, are wrong ones; that the Creator ordains what the Sanctifier prohibits?

The true solution of this question appears to lie in the very old distinction between moderation and excess,—use and abuse. It is against the whole constitution of our nature to say that the love of praise, even of the praise of man, is in itself wrong. It is absolutely impossible but that, as social beings, we must enjoy the approbation of our fellows. That we should do so is simply part of the same law which makes us enjoy their society and conversation, and feel affection toward them, and concern in their welfare. It is part of our social nature.

If there is any one principle in the system of creation which we are familiar with more than another, it is that the talents and faculties which God gives, give pleasure in the exercise of them. We see this even in animal nature. The beasts of the field, the fowls of the air, the fish of the sea, delight in the motions which the Creator has given to them; the quick flight, the rapid course, the bound, the leap, the run; they delight in the elasticity, the ease, the flexibility, with which they perform the bodily movements which belong to the species; this is their life, and they enjoy the expression of it. And man has a higher life, of which, exactly on the same principle, he enjoys the expression and the use: he has moral and intellectual faculties, powers of apprehension and reasoning, powers of observation, of memory, of speech; he delights in the exercise and use of these gifts. But there is this difference in the case of man and that of the brute creation, over and above the difference of the gifts themselves—viz. that man exerts his gifts with the consciousness that he is *seen* exerting them. As a conscious being, conscious of himself, and conscious of having others around him, he cannot help this consciousness in the exertion of his gifts. It is part of his nature. He knows that he is seen; he would not be a conscious being if he did not know this. What then, in the case of the brute creation, is simply and solely *motion*, is in his case, by the very law of his nature, a *manifestation*—the manifestation of himself to the world, the world of fellow-men around him. It is, by the necessity of the case, a *demonstration* of what he is, and what powers he has ; a demonstration to others as well as to himself. He cannot throw himself back upon the unconsciousness of the lower creation, or pretend to their kind of simplicity; all this he was precluded from when he was raised to the dignity and the responsibility and inner life of man. He is made by God a conscious being, and he cannot escape from his own nature and from the eye within. The exercise of his gifts and powers thus being by the necessity of the case a *manifestation*, must have in some degree its pleasure and excitement *as such*. It must give pleasure as being the *manifestation*, as well as being the *motion* of the faculties. And thus the whole of the moral and intellectual life of man is, not culpably on his part,—however it may *lead* to fault if not watched properly,—but by an ordinance of God, a *manifestation ;* and the metaphor of the poet is perfectly true in fact, for life *is* a stage, and God has made it so, and we cannot make it otherwise.

But though the love of praise, the desire for honour, is in itself perfectly right, there is all the difference in the mode in which it is felt and indulged. We are complex creatures, with a remarkable machinery of different and even contradictory feelings and passions within, making up that concordia discors — man. Nature does not allow us to throw ourselves into any one passion or feeling. So, in this particular case, while the love of praise is doubtless implanted within us, there is also something within us which pulls us back from it. Are we not half ashamed of it while we feel it? Is not the curb of nature strong upon the eager impulse? Is there not a principle of self-respect which challenges and *disputes* this appeal to the world outside; which summons the man homeward; which sets up a good conscience and self-approval as the great reward, and tells him to distrust other tribunals? I believe that every one, young or old, feels that inward drawback upon the love of human praise; feels this authoritative check; feels a higher principle at work within him; bows instinctively before a throne in his own heart, and knows that he stands before the Mount of God, and the tribunal of a supreme Judge, compared with whose sentence upon him the opinions of men are wholly insignificant and trifling. This, by whatever name we call it—self-respect, or conscience, or holy fear —is the counteracting principle to the love of human praise. It is the deepest principle in our nature, and is part of our very innermost self.

A strong moral character, then, attends to this principle, keeps its balance, and is not carried away by the love of human praise: a weak moral character loses its balance and is carried away by it; the man abandoning himself to that part of his nature which throws him upon the outer world for his pleasure and reward. True, it is a part of his nature, but it is a more superficial part, a lighter part than the other; it is not meant to be in power, but to be in subjection to the other. He gives it the pre-eminence.

I think that this difference in the use of a natural principle—(and I would call attention to this point as an important one in the philosophy of morals generally)

—that this difference of *degree*, as we call it, between moderation and excess,—is more than a mere difference of degree; that it is a difference of kind. Let us take the case of other appetites. One man eats and drinks as much as is proper for his health, another eats and drinks to excess; the material difference is only one of degree more or less, yet any one knows that the moral difference is one of kind, that it is a difference between temperance and gluttony. So one man is properly indignant, another is furious; this is only a difference of degree outwardly, but it is really the difference between justice and passion. So one man is prudent in money matters, another is a miser. In all these cases what we call a difference of degree is in truth a difference of kind, and it is just so in the present case. The love of praise is *in itself*, as I have said, a natural appetite; but the excess of it is corruption and disease. When that which is meant for an occasional healthy stimulant is converted into a luxury, and made our regular diet, then the boundary line is crossed, and the result is a moral effeminacy or weakening of the whole fibre of the character, it is degradation, and corruption. The man then becomes a spoilt and pampered child, depending on this perpetual excitement, and fretful unless he has it. No one can, indeed, look abroad on the world without seeing how fearfully this principle of self-manifestation, natural and necessary as it is in itself, has been abused; the frightful devastation which it has made on the field of human character, the mischief which it has caused in every department of human life. See men, instead of taking it in its time and place, and along with other principles of our nature, instead of simply responding to it as a stimulus, becoming wholly absorbed in it as a *passion*,—as if the one and sole purpose for which human life was given was the revelation of themselves to the world, their powers, gifts, and ideas, and the disclosure of their whole interior before the eyes of men;—see them eager in this process, and indomitable in it; tremblingly anxious that nothing should ever be lost, and grudging their least power or motion to privacy or home;—and what has been the result of all this? Have truth or society been substantially benefited by this excess? We may refer to this source, indeed, much eloquence and brilliance, many a fantastic theory, many an ingenious scheme and problem; but seldom the addition of one solid truth to philosophy, or one substantial step in any department of policy or knowledge.

Such reflections as these are not perhaps wholly inappropriate to this day's celebration. We cultivate the principle of emulation, as I have said, in our schools; we cannot do without it; it is necessary for developing the minds of youth; it is a providential stimulus put into our hands to apply at our discretion. Whatever risks may attend it must be faced. And perhaps the arena of a school, as it brings out the principle of emulation most strongly, so also contains the strongest correctives to it. There is no sharper curb upon the principle of display than public opinion amongst youth. In this we have a wholesome yoke, a natural self-acting discipline bearing upon any undue tendency. This coercing power may be exercised with some degree of roughness, but its general effect is good ; and perhaps there is no scene of after life which contains such strong ingredients of discipline, such potent corrections, for this temper. A large school is, indeed, for this special purpose, as for others, a most valuable initiation into actual life. It teaches the proper form and use of the desire for human honour ; it educates the natural appetite, fosters it and reins it at once ; gives it its balance, and brings it out as a manly, wholesome part of our nature, instead of a feeble and morbid excess and excrescence.

And if these reflections are at all appropriate to the sphere of a school, they are not wholly without their application either to those particular classes of society for which this institution has been established. The middle classes of this country are undoubtedly keenly alive to what we call the rewards and prizes of the social system ; they appreciate most acutely success in life. Nowhere is the maxim, that a man should rise in the world, should better himself, elevate himself in the social scale, so current and made such a home watchword. And this, perhaps, is one reason among others, why the middle classes of society are rather frowned upon by the poet and man of sentiment, and are not nearly such favourites with him as either of the stationary classes, the one below or the other above. The stationary classes, both below and above, acquire picturesque associations connected with time and custom ; they repose within their ancient landmarks, they represent former days, they rest upon old ties and relations; they are quiet, soothing, and softening features in our landscape; the poor have the charms of their poverty, and of a certain humility attaching to their station to recommend them; the rich and noble have the charms of ancient wealth and position, the poetical honours of time; but the middle classes have neither the one nor the other, but come before us as struggling uneasy masses of life; they have emerged from one position and are making their way to another, and in the interim they are without a settled shape; we turn from the repose of upper and lower life to a scene where all is in motion, and where the bustle, strife, and dust of the world are all collected.

Undoubtedly there is some truth in this contrast, and yet the middle classes of this country have an interest of their own attaching to them. Doubtless it is an *ambitious* class, nobody will deny it; it is an active class, all on the alert, and full of energy and spirit. No one can have had any dealings or acquaintance with the business type in this class, without seeing the readiness, quickness of apprehension, and power which it exhibits. And all this, I will add, is a very important reason for institutions such as these. It constitutes a call for them; for is it not of the utmost importance that such a character as this in a class, involving such power and such results for good or evil to the Church and country, should have the advantage of sound and superior training? Doubtless, unless it has, and unless the Church has some hand in that training, the Church will feel the effects of it some day. It will find that it has slipped its hold over just the most powerful class in the country, and it will find out its mistake when it is too late to correct it.

But though middle life in this country is certainly a struggle, and a very sharp one, does no interest attach to it even on that very account? Is nothing but what is stationary interesting? Is there not a poetry of motion as well as of rest? I believe that what is called the poetry of life, and the romance of real life, is more enacted in this class than in any other in society. I mean by the romance of life its ups and downs, lights and shadows, successes and disappointments. What hopes and fears, anxieties, depressions, joys, emotions of all kinds, gather or have gathered around every shop and every warehouse in every town of this country? Could they tell their history what a tale they could unfold, what a disclosure of character, what conflicts of feeling! Everything has its beginning, and what a tender thing is that beginning! What hopes and fears centre upon it! How easily may the opening promise be nipped! Through what fluctuations does the little bark of enterprise make way! What ventures must be run! "For I have set my life upon a cast, and I must stand the hazard of the die." What thousands who have staked their all upon some business project have said this to themselves! What prospects to the man himself and all his home circle are involved in the issue! Is trade vulgar in the poet's eye? Yet it is by these deep agitations of heart, these conflicts, and these emotions,—which, if they were represented properly, and to the life, upon any stage, would be thought the most real poetry,—that trade in all its departments, high and low, in all its enterprises, from the pettiest shop in the market-town to the great exchanges in the busy capitals of commerce, is conducted.

As a sphere for the formation of character then, it may fairly be questioned whether this struggling middle-class life comes at all behind either of the two spheres of life just mentioned. It has its snares,— its great snares; and stationary life has too. The humble peasant-life has the temptation to a stupid besotted indifference to everything spiritual; old-established rank has the temptation to luxurious indolence and pride; the struggling middle-class life has the temptation to the love of money and eagerness for getting on in the world. Doubtless this latter is the spiritual ruin of thousands; we see it and know it. It is the special fault of a commercial people. Still, to minds of any seriousness, or that have the least disposition to self-recollection, this very life offers many corrections to such a worldly spirit. It is remarked that sailors are superstitious because they have to deal with a very treacherous and uncertain element, from which they do not know what treatment to expect. The same kind of reason, operating in a different sphere, has often made the English trader and merchant religious. He is conversant, to a degree in which those who belong to the stationary classes are not, with the extraordinary uncertainty of human events; and in the sphere of risk and venture in which he lives (and even without morbid speculation all trade must involve a great deal of this), he is, as compared to the latter, something like what a sailor is to the landsman. There is something in such a situation which inspires a wholesome fear; he feels himself in the midst of what he cannot control, and looks with awe upon that wonderful machinery of human events in which he is so implicated, the springs of which are hidden from him, and are touched by some power above and beyond him. "Lo, he goeth by me, and I see him not: he passeth on also, but I perceive him not. Behold, he taketh away, who can hinder him? Who will say unto him, What doest thou?" Even success itself inspires fear; even the favouring wave, as it lifts him up, gives him the sense of danger; his heart sinks; he fears he knows not what, and he would fain appease the θεῖον φθονερόν with self-renouncing thoughts. Thus, at the very moment of some prosperous climax, just as the height is gained, a calm has come over him like the stillness of the grave; a feeling that all is over, and the end come; he looks behind him and before him,—on the vista of an irrevocable past, and the veil which lies over the life that remains to him, and he feels himself indeed a stranger and a sojourner upon the earth.

But whatever may be the religious effect attaching to situations of uncertainty and risk, certain it is that we have our calendar of religious merchants; witness our schools, our almshouses, our charitable institutions of all kinds. Freely they received, and freely they gave. They returned to God the money which was lent to them. That was the secret learnt by many a successful life. The youth was early launched into the world. In the morning of life he left a frugal, perhaps a humble home; but he had presentiments, and heard prophetic chimes in the distance, and music in the air; he spent the morn in successful toil; in the evening he returned home again, crowned with wealth, of which he gave his native town the benefit; and there he now reposes beneath the stone canopy, having left his benefactions to posterity to speak for him when he was gone.

If there are any, then, among the younger of those here present, as probably there are, who are soon about to quit this scene of preparation and to enter upon the business of life, and who have the feelings which naturally accompany the approach of such a change,—if there are any (and I will, among such a number, suppose it certain that there are some) who will one day attain to eminence in commerce or professional life, and who have a rising consciousness of their ability to attain it,—no one who respects Christian liberty would try to discourage or suppress such natural feelings and aims. It is God's ordinance, and it is to the great benefit of the cause of religion that Christian minds should mingle with every department of business and thought. Nor is the law of humility in our nature in any real opposition to the law of self-manifestation in the same nature, which indeed is the condition of the very development of our gifts and powers, whether in school or in real life. But there are serious cautions which I need hardly suggest to those who must be so familiar with them. There is all the difference between the world exercising and developing, and the world hardening, the mind ; there is all the difference between one kind of man of the world, and another; between one who, as he rises in life, keeps up old friendships and family ties, and remembers early lessons ;—who keeps the world outside of him, and does not let it enter into his heart ; and one who parts with his better self, and is absorbed into the world. Then let us remember that, great merits as they are, we must not think industry and activity everything. We *may* overrate them. It is true that industry at first is difficult and trying, especially in any new kind of work ; it is some time before we can adapt ourselves to it, and acquire anything like ease or skill ; but when these first difficulties are surmounted, and the habit is formed, then work becomes a pleasure. This is obviously the case with multitudes of people ; work is their amusement. They could spare it a great deal less than they could what they *call* their amusements. This is an ordinance of Providence, doubtless,—I mean, that our labour should be our enjoyment also ; but then it leads to this reflection, viewing it as a test. We look abroad on the world, and see, as a simple matter of fact, that the worst men and the best men are both great workers. Yet men of the world constantly think that industry covers everything. This one virtue satisfies them, atones for every fault, and makes them perfectly contented with themselves. The test is not the quantity of work alone, but the spirit and aim of it also. Is it not to a considerable extent true, that as man advances in life, work becomes his real play, and suffering his real work ; that a few months, or a few weeks, spent in what are beautifully called " God's prisons," do more to fit the soul for immortality than years of activity? Then beware of that formidable enemy to what is spiritual in man—*an earthly future.* True, an earthly future is part of the very life which has been given us, but, when it is a hopeful and animating future, it is very apt to supersede the spiritual future in our minds altogether. It is easy to *talk* about eternity; but the practical sense of immortality within us is really a much weaker and fainter thing than we often suppose. It is easily suppressed; it requires watchful cherishing, like a tender plant. It withdraws before strong boisterous earthly hopes,—it vanishes and hides itself, and cannot easily be called back again. God grant that this may not be the case with any of those here present, but that they may use this world as not abusing it, for "all that is of the world," *i.e.* of the world as thus abused, "the lust of the flesh, and the lust of the eyes, and the pride of life, is not of the Father, but of the world; and the world passeth away and the lust thereof, but he that doeth the will of God abideth for ever."

RELIGION THE FIRST CHOICE.

MATTHEW VI. 33.

"*But seek ye first the kingdom of God, and His righteousness; and all these things shall be added unto you.*"

IT is the favourite test of a sincere character in Scripture choosing a religious life, and the use of religious principles, as the first step, not as a last step in our course. We are indeed warned against being religious *at first only*, that is against a religion of mere impression —the seed which forthwith springs up because there is no deepness of earth, and which, because it has no root, withers away. But to choose the guidance of religious principle as a first step and not as a last one, as what is to precede our active career in life and not to come after it, is the only mode of choosing religion which Scripture says is worth anything. It is evident to common sense that such a choice as the latter is worthless. Certainly a man may lead a selfish and careless life, and at the end of it repent sincerely and change his way of living, but then he has only the last part of life to live well in. For a man at the commencement of life only to choose religion as something which is to come at the end, something which has its natural place after the active part of life is over—this is certainly a mockery offered to God. What is true at last is true at first too. And yet that this is a common mode of choosing religion we cannot doubt. It is not only that persons go on putting off from natural irresolution what they wish and in a way intend to do now; they have a plan of life in their minds, in which the use of ordinary worldly principles stands first, and the use of strictly religious principles stands last in date.

To counteract this false view of life, to forestall it by the true one, to put religion in proper possession of the field, to preach the text—" Seek *first* the kingdom of God, and his righteousness; and all these things —everything of this world that is for your good— shall be added unto you," enters into the very design of a great institution for the education of youth, such as this is. This is a subject, therefore, in keeping with the peculiar character and work of this institution, and I will follow it, therefore, into one or two particulars connected with that practical sphere of life for which, perhaps, the majority of those who are educated at this place are designed. I have, doubtless, around me many who are destined to rise and obtain eminence in that sphere, many whose abilities will be strongly developed in it, who have a capacity and aptitude for that important department of knowledge and work, of which they may at this moment be unconscious, but which will come out at the proper time. It is impossible to overrate the importance of this field of work, and the vast consequences which depend upon the choice of principles which those make who have to manage it. Those who conduct the business of the country have indeed vast issues in their hands. So much the more important, therefore, is the service which those schools perform which undertake especially the training of the men who will one day conduct it. There is no disposition, indeed, now-a-days to underrate the sphere of trade and commerce; nor is there any disposition to underrate the abilities and powers of minds which are required for success in it. Perhaps all classes of society underderstand each other better than they did in former times, and so far this is an improvement; there is less mutual depreciation. Nobody can put before him, indeed, the material with which a man of business has to deal,—its multiplicity, its changeableness, its complication, without recognising not only the solid, but the acute and penetrating properties of intellect which are necessary to deal ably with it;—the quickness of apprehension, foresight, capacity for arrangement, power of keeping a quantity of matter in the head at once; memory, presence of mind and self-collectedness, and other high qualities of the understanding. The sphere of business is indeed a great sphere, viewed simply as a field for the exertion of the intellectual powers, without reference to material results. And there are thousands of minds whose faculties are developed by it to an extent which is truly wonderful, which, probably, would not have been nearly so invigorated and expanded upon any other arena.

It would be useless, however, to shut our eyes to the great trials to which the religious principle is subject in this sphere of activity and energy; and one is that to which I have referred. And I cannot but think that this trial exists with *peculiar force* in the sphere of commerce,—I mean the temptation to defer the use of religious principles till after the struggle of life is over; till success has been gained, and those principles can no longer obstruct and slacken speed on the way to it. It must be confessed that we see all around us considerable signs of the prevalence of this place and date given to religion in life. Religion is in many cases an impediment to the use of a quicker set of means for gaining the ends which from time to time we place before us; it is apt to retard, to cut off facilities, to shut out short cuts. We do not like to be obstructed in our road; to wait for an advantage, when we see our way immediately to it by one course;—to take a more difficult path when there is an easier one. At the same time we cannot deny that religion has a place in human affairs. We therefore give it a place, but one which removes it from being in our way just at the present moment. We give it a standing ground *farther on in life.* I do not say that men put this to themselves in so many words, or that they are even definitely conscious that they hold such a view at all: but they practically adopt it; their idea of the necessities and urgencies of a life of action and of a mercantile career so possesses them that any scruples that arise whether such and such a step is strictly right, give way before it. What would appear to an impartial spectator to be inconsistent with the rights of others, and with a due regard to the welfare of others;—not coinciding even with a proper standard of honesty,—is by force of will resolved to be a law of the calling. So imperious is the necessity for the resort to certain means, in those who are in the thick of the occupation and the excitement of active life, and of working toward an object! For it must be remembered that intense occupation is excitement as well. A man who is keen in pursuit of success in any department of trade or commerce, is not in the steady and balanced attitude of a bystander toward any question as to what is right and permissible that arises in his department. His wishes, his hopes, the ardour of the race, prepossess him with a certain aspect of such points. He comes with his solution of them ready prepared, and sees nothing which he does not wish to see. There is indeed no greater excitement than *work*, when it is carried on for an object, and when it is continuous and urgent, and calls all the faculties into requisition.

It is unnecessary to give instances of the sort of liberties to which I refer, which active commercial and manufacturing life allows itself, under the pressure of this apparent necessity, and the stimulus of an object. We are but too familiar with the mention of them. They have been subjects of notice in our journals and periodicals, and of constant popular comment. I would not say—far from it—that such instances must be taken as fair samples of mercantile life, or that a class ought to be charged with the acts of individuals. Doubtless there is quite enough sterling honesty in our trade to put to shame these departures from it, and to fasten all the more blame upon them, because they are allowed by men to themselves, in spite of the force of so much bright example the other way. Still what laxity prevails, is, I am afraid, enough to show how formidable a trial of religion the impetus of commercial life is, and how great the temptation to haste to get rich.

We all know the numberless ways and shapes in which this trial meets men—the daily cases which occur in which a man may act with more regard or less regard to truth and right, according as he chooses; in which he may be exacting, take an unfair advantage, keep back the truth, turn another man's difficulties to his own account ungenerously; or may do the very reverse of all this. If he hastes to get rich, he resolves that the rule of the trade is remorseless, and opportunity is always to be snatched; and he quotes and perverts the proverb that time and tide wait for no man; the temptation to attain an end in view is such that he grudges weight to any scruple that interferes with the pursuit. Such a man may escape actual dishonesty, and yet pursue wealth in a way to contract guilt. To be hard upon others, and eager for self; to fasten immediately upon whatever offers itself for our profit—this, as a formed habit of mind, is most contrary to the Christian temper; it is incompatible with all true religion, and with a man's being in God's favour. Indeed religion utterly condemns all absorption in worldly ends, and passionate devotion to them, if it is only because it entirely shuts out spiritual ideas and aims, and prevents the whole work of grace. A man cannot serve two masters.

Now it is impossible to account for the way in

which men who make a respectable figure in the world, and profess to have a sense of the truth of religion, will allow themselves to be thus irreligiously and guiltily swallowed up in the pursuit of wealth for years, even for the whole of active life; except upon the extraordinary strength of that tendency in human nature to suppose that it may fix the date and place of religion in human life where it is convenient to it to fix them. There is a very strong disposition in men to think that they have religion at their command in this way, and can keep it at a distance as long as they please, and come to an agreement with it afterwards, when the time comes. How deep in human nature lies the thought that you may do deliberately wrong, and gain by doing so all that you want; and that you may atone for it afterwards by the good use that you will make of the advantage thus gained! A man thus flatters himself that he will gain by the wrong-doing in this world, and not lose by it in the next. There come at particular points in a man's life trying moments, when a great opportunity offers, when a new channel opens, when a great step can be made; but it involves something to which the conscience does not readily agree. Shall he then avail himself of the offer which the world makes him, or shall he forego it? shall he let the opportunity pass by? It is a testing occasion for his character; he is conscious of it, and yet he is divided in his heart. Has he sufficient faith in the moral government of God to reject it, to say to himself that it will be better for him ultimately to do right, whatever intermediate prospects it may close? He has not: and yet he cannot yield to the tempter without some understanding with himself, some point of view taken to break his fall. This then is the view on which he falls back. He will do wrong now, and will be a thoroughly good man afterwards. There shall be no mistake about the religious character which shall belong to him when he does once adopt it. He says to himself, "First of all, let me make my fortune; after that, and when I am raised in the world, I will do a great deal of good with it; I will benefit society, I will encourage religion, I will be a philanthropist; I will make the very station which I gain, by the means I now use, tell for the advantage, spiritual and temporal, of others. Religion shall be no loser by this step, she shall have all the benefit of my name, and credit, and position; I will give her all my public support; but first of all I must make my fortune." There is a passage in a Greek drama in which one of the personages shrinks irresolutely from a proposed crime which is to turn out to his own and his companion's great profit; and the other says to him, "*Dare* ——, and *afterwards* we shall show ourselves just." It is to be feared that this is the way in which many a man has spoken to his own faltering conscience, when it shrank from an unscrupulous act which promised a great worldly advancement. *Dare*, he has said to himself,—Dare to take this one step; this step will be the beginning of advancement, and when I am elevated in the world, then I shall show myself a good man, and have the reputation of one. Thus it is that people persuade themselves that religion is not made for the hurry and the struggle of life. Now, they say or they think, now, in the very thick of the struggle, they must be allowed some little liberty, afterwards it will be different; but *now* one cannot be impeded; now there must not be this check, this shackle; now it is inopportune, unsuitable to the crisis; religion must wait a little.

I say it is difficult to account for men who profess a sense of the truth of religion, devoting themselves with the passion they do, and for the number of years they do, to a worldly object, unless they have some such idea as this in their minds, by which they justify and explain their course to themselves. And yet how low and debased a conception this is of the religious character, that it should rise up *upon such a foundation*. Religion is a growth in the human mind; upon what kind of soil does it grow here? Upon the soil of a worldly heart, and the long formation of worldly habits. But it is an absurdity to think that a religious character can rise up upon such a ground; the very nature of the ground is adverse to it. It is trusting to a kind of jugglery to suppose that religion can spring up in a man out of such material as this. What has he been doing all this time but rooting himself *in* the world, making himself as much a creature of this world as he can? And what he has made himself that he is. He is not a better man because his fortune is made. It is true that when his fortune is made he has no longer the motive to use those expedients, or be absorbed in that passion of acquisition which conduced to the making it. But that is an alteration of his circumstances, not of himself. It is indeed a childish view of religion to suppose that it can rise up in the soul upon a ground which has nothing to do with the production of it; as if, as Scripture says, men should gather figs of thistles. It is even a grossly superstitious view. What greater superstition can there be than for a man to suppose that by a bargain with himself he can do away with the connection of means and ends; for a religious character has its own proper means by which it is produced; which means he has all this time been discarding. We call an idea superstitious when it contradicts plain reason; and surely this idea of his is quite against reason. It is indeed in this way that superstitious religious systems act; they make men believe that they can gain a religious character without the natural means, in the place of which they substitute some set formal means of their own devising. How irrational to suppose, when religious character is the result of trial, as much as the fruit is the growth of a tree, that trial can be dispensed with upon the understanding of the man with himself that he intends one day to be religious when there is *no* trial; as if he could alter the laws of nature. Yet this is what a man really proposes to himself who thinks religion not made for the struggle of life, but for the time after the struggle; that is, that trial is not meant to be borne at the time of trial, but after the time of trial; or, that he is ready to bear trial quite well when there is none to bear; but not when there is. Of what value can a man's goodness be which is the result of such a bargain as this?

What can it be but a profession when it does come, a respectable exterior, not an inward conformation of the man to the image of God? It will sometimes happen that a man, not really religious in heart, will enjoy the good opinion of the world, and that a sort of religious reputation even may be yielded to him, and without blame, if he makes a good profession; for it is not our part to judge others; we do not know what is in their hearts, and must therefore in our behaviour assume them to be what they profess. But all this is outward. A religious character is an inward thing. It is to be feared, however, that the outward reputation, and the credit given them by others, is sometimes abused by men *as a prospect beforehand, and as an issue foreseen* in the midst of the struggle of life; that they say to themselves that, though they may not be so strict as they ought to be now, it will all be wiped off, and men will think and speak well enough of them when they are rich and great; according to the saying just quoted. They dare to override scruples, confident in a future when they shall show themselves just.

A school, therefore, which takes especially under its care the rising business-class of the country, and gives it a strictly religious education under Church influence, performs a most important service to society; because it furnishes the only discipline which can effectually deal with this peculiar source of temptation and self-deception to which the class is exposed; because it forestalls the day of trial, and imbues youth, before the struggle of life comes, with that particular view of life which will meet the temptation; the religious view of life, which regards the whole of it, from the very commencement, as dedicated to God. Its daily system, its religious tuition, its religious services, are a perpetual solemn assertion of the text—"Seek ye *first* the kingdom of God, and His righteousness;" they utter a note of warning; they say aloud, with an accent which cannot be mistaken, to every youth here —Never do in the struggle of life that which you would not do after the success of life. Never be misled by that beguiler who whispers into the ear that religion is too rigid a rule for conducting the active, busy part of life, and comes in properly at the repose of the end, when the object is gained; never, especially, "lay the flattering unction to your soul" that anything you can do for religion and mankind when you have gained your object, can make up for wrong steps in gaining it. The trial doubtless will come to many of you; and when it does come it will not come of course exactly in the form in which I put it here in words; it will not present so distinct an alternative, it will come probably under some disguise. There will be room given you to make a wrong decision if you so will; that is part of the system of human probation. But whatever shape it takes, it will be this in substance. You will be tempted to take a point of view of your own which will allow you to do something which in your real heart and conscience you had rather not do, in consideration of your good intentions and future good services to religion.

I will mention another subject upon which a good

school training is most important. Under the religious value of such an institution as this there is included one very important piece of moral discipline and instruction, which is practically given in a large school in which the morals of boys are well moulded, and of which the aim and tone are high. And it is a piece of practical instruction which is peculiarly important for the sphere of business in which man deals with man, as competitor, as partner and associate, as employer of the labour of others in a thousand ways, some casual, some permanent; I mean the cultivation of the sense of justice. It is evident that the sense of justice wants cultivating in human nature, and is apt to be very capricious and imperfect without this cultivation. It wants some training, such exercise and practice as will give it experience of people's rights, and what is due in a variety of cases from one man to another. It wants material to work upon. You must give all the faculties of the mind material to work upon if you want them to improve. Each needs exercise, and an arena to move and exert itself in, if it is to gain any decided strength. So the sense of justice requires practising ground, so to speak. A man with the best intentions may make great mistakes in any practical department or office in which he has to transact business with men, for want of a certain experience of this kind; because his sense of justice has not had the advantage of a sphere of practice,—of cases to deal with. In consequence, he does not catch the right point of view in the cases with which he has to deal. Hence collisions in men's intercourse with others, and in the transaction of business. Men often overrate their own claims, not from selfishness entirely, but from ignorance as well, because they have not been in situations which have brought them into contact with others, and so have not learnt to measure what is their due.

I cannot be wrong in saying that this sense of justice has a most critical value in the conduct of trade; and especially in the manufacturing world, where masters have vast numbers in their employ. All trade indeed is full of disputes, in which some question of justice lies at the bottom; but the manufacturing world has contests on so large a scale, and lasting so long, that society is sometimes alarmed; because there the ground is divided into two great classes which have most important opposite interests regarding wages, and regarding length of time of work. In every strike then, there is a question of justice which lies at the bottom; and what is the proper instrument and means of deciding this question? The reply is a *sense* of justice. There must be a discriminating faculty which applies itself to the merits of the case, and weighs the claims on both sides. Each side is bound to consider what is due to the other side as well as to itself. It is true a right judgment may be resisted; but still, if there is on either side a really correct judgment, that judgment must have a tendency to work its way.

One is perhaps the more justified in referring to this want now, because, certainly, there is a disposition to think at this time, in the manufacturing and trading part of the community, that the judicial faculty has no place in this department; and that justice is the result of simple collision of interests working itself out; that it comes about as an *issue*, in fact, of opposing forces, but that it need not be the aim; that the aim of each side is to look out for itself. " We live in a selfish world, and we must look after ourselves," was the reply of a witness at a commission lately sitting. This witness was indeed a representative of the working-men; but though a master would probably not have made such a reply, it is but too likely that the idea in the minds of many employers of labour would not have very much differed from it. Indeed, the effect of repeated collisions is very apt to be the notion, on each side, that all justice is the result simply of people standing out for themselves. But to give up justice as an aim, which is what this view tends to, must still be a fundamental mistake. For the aim itself must tend straight to produce effects, and good effects. It must modify beforehand, and in the first instance, claims which, upon the other system, would only be modified after long detail and counteraction of opposite sides; and that might be done in forestalment of a struggle, which otherwise would only be the consequence of a struggle. An eye to the rights of both sides tends to cut off false claims from the first; at any rate it seizes the equitable point of view earlier in the contest, and tells men earlier when to give way, if they should have to give way,—which is a much nearer road to a settlement than each side blindly holding out for its own. The sense of justice must tend to make a quicker settlement than the struggle of forces.

Now, perhaps, there is no better place for training the sense of justice than a public school. Where a high standard is placed before youth, collected together in a large mass, it will in fact educate itself in this particular, and the education it gives itself is the best education it can have. There is, in a collected mass of youth in a school, that contrast, that rivalry, that struggle of wills and choices, that opposition of claims and rights, which early familiarises minds with the field of human rights, which makes them know by experience that there are such things as rights; and know that rights must be met and dealt with in some satisfactory way. All the disputes and contests which rise up among boys, so long as they are fairly carried on, are a training to the sense of justice. They find out what is due to themselves and due to others. And this learning is all the better for the circumstance that it does not deal rigorously with the subject, but in a large free way; that the aim is fairness in a liberal sense. There is an element of generosity in all true justice. Indeed that justice which tries to do without generosity is a very poor justice; more than the "lore of nicely-calculated less or more" is required here; for if people calculate the judicial mean too nicely they will not hit it; in their hearts they ought to go a little beyond it, or they will fall short of it. One sees persons who aim at an exact justice, with a jealousy of the slightest advance beyond it; and of all persons who attend to the matter at all, these make the greatest mistakes in justice. Indeed, true justice is a high Christian quality, and borders so closely upon charity that we cannot easily separate or distinguish these two virtues in action, and say which is justice and which is charity. The sublime portraiture of charity which St. Paul gives, is a portraiture of the temper of true justice too. Justice "rejoiceth not in iniquity, but rejoiceth in the truth ; justice envieth not, vaunteth not itself, is not puffed up, doth not behave itself unseemly, is not easily provoked." And, in the language of Scripture, justice and righteousness are one word. The good are the just —whose "path is as the shining light, that shineth more and more unto the perfect day." "The memory of the just is blessed ;" they shall come out of trouble ; unto the just no evil shall happen ; the way of the just is uprightness : Thou most upright dost weigh the path of the just. And even He who gave the new commandment of love, and who came down from heaven and emptied Himself of His glory to show His love to mankind, and save them from death by the sacrifice of Himself on the Cross, received the title of the "Just One." The Prophets "showed before of the coming of the Just One,"[1] "the Holy One and the Just," who was denied of man, because the "light shone in darkness, and the darkness comprehended it not."

Lastly, although it is allowable to mention special points in which the education given in a great religious school is likely to be of particular benefit to that important portion of society for which it is mainly designed, let us not forget the foundation of the whole,—

[1] Acts vii. 52.

that the education of this place is based upon Christian doctrine. Certainly this is not an age in which the tendency is to rest upon any foundation of mystery; although those who reject the mystery of the Gospel are obliged to fall back upon mystery of some kind, for indeed our whole being is a mystery. We are ourselves a mystery to ourselves; our will, our conscience, the sense of sin which we have, are all mysteries. The mystery of the Gospel is indeed the corresponding mystery to this inward mystery, and gives us the key to ourselves. But the key is rejected by those who say they do not want a key, and would rather have mystery end in simple astonishment and confusion than in hope and peace. It is remarkable, I say, that in an age characterised by these speculative tendencies, the greatest of our new institutions for education should take their stand upon the Gospel mystery. It is a cheering and encouraging thought that they do so. Education, indeed, upon another basis would be a mistake; and not only a doctrinal mistake, but a great and most overwhelming practical mistake. It is Christian doctrine which lays hold on the human heart, and gives the power and effect to moral teaching. If we want people to *act* upon what they know, here is the motive—the stimulus lies in the vision of another world, and the hope which such a revelation kindles. Human nature must have a prospect before it; and Christianity alone gives it a prospect. If we would have the tone of society elevated; greater conscientiousness imparted to trade; greater liberality in one class toward another; more public spirit; more benevolence; if we would have the covetous and grasping temper of commerce curbed; more contentedness in society; more peace and goodwill—the blessed result must come from the preaching of Christian doctrine.

THE INFLUENCE OF DOGMATIC TEACHING ON EDUCATION.

1 TIMOTHY, III. 15.

"The Church of the living God, the pillar and ground of the truth."

THERE are two classes of difficulties in Scripture, for one of which there must be some explanation; otherwise God Himself is represented as doing something wrong. The commands which He gives in early ages are to do things which in us would be positively wrong. Before we accept then what is said in Scripture, we must know that what is *primâ facie* wrong is not what it looks; it must be made certain that this interpretation is not necessary. Some process of reasoning there must be, because there is something wrong without it in the divine acts. The human mind must refuse to submit to anything contrary to moral sense in Scripture. So much intellectual inquiry then is really necessary: it is impossible to let an objection to God's moral nature go unanswered.

But while questions concerning morality and apparent Divine commands are among the difficulties of Scripture, no inquiry is obligatory upon religious minds in matters of the supernatural and miraculous; there is no moral question raised by the fact of a miracle, nor does a supernatural doctrine challenge any moral resistance. In the doctrine of the Incarnation, *e.g.* we see a wonderful depth of mystery, but there is no inquiry for us to institute, there is no question for us to raise; we have only to accept the mysterious truth, which is beyond our comprehension, of our Lord's ineffable and perfect nature. We dwell upon a mystery, and we have no search to make, we have no argument to construct. In the former case, while there was a *primâ facie* appearance of something actually wrong having been commanded by God under a former dispensation, it was necessary to argue in order to clear the Bible from a charge; but in a revelation of the supernatural no charge is incurred; here is profound repose; here simple faith accepts the great truths of the Gospel; and, while the historical portion of Scripture cultivates a succession of inquiries which belong to its territory, the Gospel offers its sacred truth unreservedly to love and faith.

We thus see the mind going on in two totally different tracks, according as some question is laid before it in history, which compels the reader of Scripture to see something that has to be explained; or, according as it is a mystery of the Gospel, which does not require explanation. There is nothing inconsistent in these two lines of thought with each other. There must be a spirit of intellectual inquiry in the study of Scripture whenever there is a question legitimately to rouse it. In the Old Testament the question of God's former modes of acting, which we do not see now, but which did then prevail in the world, cannot be dismissed.

It must be met. But because we have to argue questions, and disturbing questions, when they arise in Scripture, we need not, therefore, give up simple faith upon its proper ground.

When public school education was first renovated, and made a fresh start in this country many years ago, it did so under the eye of a great man, in whose memory we all here feel interest. And, perhaps, it is not without its importance just now that the religious influence under which that great movement was conducted should be taken notice of. I say that we should form a proper estimate of it, because the religious character of the movement was so conspicuous in the whole of it; and therefore it will be of some importance to ascertain what that religion was, and the creed on which it was built. In Arnold, then, we have undoubtedly a man who was ready to take up controversy on critical subjects relating to Scripture, and who laid down new views with great boldness, and sometimes without a sufficient consideration. He entered very strongly into the Old Testament question of the Divine commands which run counter to our ideas of sound morals; and he applied solutions to some of the enigmas of the Old Testament from which people in general justly dissented.

But while there was one part of the ground of Scripture upon which he appeared as an investigator and an inquirer into truth, upon another part, and by far the most important part, he took his place as a simple believer, accepting all the doctrines of the Gospel without a question, and taking his stand with an absolute repose and an unhesitating and unwavering faith upon the supernatural mysteries of Christianity. The Old Testament questions upon which he decided with too great haste, still in fact left open to him the whole body of the great doctrines of Christianity for steadfast adherence and devout and simple belief. He had a loyal attachment to the principle of faith, a firm allegiance to it as the genuine making of the man, raising him from a lower to a higher life; and he accepted it heartily, as expressed in a primitive framework, and in a form of sacred words. His contemporaries were keenly alive to his errors of judgment in this Old Testament controversy, and were too much turned away by them from a true acknowledgment of the weight of his doctrinal teaching in the school chapel. But it ought to be said that he combined singular independence of mind, chivalry, and ardour in the pursuit of truth with the most noble expression of doctrine; and that not only doctrine itself received a magnificent expression under his treatment, but that every collateral thought which gives support to supernatural truth and the hold of the mind upon it, was fostered and cherished in his mind. He had no idea of truth being left floating to find a new foundation where it could; but with him it was an understood thing that education must be founded upon religion, and that the religion upon which it was founded was a truth of fact. He stood upon the rock of the Nicene Creed, and, standing upon that sacred deposit, he had no fear for the working out of his plans and method.

For without a religion to stand on, what was a school but an experiment, without any guarantee for higher training in it; a whole mass of human nature taken in and turned out again, without any hold being obtained over it, and nothing except its own humorous waywardness and impulse being conspicuous. In the trial of strength Arnold wanted a faith that would be a yoke, that would claim a supremacy by the certainty of its convictions, and hold the school together in the bonds of a true growth, so that he might claim for the school something of the higher union—" For as the body is one, and hath many members, and all the members of that one body being many are one body: so also is Christ:"—all grows together from one root of doctrine, and that is the doctrine of Christ crucified. "The savage," he says, "and the half-civilised man thinks that he can bribe God to forgive him by costly or painful sacrifices; the philosopher thinks that sacrifices are not needed. But He who is in the bosom of the Father has declared to us that evil must cease to be evil, or that it must be destroyed from out of the kingdom of God; that God's love to us would not spare even His own Son to save us from destruction, but that God's holiness must have destroyed us—yea, must and will now destroy us—if we lay not hold of the redemption which He has offered us. This is the love of God, not to pass over our sins, but to give His own Son to be the propitiation for our sins. And this proof of His love shows what must come to us if we refuse the propitiation thus offered. This, if it fully entered into our minds, if believed with an undoubting and unwavering faith, must, indeed, save us all." Thus, on the one hand, strong and urgent on the duty of intellectual inquiry, always reminding us that difficulties are not to be passed over, and that this only makes weak men,—whereas faith requires acts of minds of energy and power,—on the other hand, he holds to the faith of Nicæa. His language is the primitive language. He puts force into it, and does not use it with reluctance and unwillingness; but he uses it as the foundation of his school and its teaching.

And his thought is primitive not only when he lays down doctrine, but when he deals with the ethics which are favourable to doctrine, and points out to men how their minds must be trained, and general principles implanted, if you are to have a particular creed implanted in people's hearts and taking root there. It is this subsidiary advice impressing moral ideas upon men, with a view to faith and in aid of faith, which is so charged with the *animus* of faith and is so strong with sacred bias. One observes now that the idea of a victorious faith is a great deal given up in many quarters. The notion is that if Faith conquers, she does it by being unfair, and that she gets more than she ought to have. There must be nothing gained by Faith from within, by the strength of her own spirit, by her own courage enabling her to face difficulties and so bringing her out of them. In order to be intelligent faith, Faith must always be beaten; acknowledging herself wrong, she is then sound and healthy. Now, this is not the teaching of Arnold. The usual conclusion into which people slide now if there is any difficulty as to faith, if faith feels charged with too heavy a burden, and the favourite expedient is—drop one part of it; you will be astonished to find what a relief it is, and how cheerfully you bear the other part. The whole defect of faith is made to consist in the weight of the load imposed, in having too much to put up with.

But, now, the principle that Arnold lays down is the counter principle—that faith must struggle from within, not be eased in every case and have weight taken off from without. What you want is not to have a truth taken off from your weight, but to have a new strength inserted in your belief. "You see," he says, "what it is that is wanted— namely, to make notions wholly remote from your common life take their place in your minds as more powerful than the things of common life—to make the future and the unseen prevail over what you see and hear now around you. I know indeed," he continues, "of one thing which would effect this in an instant. Let any one of you be dangerously ill, let his prospects of earthly life be rendered less than uncertain, then he would soon think far more of the unseen world than of the world around us." The principle upon which such a question is put is, of course, that the mind is, in the regular and legitimate course of things, the stimulus to its own faith, and that it can impart strength to its own belief, if it will take the trouble. It must be considered that faith is freshened by acts of faith—by doing things which naturally follow from faith. "Assuredly," he says, "the faith you find at once so uninteresting and so hard to understand cannot be the ruling principle of your lives—you cannot in any sense be walking by faith. And therefore I have thought that it might be well to say a few words as to the means of gaining this faith; to tell you how you may, with God's blessing, come to understand and love it, and to act upon it, just as naturally as we now act every day, from some motive of worldly pleasure or pain."

Coleridge has a great maxim—that "to restore a commonplace truth to its first uncommon lustre, you need only translate it into action." That is to say, in proportion as you make truth a thing that stirs you, you give it a newness; you recommend it to your belief, it strikes home to you. Arnold's great wish was for a real belief, not a mere belief of words; but he did not think this was to be gained by making a doctrine less supernatural, but by making the mind itself more aspiring; not by lowering the truth, but by raising the mind. He considered that the mind was to be trained to faith of set purpose, and by distinct inculcation of all the imagery of faith upon its attention. "A child," he says, "may be soon taught to love his Saviour, and will listen with great eagerness when he hears how Jesus Christ came down from heaven for his sake, how He lived in poverty and sorrow, and died a cruel death, that we might be made for His sake everlastingly happy. . . . . Nay, even the third great truth which the Gospel teaches us, the sanctification of our hearts by the Holy Spirit, can be and often is practically taught to very young children, when they are taught to pray that God will make them good." We are reminded in his general vein of religious thought much of Mr. Keble. The faith of a child was the pattern of a grown-up man's faith with both of them. He shows us in an especial way his sympathy with a child's mind in the reception of matters of faith; he takes in the whole idea that is in the child's mind, and sees how much there is in it which is exactly the same in the child and in himself. He stops short where he must, and the child stops short. Both of them believe and rest in mysteries of faith, in the one way in which they must, as they are imparted to them by the Divine Spirit.

Arnold did not attempt to penetrate supernatural truth, and saw that as a child received it, so did a man; it was beyond both. He valued the first fresh acquaintance of the child with mystery, with truth above nature. He saw the naturalness of faith; how the first impulse of nature was to accept the Gospel, and how the whole intellect of the child rose with the truths which it embraced. He had always deep in his mind an image of believing childhood, and with this association and sentiment was the whole structure of his dogmatic language linked: dogmatic language was so far child's language, that it only put into words what was above our understanding. The language of the Council of Nicæa is coupled in his mind with the language of childhood. Nature so clearly fitted him to be a preacher of Christianity, and the supernatural doctrines of Christianity, that such a witness to the Supernatural Man Christ Jesus cannot but arrest us.

He has a joy and pride in the declarations of the Gospel which bespeak a real belief; the very frame of his language shows it.

And now, why have I gone back to the activities of former days, and to the original of the great public education movement? It is that we may see the unity of the movement from first to last. It began with a remarkable alliance of education and religion, and that alliance has continued. Making allowance for the different modifications which a great principle contracts in the course of its advance, this is the same powerful combination that it was. We here feel that we are carrying out a great work, and not only that we are carrying out a great work, but that we are carrying out the same great work that first arrested attention, as a renovation of the educating power of the country, more than thirty years ago.

This institution is the head, indeed, of a subordination of schools; and we have in him who has had to superintend this large formation a singular and special fitness for such a work—such as marks him for it. The vast materials which enter into such a plan would, unless they had found a head that could give them place, and arrange their operations in a scheme, have issued in a general medley; but he who is at once the head and the founder of this whole system has conducted it successfully, and gathered all its resources into one efficient plan. And one of the great qualifications for this arduous work has been the patience with which he has borne the imperfections of his plan in process of its forming; the gradual way in which he has been enabled to deal with the rising claims of each part of the growth, teaching every part of the whole to do with as little as it can for the interim, while it was only in a provisionary state. First, the building was raised with only its necessary walls and roof, and rooms to shelter scholars and masters; then a hall rose, then a library, then a chapel. There was no hurry to make everything perfect at once; everything took its time; and its place in the arrangement came as it was allowed for in the general plan. It required one who was endowed with great capacity for action to collect all the minds together, and fit them into their proper positions in the working order of a large plan, uniting many institutions. To put together such materials required gifts, the use and employment of which must have constituted their own reward in a great measure, for all capacities and fitnesses take a pleasure in their own exercise; but it must at the same time have thrown a great weight on the mind, and imposed a life of labour and pressure, and incessant calls upon the attention.

It must strike any one who contemplates the map of life, that many different kinds of lives have leading attributes in common. One man is a statesman, another man a traveller and discoverer, another man a man of business, another a schoolmaster, and so on; all these forms of life seem to come to much the same thing as far as regards labour. A life labour must go along with all this class of lives. Wherever there are things to be done, carefully and with due regard to time and place; wherever there is character

Dogmatic Teaching on Education. 343

to be studied and judged truly; wherever there is accurate observing, and expeditious doing, there is labour. All lives that undertake objects and make themselves difficult have much in common and do much similar kind of mental work. I take up the travels of Dr. Livingstone—it strikes me very soon that bodily toil is the least of his labours; I see him in the thick of a problem, he has a piece of reasoning to get through that taxes severely all his powers. Who is to put together the action of all these forces, and get at the old secret of the world and the key of a continent? The great traveller is a reasoner as much as a traveller, working hard in the inside of his brain, putting things together—rivers, and forests, and lakes: the outflowing of bogs, the forming of inundations. With these he reasons, a whole argument is working up into form in his mind, he is full of a problem. Here, then, is the same kind of work of mind haunting a traveller which besets a sedentary student: while a life which is connected with founding institutions carries its own high qualities, its perseverance, its patience and equanimity, its power of gathered attention to a large field of action, upon its face.

Let us now turn to the work of the day. We are to lay the foundation of a new church. For the completion of the splendid design we must look forward another year; we have to do now with the severe, yet sterling and fit and costly foundation, worthy of its end. Laid deep in the hill side, it typifies the ancient Creed. The cause of education has been, and will continue to be, a missionary cause; religion has become by use the natural ally of education, and so long as education goes on, so long it must support the Christian Creed. This is its natural work. It cannot avoid doing it. There is a great power in this country, a power which is part of progress, and implicates the future, which has signed a compact with the Creed. Education in its popular aspect can no more give up the Creed than it can give up the classics. It is true the law may alter, and legal constitutions may change from one system to another, and they may shake off the yoke of the Act of Uniformity. But education as commending itself to the people, and conducted by a popular impulse, must go on as it has done, taking religion along with it by a voluntary partnership. And both mutually benefit by the alliance.

You may, indeed, offer an education without a religious creed, and you may offer all the material of knowledge, but without a creed you have not the natural recipient of education. Religion gives the power of receiving education; it provides that seriousness and weight in the young mind, which knows how to lay hold of the resources to the enjoyment of which it is admitted. How does any solemn thought, any impressive sight, any memento of greatness, any gleam of nature, any opening in the sky, set us forward in the work of life, give us a start in some particular undertaking that we have to enter upon! Well then, that which furnishes the higher start in the general work of education is religion. In works of fiction there is a moment which makes the character; the creator of the work of art who wields all the resources of moral description, of sentiment and imagery, may have striven with his idea in vain ; he buffets the air with words, and loads the ground of the drama with structures of scenes of conversations, but for all that the character is not yet drawn, and he has that in his mind which is not expressed. His effort is to strike it out, and to shape it, and it will not come into shape ; but a moment brings it out, and the person stands before you. That ideal in the world of school creation is the Creed. At once a school becomes something else; something it gains of an end above nature, of a supernatural end of its own work. The rank of all work is raised, and the scholar is raised with his work. The school belongs to the ages that are past, and is part of the chain of forts and defences of Christianity.

NOTE TO PAGE 27,—THE SYLLABUS.

THE reply of the Section of the Theological Faculty of Munich (1869) takes advantage of the negative form of the Syllabus—that it is a list of condemned *errors*, to throw a convenient ambiguity upon the *truths* which the Syllabus does, and which the Council will, proclaim. "The Syllabus errorum," I quote from the reply, "censured a number of theses and designated them as errors, without distinctly stating which of the different views included in the range of the contradictory views is to be considered the true one." But to say this is to forget that to any distinct proposition which is declared false, there is a contrary distinct proposition which is, by the force of the other's falsity, declared true. Let the proposition, *e.g.* be, theft is right; which proposition is condemned: it is absurd to say that the contrary of the proposition that theft is right is "a range of different views," and that we "nowhere distinctly state which of the different views included in this range of contradictory views is to be considered the true one." We take, then, the propositions in the Syllabus: "The Church hath not the right to apply force, and—the temporal power of the Episcopacy is the gift of the State, and may be recalled by the State when it likes;" which propositions are declared false: it is evident that this condemnation of itself declares two contrary propositions true—viz. "The Church *hath* the right of applying force: and The temporal power of the Episcopacy is *not* the gift of the State, and may not be recalled by the State."

The political subject-matter of the decrees again is appealed to, as a guarantee not of fact that they will not be, but as a philosophical reason why "they would not be proclaimed as directly revealed and traditional dogmas;" they are excluded, it is said, "to a great extent by their very nature from being so." The unfitness of such material from its very nature for dogma, would be indeed a most excellent and cogent reason for declining to enunciate it as such; but it is unhappily no reason at all why, being enunciated as such, it will not be such. That ought to have been thought of first; it will be too late to revert to the subject-matter when the dogma is made. Again, recourse is had to all the resources and capacities of ambiguity in what constitutes an *ex cathedra* utterance of the Pope. The Pope may have distinctly pronounced a proposition to be an article of faith; but has he done so under all the conditions which theologians have a right to require? and among the conditions they have a right to require if they see occasion for it, is a "more mature consideration of the point to be defined according to the rules of Holy Writ and ecclesiastical tradition." But if, after the formal declaration of a dogma by the Pope, theologians have the right to consider first whether the subject-matter admits of a dogma, and secondly, whether the Pope has bestowed sufficient consideration on the matter; we must ask, with all deference to the admirable discreetness of these theologians, what has become of, and what is contained in, Papal Infallibility? It cannot certainly particularly signify in what quarter—whether a Pope with, or a Pope without a Council—*such* an Infallibility resides.

THE END.

Printed by R. & R. CLARK, *Edinburgh*

NEW BOOKS AND NEW EDITIONS

IN COURSE OF PUBLICATION BY

MESSRS. RIVINGTON
WATERLOO PLACE, LONDON

And at Oxford and Cambridge

April 1876

The Child Samuel. A Practical and Devotional Commentary on the Birth and Childhood of the Prophet Samuel, as recorded in 1 Sam. i., ii. 1—27, iii. Designed as a Help to Meditation on the Holy Scriptures for Children and Young Persons. By **Edward Meyrick Goulburn**, D.D., Dean of Norwich.
Small 8vo. *[Nearly ready.*

The Principal Ecclesiastical Judgments delivered in the Court of Arches, 1867-1875. By the Right Hon. Sir **Robert Phillimore**, D.C.L.
8vo. 12s.

Thirty-two Years of the Church of England, 1842-1875: The Charges of Archdeacon Sinclair. Edited by **William Sinclair**, M.A., Prebendary of Chichester, Rector of Pulborough, late Vicar of S. George's, Leeds. With a Historical Introduction by **Robert Charles Jenkins**, M.A., Hon. Canon of Canterbury, Rector and Vicar of Lyminge.
8vo. *[In the Press.*

Sermons Preached chiefly before the University of Oxford. By **J. B. Mozley**, D.D., Canon of Christ Church, and Regius Professor of Divinity in the University of Oxford.
8vo. *[Nearly ready.*

Rudiments of Theology. A First Book for Students. By **John Pilkington Norris**, B.D., Canon of Bristol, and Examining Chaplain to the Bishop of Manchester, Author of "Key to the Four Gospels," "Key to the Acts of the Apostles," &c.
Crown 8vo. 7s. 6d.

A Selection from the Lectures delivered at St. Margaret's, Lothbury. By the Rev. **Henry Melvill**, B.D., late Canon of St. Paul's, and Chaplain in Ordinary to the Queen.
New Edition. Crown 8vo. 5s. *[In the Press.*

[B—502]

London, Oxford, and Cambridge

Life of Robert Gray, Bishop of Cape
Town and Metropolitan of the Province of South Africa. Edited by his Son, the Rev. Charles Gray, M.A., Vicar of Helmsley, York.

With Portrait and Map. Two Vols. 8vo. 32s.

The Compendious Edition of the Annotated Book
of Common Prayer, forming a concise Commentary on the Devotional System of the Church of England. By the Rev. John Henry Blunt, M.A., F.S.A., Editor of the "Dictionary of Sects and Heresies," &c., &c.

Crown 8vo, 10s. 6d.; in half-morocco, 16s.; or in morocco limp, 17s. 6d.

The Life of Worship. A Course of Lectures.
By the Rev. George Body, B.A., Rector of Kirkby Misperton, Author of "The Life of Temptation" and "The Life of Justification."

Crown 8vo. [*In the Press.*

The Light of the Conscience. By the
Author of "The Hidden Life of the Soul," &c., with an Introduction by the Rev. T. T. Carter, M.A., Rector of Clewer, Berks.

Crown 8vo. 5s.

Morning Notes of Praise. A Series of
Meditations upon the Morning Psalms. Dedicated to the Countess of Cottenham. By Lady Charlotte-Maria Pepys.

New Edition. Small 8vo. 2s. 6d.

Quiet Moments; a Four Weeks' Course
of Thoughts and Meditations before Evening Prayer and at Sunset. By Lady Charlotte-Maria Pepys.

New Edition. Small 8vo. 2s. 6d.

Life of Archbishop Fénelon. By the
Author of "Life of S. Francis de Sales," "Life of Bossuet," "A Dominican Artist," &c.

Crown 8vo. [*In the Press.*

The Mystery of Christ: Being an Examination
of the Doctrines contained in the first three Chapters of the Epistle of Paul the Apostle to the Ephesians. By George Staunton Barrow, M.A., Rector of Knight's Enham, Hants.

Crown 8vo. [*In the Press.*

London, Oxford, and Cambridge

Manuals of Religious Instruction. Edited

by John Pilkington Norris, B.D., Canon of Bristol, Church Inspector of Training Colleges, and Examining Chaplain to the Bishop of Manchester.

The OLD TESTAMENT.
The NEW TESTAMENT.
The PRAYER BOOK.

Three Volumes complete. Small 8vo. 3s. 6d. each. Or each Volume in Five Parts, 1s. each Part.

A Commentary, Expository and Devotional,

on the Order of the Administration of the Lord's Supper, according to the Use of the Church of England, to which is added an Appendix on Fasting Communion, Non-Communicating Attendance, Auricular Confession, the Doctrine of Sacrifice, the Eucharistic Sacrifice. By **Edward Meyrick Goulburn**, D.D., Dean of Norwich.

Sixth Edition. Small 8vo. 6s.
Also, a Cheap Edition, uniform with " Thoughts on Personal Religion," and " The Pursuit of Holiness." 3s. 6d.

Liber Precum Publicarum Ecclesiæ

Anglicanæ. A Gulielmo Bright, D.D., et Petro Goldsmith Medd, A.M., Presbyteris, Collegii Universitatis in Acad. Oxon. Sociis, Latine redditus.

New Edition, with Rubrics in red. Small 8vo. 6s. [*In the Press.*

Bible Readings for Family Prayer.

By the Rev. **W. H. Ridley**, M.A., Rector of Hambleden, Honorary Canon of Christ Church, Oxford.

Crown 8vo.

Old Testament—Genesis and Exodus. 2s.
Four Gospels, 3s. 6d. { St. Matthew and St. Mark. 2s.
{ St. Luke and St. John. 2s.
The Acts of the Apostles. 2s.

Ars Pastoria. By Frank Parnell, M.A.,

Rector of Oxtead.

Small 8vo. 2s.

Short Devotional Forms, for Morning,

Night, and Midnight, and for the Third, Sixth, Ninth Hours and Eventide of each Day of the Week. Arranged to meet the Exigencies of a Busy Life. By **Edward Meyrick Goulburn**, D.D., Dean of Norwich.

Fourth Edition. 18mo, cloth limp, 1s. 6d.

London, Oxford, and Cambridge

Meditations on the Life and Mysteries

of Our Lord and Saviour Jesus Christ. From the French. By the Compiler of "The Treasury of Devotion." Edited by the Rev. T. T. Carter, M.A., Rector of Clewer, Berks; Honorary Canon of Christ Church, Oxford.

Crown 8vo.

Vol. I.—THE HIDDEN LIFE OF OUR LORD. 3s. 6d.
Vol. II.—THE PUBLIC LIFE OF OUR LORD. *Two Parts,* 5s. *each.*
Vol. III.—THE SUFFERING LIFE, AND THE GLORIFIED LIFE, OF OUR LORD. 3s. 6d.

A Christian Painter of the Nineteenth

Century: being the Life of Hippolyte Flandrin. By the Author of "Life of S. Francis de Sales," &c., &c.

Crown 8vo. 7s. 6d.

The Treasury of Devotion: a Manual

of Prayers for General and Daily Use. Compiled by a Priest. Edited by the Rev. T. T. Carter, M.A., Rector of Clewer, Berks.

New Edition, in Large Type, Crown 8vo, 5s.; *or in morocco limp,* 10s. 6d. *The Smaller Edition, Imperial 32mo,* 2s. 6d.; *cloth limp,* 2s., *or bound with the Book of Common Prayer,* 3s. 6d.

Dictionary of Sects, Heresies, Ecclesi-

ASTICAL PARTIES, AND SCHOOLS OF RELIGIOUS THOUGHT. By various Writers. Edited by the Rev. John Henry Blunt, M.A., F.S.A., Editor of the "Dictionary of Doctrinal and Historical Theology" and the "Annotated Book of Common Prayer," &c. &c.

Imperial 8vo, 36s. *In half-morocco,* 48s.

Bossuet and his Contemporaries. By the

Author of "Life of S. Francis de Sales," "A Dominican Artist," &c.

Crown 8vo. 12s.

The Holy Angels: Their Nature and

Employments, as recorded in the Word of God.

Small 8vo. 6s.

Some Elements of Religion. Lent Lec-

tures. By Henry Parry Liddon, D.D., D.C.L., Canon of St. Paul's, and Ireland Professor of Exegesis in the University of Oxford.

Second Edition. Crown 8vo. 5s.

London, Oxford, and Cambridge

Life, Journals, and Letters of Henry
Alford, D.D., late Dean of Canterbury. Edited by his Widow.
With Portrait. New Edition. Crown 8vo. 9s.

Selection from the Sermons preached
during the latter Years of his Life, in the Parish Church of Barnes, and in the Cathedral of St. Paul's. By **Henry Melvill**, B.D., late Canon of St. Paul's, and Chaplain in Ordinary to the Queen.
Two Volumes. Crown 8vo. 5s. each. Sold separately.

A Plain Statement of the Evidence
of Scripture and Tradition on Church Government. By the Rev. **John Mitchell**, M.A.
Small 8vo. 2s.

The Gospel of the Childhood: a Practical
and Devotional Commentary on the Single Incident of our Blessed Lord's Childhood (St. Luke ii. 41, to the end); designed as a Help to Meditation on the Holy Scriptures, for Children and Young Persons. By **Edward Meyrick Goulburn**, D.D., Dean of Norwich.
Second Edition. Square 16mo. 5s.

The Chorister's Guide. By W. A. Barrett,
Mus. Bac. Oxon., of St. Paul's Cathedral, Author of "Flowers and Festivals."
Second Edition. Square 16mo. 2s. 6d.

Notitia Eucharistica: a Commentary,
Explanatory, Doctrinal and Historical, on the Order for the Administration of the Lord's Supper, or Holy Communion, according to the use of the Church of England. With an Appendix on the Office for the Communion of the Sick. By **W. E. Scudamore**, M.A., Rector of Ditchingham, and formerly Fellow of St. John's College, Cambridge.
Second Edition, revised and enlarged. 8vo. 32s.

The Last Three Sermons preached at
Oxford by **Philip N. Shuttleworth**, D.D., sometime Lord Bishop of Chichester. Justification through Faith—The Merciful Character of the Gospel Covenant—The Sufficiency of Scripture a Rule of Faith. To which is added a Letter addressed in 1841 to a Young Clergyman, now a Priest in the Church of Rome.
New Edition. Small 8vo. 2s. 6d.

London, Oxford, and Cambridge

The Guide to Heaven: a Book of Prayers

for every Want. (For the Working Classes.) Compiled by a Priest. Edited by the Rev. T. T. Carter, M.A., Rector of Clewer, Berks.

New Edition. Imperial 32mo, uniform in size with "The Treasury of Devotion." 1s. 6d., or cloth limp, 1s.

An Edition in Large Type. Crown 8vo, 1s. 6d., or cloth limp, 1s.

Sermons on the Epistles and Gospels

for the Sundays and Holy Days throughout the Year. By the Rev. Isaac Williams, B.D., Author of a "Devotional Commentary on the Gospel Narrative."

New Edition. Two Volumes. Crown 8vo. 5s. each. Sold separately.
Vol. I.—ADVENT TO WHITSUNTIDE.
Vol. II.—TRINITY TO ALL SAINTS' DAY.

Voices of Comfort.

Original and Selected, edited by the Rev. Thomas Vincent Fosbery, M.A., sometime Vicar of St. Giles's, Reading, Editor of "Hymns and Poems for the Sick and Suffering."

Second Edition. Crown 8vo. 7s. 6d.

Henri Perreyve.

By A. Gratry, Prêtre de l'Oratoire, Professeur de Morale Evangélique à la Sorbonne, et Membre de l'Académie Française. Translated, by special permission, by the Author of "Life of S. Francis de Sales," &c. With Portrait.

New and Cheaper Edition. Crown 8vo. 6s.

Out of the Body.

A Scriptural Inquiry. By the Rev. James S. Pollock, M.A., Incumbent of S. Alban's, Birmingham.

Crown 8vo. 5s.

The Young Churchman's Companion to

the Prayer Book. By the Rev. J. W. Gedge, M.A., Diocesan Inspector of Schools for the Archdeaconry of Surrey.

Part I.—MORNING AND EVENING PRAYER AND LITANY.
Part II.—BAPTISMAL AND CONFIRMATION SERVICES.
Part III.—THE OFFICE OF HOLY COMMUNION. [*In preparation.*

18mo, 1s. each; or in paper Cover, 6d.

Thoughts on Personal Religion;

being a Treatise on the Christian Life in its Two Chief Elements, Devotion and Practice. By Edward Meyrick Goulburn, D.D., Dean of Norwich.

New Presentation Edition, elegantly printed on Toned Paper.
Two Vols. Small 8vo. 10s. 6d.
An Edition in one Vol., 6s. 6d.; also a Cheap Edition, 3s. 6d.

London, Oxford, and Cambridge

Of the Imitation of Christ. In Four Books.

By Thomas à Kempis. An entirely New Translation. Forming a Volume of the "Library of Spiritual Works for English Catholics."

Small 8vo. Elegantly printed with Red Borders, on Extra Superfine Toned Paper. 5s.

The Christian Year. Thoughts in Verse

for the Sundays and Holy-Days throughout the Year. Forming a Volume of the "Library of Spiritual Works for English Catholics."

Small 8vo. Elegantly printed with Red Borders, on Extra Superfine Toned Paper. 5s.

The Spiritual Combat. Together with the

Supplement and the Path of Paradise. By Laurence Scupoli. A New Translation. Forming a Volume of the "Library of Spiritual Works for English Catholics."

Small 8vo. Elegantly printed with Red Borders, on Extra Superfine Toned Paper. 5s.

The Devout Life. By Saint Francis of

Sales, Bishop and Prince of Geneva. A New Translation. Forming a Volume of the "Library of Spiritual Works for English Catholics."

Small 8vo. Elegantly printed with Red Borders, on Extra Superfine Toned Paper. 5s.

Dictionary of Doctrinal and Historical

Theology. By Various Writers. Edited by the Rev. John Henry Blunt, M.A., F.S.A., Editor of "The Annotated Book of Common Prayer," &c.

Second Edition. Imperial 8vo, 42s. *In half morocco,* 52s. 6d.

A Book of Litanies, Metrical and Prose,

with an Evening Service. Edited by the Compiler of "The Treasury of Devotion."

32mo, 6d. *; or in paper Cover,* 4d.
The Metrical Litanies separately, 5d. *; or in paper Cover,* 3d.

An Edition of the complete Work, with accompanying Music. Arranged under the Musical Editorship of W. S. Hoyte, Organist and Director of the Choir at All Saints', Margaret Street, London. 4to. 7s. 6d.

Allegories and Tales. By the Rev. W. E.

Heygate, M.A., Rector of Brighstone.

Crown 8vo. 5s.

London, Oxford, and Cambridge

Notes on the Greek Text of the Gospel

according to S. Luke. By the Rev. **Arthur Carr**, M.A., Assistant-Master in Wellington College, late Fellow of Oriel College, Oxford.

Crown 8vo. 6s.

Prayers and Meditations for the Holy

Communion. By **Josephine Fletcher**. With a Preface by **C. J. Ellicott**, D.D., Lord Bishop of Gloucester and Bristol.

With Rubrics in red. Royal 32mo. 2s. 6d.
Cheap Edition. 32mo, cloth limp, 1s.

Words to Take with Us: a Manual of

Daily and Occasional Prayers, for Private and Common Use. With Plain Instructions and Counsels on Prayer. By **W. E. Scudamore**, M.A., Rector of Ditchingham, and formerly Fellow of St. John's College, Cambridge.

Fourth Edition. Small 8vo. 2s. 6d.

The Hidden Life of the Soul. From the

French. By the Author of "A Dominican Artist," "Life of Madame Louise de France," &c. &c.

New and Cheaper Edition. Small 8vo. 2s. 6d.

Our Mother Church; being Simple Talk

on High Topics. By **Anne Mercier**.

New Edition. Small 8vo. 3s. 6d.

The Mystery of the Temptation: a Course

of Lectures. By the Rev. **W. H. Hutchings**, M.A., Sub-Warden of the House of Mercy, Clewer.

Crown 8vo. 4s. 6d.

The Life of Justification: a Series of Lec-

tures delivered in Substance at All Saints, Margaret Street. By the Rev. **George Body**, B.A., Rector of Kirkby Misperton.

Fourth Edition. Crown 8vo. 4s. 6d.

The Life of Temptation: a Course of Lec-

tures delivered in Substance at S. Peter's, Eaton Square; also at All Saints, Margaret Street. By the Rev. **George Body**, B.A., Rector of Kirkby Misperton.

Third Edition. Crown 8vo. 4s. 6d.

London, Oxford, and Cambridge

Immanuel: Thoughts for Christmas and other Seasons; with other Poems. By **A. Middlemore Morgan, M.A.**
Small 8vo. 6s.

Directorium Pastorale. The Principles and Practice of Pastoral Work in the Church of England. By the Rev. **John Henry Blunt, M.A., F.S.A.**, Editor of "The Annotated Book of Common Prayer," &c. &c.
New Edition. Crown 8vo. 7s. 6d.

The Pursuit of Holiness: a Sequel to "Thoughts on Personal Religion," intended to carry the Reader somewhat farther onward in the Spiritual Life. By **Edward Meyrick Goulburn**, D.D., Dean of Norwich.
Fourth Edition. Small 8vo. 5s. Also, a Cheap Edition. 3s. 6d.

Ecclesiastes: the Authorized Version, with a running Commentary and Paraphrase. By the Rev. **Thos. Pelham Dale**, M.A., Rector of St. Vedast with St. Michael, City of London, and late Fellow of Sidney Sussex College, Cambridge.
8vo. 7s. 6d.

The Divinity of our Lord and Saviour JESUS CHRIST; being the Bampton Lectures for 1866. By **Henry Parry Liddon**, D.D., D.C.L., Canon of St. Paul's, and Ireland Professor of Exegesis in the University of Oxford.
Seventh Edition. Crown 8vo. 5s.

Sermons Preached before the University of Oxford. By **Henry Parry Liddon, D.D., D.C.L.**, Canon of St. Paul's, and Ireland Professor of Exegesis in the University of Oxford.
Fourth Edition. Crown 8vo. 5s.

Plain Sermons preached at Brighstone. By **George Moberly, D.C.L.**, Bishop of Salisbury.
Third and Cheaper Edition. Crown 8vo. 5s.

The Annotated Book of Common Prayer; being an Historical, Ritual, and Theological Commentary on the Devotional System of the Church of England. Edited by the Rev. **John Henry Blunt**, M.A., F.S.A.
Sixth Edition, Revised. Imperial 8vo, 36s. In half-morocco, 48s.
[This large edition contains the Latin and Greek originals, together with technical Ritual Annotations, Marginal References, &c., which are necessarily omitted for want of room in the "Compendious Edition."]

London, Oxford, and Cambridge

The Reformation of the Church of
England ; its History, Principles, and Results. A.D. 1514-1547. By the Rev. John Henry Blunt, M.A., F.S.A., Editor of "The Annotated Book of Common Prayer," and "The Dictionary of Doctrinal and Historical Theology," &c., &c.
Third Edition. 8vo. 16s.

Household Theology : a Handbook of Religious Information respecting the Holy Bible, the Prayer Book, the Church, the Ministry, Divine Worship, the Creeds, &c. &c. By the Rev. John Henry Blunt, M.A., F.S.A.
New Edition. Small 8vo. 3s. 6d.

The New Mitre Hymnal; adapted to the Services of the Church of England.
32mo. 1s. 6d. Cloth limp. 1s.
An Edition with Tunes. Royal 8vo. 5s.

The Prayer Book Interleaved. With Historical Illustrations and Explanatory Notes, arranged parallel to the Text. By the Rev. W. M. Campion, D.D., Fellow and Tutor of Queen's College, and Rector of St. Botolph's, Cambridge, and the Rev. W. J. Beamont, M.A., late Fellow of Trinity College, Cambridge. With a Preface by the Lord Bishop of Winchester.
Eighth Edition. Small 8vo. 7s. 6d.

The Book of Church Law; being an Exposition of the Legal Rights and Duties of the Clergy and Laity of the Church of England. By the Rev. John Henry Blunt, M.A., F.S.A. Revised by Walter G. F. Phillimore, B.C.L., Barrister-at-Law, and Chancellor of the Diocese of Lincoln.
Crown 8vo. 7s. 6d.

Mazzaroth; or, the Constellations. By Frances Rolleston.
Royal 8vo. 12s.

The Catholic Sacrifice. Sermons Preached at All Saints, Margaret Street. By the Rev. Berdmore Compton, M.A., Vicar of All Saints, Margaret Street.
Crown 8vo. 5s.

The Knight of Intercession, and other
Poems. By the Rev. S. J. Stone, M.A., Pembroke College, Oxford.
Third Edition, revised and enlarged. Small 8vo. 6s.

London, Oxford, and Cambridge

Sacred Allegories. The Shadow of the

Cross—The Distant Hills—The Old Man's Home—The King's Messengers. By the Rev. W. Adams, M.A., late Fellow of Merton College, Oxford.

With numerous Illustrations.
New Edition. One Vol. Crown 8vo. 5s.
The four Allegories separately. Small 8vo. 1s. each.

A Companion to the New Testament.

Uniform with "A Companion to the Old Testament."
Small 8vo. [*In the Press.*

The Greek Testament. With a Critically

Revised Text; a Digest of Various Readings; Marginal References to Verbal and Idiomatic Usage; Prolegomena; and a Critical and Exegetical Commentary. For the use of Theological Students and Ministers. By **Henry Alford**, D.D., late Dean of Canterbury.

New Edition. Four Volumes. 8vo. 102s.
The Volumes are sold separately, as follows:—
Vol. I.—THE FOUR GOSPELS. 28s.
Vol. II.—ACTS TO II. CORINTHIANS. 24s.
Vol. III.—GALATIANS TO PHILEMON. 18s.
Vol. IV.—HEBREWS TO REVELATION. 32s.

Genesis. With Notes. By the Rev. G. V.

Garland, M.A., late Vicar of Aslacton, Norfolk. [The Hebrew Text, with Literal Translation.]

Parts I. to X. 8vo. In paper Cover, 6d. each.

Short Sermons on the Psalms, in their

order, preached in a Village Church. By **W. J. Stracey**, M.A., Rector of Oxnead and Vicar of Buxton, Norfolk, formerly Fellow of Magdalene College, Cambridge. Psalms I—XXV.

Small 8vo. 5s.
Vol. II., containing Psalms XXVI—LI. [*In the Press.*

The Athanasian Creed. An Examination

of Recent Theories respecting its Date and Origin; with a Postscript, referring to Professor Swainson's Account of its Growth and Reception, which is contained in his Work entitled "The Nicene and Apostles' Creeds, their Literary History." By **G. D. W. Ommanney**, M.A., Vicar of Draycot, Somerset.

Crown 8vo. 8s. 6d.

London, Oxford, and Cambridge

Yesterday, To-day, and For Ever:
A Poem in Twelve Books. By **Edward Henry Bickersteth**, M.A., Vicar of Christ Church, Hampstead.

Tenth and Cheaper Edition. Small 8vo. 3s. 6d.
A Presentation Edition, with red borders. Small 4to. 10s. 6d.

The Holy Catholic Church; its Divine
Ideal, Ministry, and Institutions. A Short Treatise. With a Catechism on each Chapter, forming a Course of Methodical Instruction on the subject. By **Edward Meyrick Goulburn**, D.D., Dean of Norwich.

Second Edition. Crown 8vo. 6s. 6d.

The Religion of the Christ: its Historic
and Literary Development considered as an Evidence of its Origin. Being the Bampton Lectures for 1874. By the Rev. **Stanley Leathes**, M.A., Minister of St. Philip's, Regent Street, and Professor of Hebrew, King's College, London.

8vo. 12s.

The First Chronicle of Æscendune. A
Tale of the Days of St. Dunstan. By the Rev. **A. D. Crake**, B.A., Chaplain of All Saints' School, Bloxham, Author of the "History of the Church under the Roman Empire," &c., &c.

Crown 8vo. 3s. 6d.

Alfgar the Dane, or the Second Chron-
icle of Æscendune. A Tale. By the Rev. **A. D. Crake**, B.A., Chaplain of All Saints' School, Bloxham, Author of the "History of the Church under the Roman Empire," &c., &c.

Crown 8vo. 3s. 6d.

The Annual Register: a Review of Public
Events at Home and Abroad, from the Years 1863 to 1875.

8vo. 18s. each.

London, Oxford, and Cambridge

Library of Spiritual Works for English
Catholics.

It is hoped that the "Library of Spiritual Works for English Catholics," which will comprise translations, compilations, and other works, will meet a need which has long been felt. As the devotional life of the Church of England has increased, so the demand for spiritual treatises has become more and more urgent, and has arisen from all classes of society. This series of books, some well-known, some already oftentimes translated, and others, it may be, yet to be presented for the first time in an English dress, is intended to meet this want.

The aim of the translators is twofold. First, to provide the reader with a fair rendering of the original as far as possible unmutilated. It has been a common complaint of late, that translations have been marred by the absence of parts of the original, the exclusion of which a more intelligent view of Catholic devotion in the present day has rendered unnecessary. In these editions these omissions have been to a great extent supplied; yet at the same time any term or expression which may come under the imputation of being "un-English" has been reduced, as far as may be without destroying the thought, to its equivalent in Anglican phraseology and belief. Secondly, to translate the original into ordinary English, and thus to avoid the antiquated and stilted style of writing, which often makes books of this kind distasteful, or even sometimes unintelligible.

Elegantly printed with red borders, on extra superfine toned paper.
Small 8vo. 5s. each.

OF THE IMITATION OF CHRIST. In 4 Books. By **Thomas à Kempis**. A New Translation.

THE CHRISTIAN YEAR: Thoughts in Verse for the Sundays and Holydays throughout the Year.

THE SPIRITUAL COMBAT; together with the Supplement and the Path of Paradise. By **Laurence Scupoli**. A New Translation.

THE DEVOUT LIFE. By **Saint Francis of Sales**, Bishop and Prince of Geneva. A New Translation.

The Volumes can also be had in the following extra bindings:—

	s.	d.
Morocco, stiff or limp	9	0
Morocco, thick bevelled sides, Old Style	12	0
Morocco, limp, with flap edges	11	6
Morocco, best, stiff or limp	16	0
Morocco, best, thick bevelled sides, Old Style	19	6
Russia, limp	11	6
Russia, limp, with flap edges	13	6

Most of the above styles may be had illustrated with a beautiful selection of Photographs from Fra Angelico, 4s. 6d. extra.

CHEAP EDITIONS.

32mo, cloth limp, 6d. each, or cloth extra, 1s. each.

Of the Imitation of Christ.
The Spiritual Combat.
The Hidden Life of the Soul.
Spiritual Letters of Saint Francis of Sales.
The Christian Year.

[*Other Volumes are in preparation.*]

London, Oxford, and Cambridge

New Pamphlets

Bishop Wilberforce. A Sermon preached at the Parish Church of Graffham, Sussex, on its Reopening after Restoration, Nov. 2, 1875. By **H. P. Liddon, D.D.**, Canon of St. Paul's, and Ireland Professor at Oxford.
8vo. 1s.

The Church's Need of more Workers. A Sermon preached at S. Mary Magdalene, Paddington, on Septuagesima, 1876, in behalf of the Ordination Candidates Exhibition Fund. By **Robert Gregory**, M.A., Canon of S. Paul's.
8vo.

In Memoriam. James Graham Goodenough, R.N. A Sermon preached on the second Sunday after the Epiphany, 16th January 1876, at All Saints, West Bromwich. By the Hon. and Rev. **Algernon Stanley**, sometime Assistant Curate of that Parish.
8vo. 1s.

The Future Supply of Clergy for the Service of the Church of England, considered in a Letter addressed, by permission, to the Right Hon. W. E. Gladstone, M.P. By the Rev. **George Broadley Howard**, sometime Scholar of S. John's College, Cambridge.
8vo. 1s.

Everlasting Punishment. Is the Popular Doctrine de Fide? and if not, is it True? Considered in a Letter to the Right Hon. W. E. Gladstone, M.P. By the Rev. **F. N. Oxenham**, M.A.
8vo. 2s. 6d.

Papal Infallibility. Reasons why a Roman Catholic cannot accept the Doctrine of Papal Infallibility as defined by the Vatican Council. By a Roman Catholic Layman.
8vo. 2s.

The Infallible Church and the Holy Communion of Christ's Body and Blood. Correspondence between Lord Redesdale and Cardinal Manning in the *Daily Telegraph*.
8vo. 6d.

Further Correspondence between the same.
8vo. 6d.

Opening of the Diaconate to Persons Engaged in Professions and Trades. A Paper read at a Clerical Meeting. By the Rev. **G. W. Pearse**, Rector of Walton, Bucks.
8vo. 6d.

London, Oxford, and Cambridge

New Pamphlets

A Form of Prayer to be
used upon St. Andrew's Day, or upon any of the Seven Days next following. Being the Day or Days of Intercession for a Blessing upon the Missionary Work of the Church. Prepared by a Joint Committee for the Two Houses of the Convocation of Canterbury.

Royal 32mo. 1d.

An Additional Order for
Evening Prayer on Sundays and Holy Days throughout the Year, taken from the Holy Scriptures and the Book of Common Prayer. Prepared by the Lower House of Convocation of the Province of Canterbury.

[*This Form has already been approved for use in their Dioceses by the Bishops of Ely, Exeter, Hereford, Llandaff, Lichfield, Lincoln, Oxford, Rochester, St. Asaph, Salisbury, Winchester, and Worcester.*]

Royal 32mo. 2d.

The Shortened Order for
Morning and Evening Prayer daily throughout the Year, except on Sunday, Christmas Day, Ash-Wednesday, Good Friday, and Ascension Day, with "The Act of Uniformity Amendment Act."

Royal 32mo. 1d.

On the Sacrament of the
Lord's Supper. By The Plain Man's Friend.

Tenth Edition. Crown 8vo. 4d.

Holy Places. A Sermon
Preached in Worcester Cathedral on the Occasion of the Anniversary Festival of the Three Choirs, on Thursday, September 23, 1875. By **Edward Bickersteth, D.D.**, Dean of Lichfield.

8vo. 6d.

On the Excessive Rating of
Tithe Rentcharge. A Paper read in the Economy and Trade Section of the Social Science Association at Plymouth, September 1872. By the Rev. **R. Hobhouse**, Rector of St. Ive, near Liskeard.

Second Edition. 8vo. 6d.

Short Addresses on the
Holy Communion. Delivered during the Lincoln Mission, February, 1876, in the Parish Church of S. Peter's-in-Eastgate. By the Rev. **A. Babington**, Head Master of the Lincoln Grammar School.

8vo. 6d.

The Bishop's Oath of
Homage. By **John Walter Lea**, B.A., &c., Fellow of the Royal Historical Society. Dedicated by permission to the Right Rev. the Lord Bishop of Winchester.

8vo. 1s.

London, Oxford, and Cambridge

MESSRS. RIVINGTON *issue the undermentioned Lists, which may be had gratis and post free* :—

CLASSIFIED CATALOGUE OF BOOKS SELECTED FROM THEIR PUBLICATIONS.

LIST OF NEW BOOKS IN COURSE OF PUBLICATION.

LIST OF BOOKS FOR SCHOOLS AND COLLEGES.

MONTHLY CLASSIFIED LIST OF ALL NEW BOOKS PUBLISHED IN THE UNITED KINGDOM AND ON THE CONTINENT.

CATALOGUE OF A SELECTION FROM THEIR EDITIONS OF THE BIBLE, PRAYER BOOK, ETC., AND THEIR DEVOTIONAL WORKS, IN EXTRA BINDINGS.

RIVINGTONS: WATERLOO PLACE, LONDON;
and at Oxford and Cambridge.

www.ingramcontent.com/pod-product-compliance
Lightning Source LLC
Chambersburg PA
CBHW020259240426
43673CB00039B/647